ADVANCE PRAISE FOR PREGNANT PICTURES

"*Pregnant Pictures* presents a revolutionary body of images and analyses. What an astonishing archive Matthews and Wexler have assembled! Scholars and artists will be making reference to this book for years to come."
   —Wayne Koestenbaum, author of *Jackie Under My Skin: Interpreting an Icon*

"This book establishes pregnant pictures as a genre and pregnancy itself as a shape and an experience worthy of aesthetic attention. As elastic as the pregnant bodies they portray, these photos encompass and express the multiple dimensions of pregnancy and the many subtleties of the pregnant woman, from the archetypal to the idiosyncratic. A stunning collection and a fascinating analysis!"
   —Robbie Davis-Floyd, author of *Birth as an American Rite of Passage*

"In tracing pictures of pregnancy in modernist art photography, childbirth books, medical texts, advertising images and family photographs, Wexler and Matthews reveal the shifting social attitudes about pregnancy in the twentieth century. Inventing a vocabulary to discuss forms of representation that have remained as invisible in popular as in academic discourse, they have offered us a stunning collection of images, and a wonderful introduction to a new feminist photographic theory and practice."
   —Marianne G. Hirsch, author of *Family Frames: Photography, Narrative and Postmemory*

"This book is one of the most important publishing events of the turn of the millennium, particularly in its unleashing of the cultural taboo against visual representations of the pregnant maternal body. Cultural inquiry about the invisibility of that most visible body, one that literally breaks through the private to the public, is itself just now breaking out of obscurity. Matthews and Wexler's important book will undoubtedly inspire further research, speculation, and visual production."
   —Andrea Liss, author of *Trespassing Through Shadows: Memory, Photography, and the Holocaust*

D1561052

November, 2020
For Franny
and David
and baby Leo
with LOVE ♡
from Laura

PREGNANT PICTURES

Sandra Matthews and *Laura Wexler*

ROUTLEDGE
A MEMBER OF THE TAYLOR & FRANCIS GROUP
NEW YORK AND LONDON

Published in 2000 by
Routledge
29 West 35th Street
New York, NY 10001

Published in Great Britain by
Routledge
11 New Fetter Lane
London EC4P 4EE

A member of the Taylor & Francis Group

Designed by D. Thorne@hotwater
Printed in the United States of America on acid-free paper.

10 9 8 7 6 5 4 3 2 1

Library of Congress Cataloging-in-Publication Data
Matthews, Sandra.
Pregnant pictures / by Sandra Matthews and Laura Wexler.
    p.   cm.
Includes bibliographical references.
ISBN 0-415-90449-8 (hardback)
ISBN 0-415-92120-1 (paperback)
1. Pregnant women—Portraits. 2. Portrait photography.
I. Wexler, Laura. II. Title.

TR681.P67.M38   2000
779'.27—dc21   99-053026

For Matthew and Rina, Thomas and Rebecca

Contents

Acknowledgments

Pregnant Pictures took many years to deliver and a number of individuals played crucial roles in keeping the project viable along the way. Jill Lewis got us started by inviting us to give a joint seminar on women and creativity at Hampshire College, where the interest encouraged us to take our ideas further. Elisabeth Young-Bruehl generously lent her support early on and Maureen MacGrogan, then at Routledge, enthusiastically signed a book contract with us although the project was just in its initial stages. Later, Bill Germano, Gayatri Patnaik and Amy Reading expertly shepherded the book to completion. Anthony Mancini oversaw design and production with an astute eye and a great deal of patience. We are very grateful for their vision and sustenance.

We are grateful also to colleagues who read drafts of the manuscript and offered constructive criticism, suggestions, and encouragement. Henry Abelove, Nancy Armstrong, Rosemary Balsam, Nancy Cott, Elizabeth Dillon, Ann DuCille, Joan Hedrick, Margaret Homans, Gertrude Hughes, Indira Karemcheti, L. Brown Kennedy, Joel Pfister, Barbara Sicherman and Lynn Wardley each made important observations at different points along the way. Naomi Rogers and Susan Tracy thoughtfully critiqued the medical chapter while Pamela Allara, Judith Fryer Davidov, Andrea Liss and Meredith Michaels read and responded attentively to the manuscript as a whole. Elspeth Brown, Liza Grandia, Sura Levine, Michael Lesy, Lynn Reiser, Rachel Roth, Mary Russo and Susan Sawyer provided helpful ideas, information, and generous responses to our inquiries. In addition, Gail Hornstein and the community of women scholars at the Five College Women's Studies Research Center as well as the community of psychoanalysts and friends at the Muriel Gardiner Society for Psychoanalysis & Humanities at Yale University provided welcome feedback and validation. *Pregnant Pictures* is stronger for all their contributions.

Audiences at Hampshire College, Yale University, the American Studies Association, the Society for Photographic Education, and the Women in Photography National Conference responded generously to our work. We wish to thank the organizers of these events for the opportunity to speak, and the many listeners who came forward with pregnant pictures of their own.

As the book took shape, our growing archive of photographs required constant tending—research to find images, organization of the images, and the lengthy procedure of requesting permission to use images from a wide variety of sources. We were fortunate to have able and dedicated assistants at several points in the process. Joshua Beckman, a Hampshire College student when he began to work with us and now a recognized poet and book artist, was deeply involved in the project during its initial phase. Joshua found some of our most interesting images and fundamentally expanded the visual base of the archive. In the last stages Adam Shemper, also a former Hampshire student who is now an accomplished writer and photographer, worked on the difficult extended task of securing permissions, and in the process retrieved lost photographers and found wonderful last-minute visual material. In between, Mara Benjamin, Sandeep Ray, and Esme Howard contributed research and organizational skills. Three Mellon Faculty Development Grants from Hampshire College and an A. Whitney Griswold Faculty Research Fund Grant from Yale University helped to underwrite their labor. Linda Anderson of the Yale Women's and Gender Studies Program was instrumental in truly finalizing the myriad picture-related tasks. Her tremendous energy and gift for organization provided the final coordination needed to finish the project.

Sharon Mayberry, Helen Smith and Rita Watson offered helpful editorial suggestions at several points. Karen Hsu provided expert image scans. The physical production of the manuscript from writing done over time on a number of different computers was a daunting task aided immensely by Harriet Boyden's and Kelly Taylor's wizardry.

Pregnant Pictures was published with the assistance of the Frederick W. Hilles Publications Fund of Yale University. We are grateful for this generosity.

Our friends and families have been truly supportive throughout. We would like particularly to thank Norbert Goldfield and Bruce Wexler, who have withstood the seemingly endless stresses and intrusions of this endeavor with abiding interest and good will. And especially we would like to recognize Matthew Goldfield, Rina Goldfield, Thomas Wexler and Rebecca Wexler, whose coming into being inaugurated our quest for pregnant pictures. This book is dedicated, with love and thanks, to them.

Introduction

In 1987, when photographer Sandra Adams, then in her early 30s, learned that she was pregnant with her first child, among the many emotions that she felt was a new kind of fear. She was afraid of the changes the pregnancy portended for her own life. She worried that impending motherhood would swallow up the woman and the artist she knew to be herself.

Sandra Adams was far from alone in this trepidation. Many pregnant women share a dread of personal obliteration and worry about the irreversible character of motherhood even as they may be looking forward to assuming the role. This anxiety can be repeated over successive pregnancies, as the coming of each new baby threatens to destabilize a woman's recently reconstructed sense of self, barely accommodated to the present demands of her family. Yet this dread is one of the many subjective experiences of pregnancy that are not often represented. What was unusual about Adams was that she chose to express her ambivalent feelings and found a unique way to represent them.

Adams constructed a series of female dolls, "effigies," each bearing a photograph of her face. She used the camera's capacity for mechanical reproduction to create small replicas of herself, ironically simulating human reproduction. She then furnished the dolls with symbolic objects, put them in coffinlike wooden "effigy boxes," and gave them to a group of her friends and colleagues. In an accompanying letter she explained that the dolls represented qualities of herself that she did not want to lose and that she was asking them to safeguard. She thus called on her community not to affirm her in her new role as a mother, but to retain an image of her as a separate self as she crossed the line into motherhood.

Adams' photographs of the effigy boxes focus on the psychological interior rather than the body of the pregnant woman. They represent pregnancy as a fragmenting state of transition and suggest that we ought not assume what a pregnant woman feels while "expecting."

Her effigies also suggest a further question: what *is* a photograph of pregnancy anyway? And, how are we to articulate and interpret its meanings? These questions have engaged us since we began the *Pregnant Pictures* project in the mid-1980s. At that time we were both junior faculty in the Five College area of Western Massachusetts, Sandra at Hamphire College and Laura at Amherst College. Career opportunities had begun to open up for women in the academy, but only recently and with far more difficulty than might have been anticipated. Childbearing and the demands of the professional clock were on a direct colli-

Sandra Adams, untitled, 1987

sion course, but nonetheless we had both recently given birth to children, bringing logistical difficulties and professional tensions as well as added joy and personal satisfaction to our lives. We couldn't help but note the gap between our
actual experiences of pregnancy, family and work, and the photographs of pregnancy available to us. We felt a need for images that might help us to better
understand how to think about our own experiences. It struck us as an unfortu-
nate omission that feminist work on the representation of the female body
almost entirely disregarded the pregnant female body while available images of
the pregnant body seemed divorced from feminist insight. Such a marked avoidance of the politics of contemporary pregnancy disguised the fact that we, like
the majority of men and women in the world, did not experience "the female
body" as never pregnant. Increasingly, it seemed to us that the few photographs
of pregnant women we did encounter projected a fictive version of maternity
contradictory to the social terrain of pregnancy which we inhabited.

We also sensed that our desire for more for more and different representations
went beyond our own personal hunger. For women, being imaged and viewed
has most often meant being kept in place. Yet being shielded from view, as pregnant women have most often been, implies a problematic social invisibility.

Invited to give a joint presentation on photography in a seminar series entitled "Women and Creativity," we determined upon a specific interpretation of
women's "creativity"—childbearing. We feared that making representations of
pregnancy the topic of a scholarly talk might be as untoward professionally as
our pregnancies themselves had been. Yet the topic offered the prospect of better integrating our personal concerns with our professional work and thereby
pushing the boundaries of both. We were inspired by the superb work and collaborative practice of feminists from the British cultural studies movement such
as Griselda Pollock, Jo Spence, Simon Watney and Patricia Holland, and by pioneering sociologists Ann Oakley, Rosalind Petchesky, Erving Goffman and
Barbara Norfleet in England and the United States.

Pregnant Pictures began in that search for photographs of pregnancy. We
looked especially for photographs that could elucidate complex cultural meanings of pregnancy, providing points of connection between women's individual
experiences and social ideas about reproduction. Our collection of pictures grew,
like most collections, in an eclectic fashion. We combed art libraries, medical
libraries, small local libraries and bookstores for art, medical, and instructional
photographs. We advertised in *Afterimage*, a journal of contemporary photography, film and video, for unpublished contemporary art photography, and in
Mothering magazine for personal snapshots of pregnancy. We put notices in clinics and on community bulletin boards. We put ourselves on the mailing lists of
numerous maternity clothing businesses in order to receive their catalogues.

With the help of research assistants we did many hours of telephone research, followed up with letters. One of our most important sources of pictures came from the public slide lectures that we gave throughout the *Pregnant Pictures* project. Our audiences always responded with suggestions and donations of more images, and helped to expand our network of picture sources. By now our archive is perhaps the most extensive collection of photographs of pregnant women in existence. It is proof of how many representations of pregnant women do, in fact, exist.

Yet we are aware, at the same time, that our collection of photographs is necessarily partial, limited both by chance and design. For example, we deal only briefly with photographs oriented toward public health and policy issues, found on posters and in brochures, and hardly at all with pornographic photographs of the pregnant body. While at first we thought we would study a continuum of reproductive photographs including representations of pregnancy and childbirth, soon we realized that photographs of pregnancy and photographs of birth do very different cultural work. Photographs of birth are records of a public drama that quickly shifts focus from the birthing woman to the emerging baby and others in attendance. They are usually intense and cathartic, readily grasped by the viewer in terms of action and spectacle. Photographs of pregnancy, on the other hand, are somehow more opaque. They seem resistant to the viewer's visual mastery, and are often awkwardly situated in relation to the familiar strategies of visual objectification. Their very awkwardness and seeming muteness calls for further exploration.

In this way we discovered a central line of analysis that is woven throughout the book: the importance of different modalities of looking. Photographs of pregnancy are constrained in number and kind because of the complicated sexuality of the pregnant woman and the viewer is also constrained because of debates over reproductive practices. Looking at the pregnant figure is not simple.

Four principal modes of looking are woven through the image domains of art and advertising, medical textbooks and instructional manuals, family photographs, popular magazines, and public policy documents that are examined in this book. They are *scopic looking, instrumental looking, clinical looking* and *iconic looking*. These modes, used in viewing many kinds of photographs, raise particular issues for the consumption of images of pregnancy.

The scopic and the instrumental modes are by far the most fundamental and pervasive. The scopic mode positions the female figure as a sight for voyeuristic appropriation, while instrumental looking intends to make the figure of the woman available as a source of useful information. Clinical looking at the female body is associated with medical photography. The iconic mode of looking adheres to specific images of women that carry a collective cultural weight. Each mode may commonly include aspects of the others, but is distinct in constructing a different address to the viewer. The distinction between modes rests in how the viewer approaches the image and apprehends its meaning. The viewer is in turn guided by the way that the photographer has structured the image, and the context in which the image is placed. It may be useful to have the following rather schematic guide to the ideological effects of each:

Scopic looking gives the viewer a sense of vicarious mastery over the scene portrayed. It is based on cultural premises of "occularism," in Martin Jay's terminology, that equate vision with knowledge, and it flourishes especially in the context of modernism.

Instrumental looking uses images to serve specific needs the viewer has for information, stimulation and reassurance. Photographs found in self-help manuals are good examples.

Clinical looking establishes a formal sense of distance that permits the viewer to cross conventional boundaries of privacy to gaze at the physical condition of a body that is pictured.

Iconic looking distills cultural meaning from specific images and connects individual spectators to a collective sense of social formations.

Each viewing mode, like each image domain, performs distinct cultural work. Each positions the viewer differently. These modes also shift over time. And although each mode has its limits, each also allows for representation to be extended in some ways that the others do not.

Imaging the *pregnant* body challenges each of these modes of looking. For instance, to present the nonpregnant female body as an object of desire is a central, defining aspect of the scopic mode. But historically, the pregnant female body has not been freely depicted as desirable, and it also has not been often represented in the scopic mode. The pregnant body has more often been viewed clinically or instrumentally. The contemporary widespread circulation of representations of the pregnant body in public as scopic images of desire and even as icons, such as Annie Leibovitz's famous pictures of pregnant Demi Moore, is a very recent development.

The circumstances of production and consumption (context) and these modes of addressing the spectator (looking relations) are critical to our analysis of the photographs in this book.

Because our archive of photographs is so interdisciplinary and heterogeneous, it offers a special opportunity to demonstrate the different ways in which photographs can be used by viewers, including specifically female viewers. However, we do not attempt to generalize about any connections between the sex or gender of the *photographer*, and the characteristics of the photographs.

Each chapter in *Pregnant Pictures* deals, in turn, with what we have come to term the "image domains" of modernist and postmodernist art photography, family photographs, medical photography, photography in childbirth manuals, photographic advertising for maternity clothing, public policy photographs and photography in popular magazines. Each domain performs distinct cultural work, yet we have tried to show that there are important points of interconnection among them.

The chronology of *Pregnant Pictures* runs from the late 1800s to the 1990s, but our emphasis is on post–WWII photographs. Also, we have focused on images that were made or circulated in the United States, and have attempted to draw connections between changes in the representation of pregnancy, and shifting attitudes and practices within U.S. culture. While we believe that a comparative study that reaches beyond the borders of the United States would be instructive, that lies beyond the scope of our project. Yet we do attempt to acknowledge certain important influences and images from abroad that we know have had an impact on U.S. attitudes and practices.

The decade during which we have written this book has seen significant change in the technologies associated with both photography and pregnancy. During this time, the biology of human reproduction has become increasingly compartmentalized in ways that potentially remove it from the bodies of women. Simultaneously pregnancy has become possible in previously impossible bodies—postmenopausal women, for example. Heterosexual intercourse is no longer a necessary correlate of pregnancy, and this separation of reproduction from sexuality has been incorporated into the mainstream public understanding of pregnancy. Research into cloning, the development of artificial uteri, and cross-species genetic transfer is proceeding apace. Human reproduction, loosened, although not yet released, from its bodily context has found a new place in the laboratory, raising many questions about who profits from these procedures and who is, or is not, monitoring them. Concurrently, medical imaging has undergone its own computerized revolution, and the inside of the living body is now visible by means of PET, MRI, and ultrasound scanning to a previously unknown standard of detail. At the same time computer imaging has stretched the indexical bond between objects and their representations. Many people fear that the mother is being erased by a visual culture that increasingly privileges images of free-floating fetuses.

Yet during this same decade, photographs of pregnant women have also emerged into public print culture, crossing the boundaries of private and public. Rather than being erased, we have found pregnant women to be increasingly visible. In our research, we have stopped short of fully using the resources of the Internet, but in this context too photographs of pregnant women are rapidly being disconnected from their prior contexts and finding a new place in cyberspace, where questions of profit and control also abound.

As we worked on this book, the phrase "pregnant pictures" took on a set of meanings far beyond the literal ones. It became clear that photographs of pregnancy participate in cultural contestation over rapidly changing scenarios of social life. Like Sandra Adams, we hope the pictures gathered here and our analyses will provoke discussion of these changes. We hope too that they will encourage the recovery and creation of even more representations of the pregnant subject as an active and authoritative social being.

I) THE SUBJECT OF PREGNANCY

> The library card catalogue contains dozens of entries under
> the heading "pregnancy": clinical treatises detailing signs of
> morbidity; volumes cataloging studies of foetal development,
> with elaborate drawings; or popular manuals in which
> physicians and others give advice on diet and exercise for the
> pregnant woman. . . . Except perhaps for one insignificant
> diary, no card appears listing a work which, as Kristeva puts it
> (1980, p. 237), is "concerned with the subject, the mother as
> the site of her proceedings."
>
> —Iris Marion Young

WHY PREGNANT PICTURES?

What has photography, apotheosis of the visible, to do with pregnancy, the very
archetype of the hidden? Why a book about images of a temporary state of the
body, the very mention of which is apt to be awkward, if not actually aversive?
Pregnancy currently occupies a marginalized and devalued discursive space even
while, as a fashionable topic, "the body" and "the new reproductive technologies"
gain ever-increasing glamour. Popular notions of pregnancy are carnal, often sentimental; sometimes they are even grotesque. The physical productions of the
pregnant body are indiscreet—a subject for the doctor's office, the bedroom and
the private talk of women. The swollen womb is an atavistic protuberance of body
fluid, blood and tissue. Camera work, on the other hand, is tasteful, an appropriate topic for the dinner table conversation, the museum symposium, the chic
magazine. The photograph is a sleek and glossy surface, a weightless skin. What
is the impulse that would seek to implicate these two so firmly with one another
and then to dwell on their conjunction? Why the subject of pregnant pictures?

Our initial concern was to recover traces of the pregnant subject herself, that
is, the pregnant woman as an individual. We were astonished at the shortage of
visual images of a bodily event as fundamental and important as pregnancy.
There were very few images of pregnant women in public visual culture, such as
art books and galleries, newspapers, magazines, posters and advertisements.
When public photographs of pregnant women *could* be found, the pregnancy
had often been dealt with in an extremely limited, idealized and dehistoricized
way. The images themselves had usually been highly stylized and sequestered

into specialized viewing arenas such as medical textbooks or maternity clothing catalogues. Clearly, the public representation of pregnancy was a site of cultural anxiety, and pregnant women saw not only very few, but also very constricted reflections of themselves. We wanted to supply a broader and more meaningful collection of pictures.

At the same time, the question—how can society reflect more probingly upon the meaning of pregnancy in the context of a rapidly changing biological foundation?—grew increasingly important to our project. Socially specific and historically contextualized representations do exist, but they reach very limited groups of viewers. This is important because just as the pregnant woman as an individual constructs her sense of self in part from images of herself, so does our society derive a sense of collectivity from the images it constructs and circulates. The ways that photographs of pregnancy have appeared and changed over time reveal pregnant pictures as social pictures—representations not only of a dramatic change in the state of the female body itself, but of important changes in the social institutions that contextualize and give meaning to that body, such as medicine, law and education.

It rapidly became clear that an historical narrative was vital not only to connect individuals with images of pregnancy, but images of pregnancy with the social changes that give them meaning. How and why do photographs of pregnancy circulate in public visual space? Historically, three principal factors have curtailed photographic representation of pregnant women: pregnancy's complicated relation to subjectivity, to sexuality, and to the social struggle for control over reproduction—in simple terms, language, sex and politics. In each case, absence of the images of pregnancy suppresses the complexity of these factors.

PREGNANT SUBJECTS

Most women must deal at some point in their lives with the possibility, impossibility, or fact of becoming pregnant. Pregnancy can be a longed-for or feared event, it can be planned or accidental, the fruit of a loving relationship or a violent rape. Once a clear indication of sexual activity, pregnancy is now quite commonly initiated a-sexually. Even a desired, "natural" pregnancy is a complicated physical, psychological and social passage, both intensely private and unavoidably public. A lost or feared or technologically enhanced pregnancy thrusts the woman into a variety of roles that she may never have imagined. Pregnancy links the most intimate aspects of a woman's body with ideas about the well being of the social body.

Yet, what can be said about the pregnant woman as subject? What is written often has a curiously muffled and saccharine or even punitive character. Pregnancy has long been seen as an exemplary instance of the analogy between women and nature that anthropologist Sherry Ortner proposed, in her essay "Is

Woman to Man as Nature is to Culture?" (1974), as the justification for "cultural language and imagery [to] continue to purvey a relatively devalued view of women."[1] Alternately she has been identified as a sociopath whose insistence upon drinking, smoking, taking drugs and having unprotected sex forces the government to discipline her on behalf of the civil rights of her fetus, charging to "women's expense" the "costs of fetal rights," as both Rachel Roth and Cynthia Daniels have argued.[2] Recently, the pregnant woman also has been featured as the occasion for a tremendous burst of scientific knowledge, and portrayed as a grateful consumer, passively pleased with the options presented by the new reproductive technologies.

But establishing and maintaining a pregnancy most often takes consciousness and work. Maria Mies points out that throughout history women "did not simply breed children like cows, but they appropriated their own generative and productive forces, they analyzed and reflected upon their own and former experiences and passed them on to their daughters. This means that they were not helpless victims of their bodies' generative forces, but learned to influence them, including the number of children they wanted to have."[3] The erasure of this history of conscious work in pregnancy undermines women's knowledge of themselves as pregnant subjects, and underplays their agency as central figures in the changing cultural drama of reproduction.

Selfhood and Alienation

Some feminist writers have tried to enhance appreciation of the work of pregnancy even though they have feared essentializing women's biological role and equating it with her social prospects. In the late nineteenth century a large number of advocates for women's rights were drawn to the cause of "voluntary motherhood," meaning planned and wanted pregnancies. Voluntary motherhood was, as Linda Gordon sees it, "a political statement about the nature of *involuntary* motherhood and childrearing."[4] These activists wanted not so much to limit pregnancy as to make it more comfortable and respected within the structures of conventional marriage and family.

In the early twentieth century Margaret Sanger's humanitarian activism was an expression of women's drive further to represent their own needs and desires concerning pregnancy within the family, especially its economic impact. This required, in turn, a much broader (and at the time illegal) social distribution of knowledge about reproduction and contraception among the poor. But Sanger also feared immigrant population growth, which made pregnancy to her a social concern more than an issue of subjectivity.

A generation and more later, in 1949 and 1970, Simone de Beauvoir and Shulamith Firestone articulated changed meanings of pregnancy in the context of second-wave feminism. They came to largely negative conclusions about the impact of pregnancy and the institution of family upon women. If women are ever to be active in the world, pregnancy seemed to these writers an almost insurmountable barrier. Both assumed that the pregnant woman fundamentally had no chance for autonomous subjectivity. Beauvoir felt that pregnancy obliterated transcendence in bodily servitude to the family and the species. Fertility was bad enough. "Woman is adapted to the needs of the egg, rather than to her own requirements," Beauvoir asserted. "It is during her periods that she feels her body most painfully as an obscure, alien thing; it is, indeed, the prey of a stubborn and foreign life that each month constructs and then tears down a cradle within it; each month all things are made ready for a child and then aborted in the crimson flow."[5] Conception only made things worse:

> Woman experiences a more profound alienation when fertilization has occurred and the divided egg passes down into the uterus and proceeds to develop there. True enough, pregnancy is a normal process, which, if it takes places under normal conditions of health and nutrition, is not harmful to the mother; certain interactions between her and the fetus become established which are even beneficial to her. In spite of an optimistic view having all too obvious social utility, however, gestation is a fatiguing task of no individual benefit to the woman but on the contrary demanding heavy sacrifices. It is often associated in the first months with loss of appetite and vomiting, which are not observed in any female domesticated animal and which signalize the revolt of the organism against the invading species.[6]

Beauvoir's conclusion to this rather frightening train of thought was that "woman, like man, is her body; but her body is something other than herself."[7]

Firestone was not content simply to describe the physical and psychological burdens of pregnancy. "Pregnancy is barbaric," she declared, and called for the "freeing of women from the tyranny of their reproductive biology by every means available" as the "first demand for any alternative [i.e., socialist] system."[8] Firestone envisioned a time when the "potentials of modern embryology, that is, artificial reproduction," would contribute to the "diffusion of the childbearing and child-rearing role to the society as a whole."[9] And although this possibility seemed "so frightening that [it is] seldom discussed seriously," Firestone was willing to consider these "new alternatives" to a "fundamentally oppressive biological condition that we only now have the skill to correct."[10] In her positive valuation of the liberatory possibilities of the new reproductive technologies she was prescient, although perhaps too sanguine about the "elimination of sexual classes" that would necessarily follow women's "seizure of control of *reproduction*" and destruction not just of "male *privilege* but of sex *distinction* itself."[11]

In fact, in their negativity toward pregnancy within the patriarchal family, both Beauvoir and Firestone made courageous and important contributions toward opening up a fuller, more differentiated discourse on women's social agency in childbearing, or lack of it. But they tended to mistrust that women could ever truly construct an active political role that would include pregnancy. They spoke not as, but on behalf of, pregnant women.

A Voice of Her Own

In the 1970s, French psychoanalyst Julia Kristeva and American poet and social activist Adrienne Rich began to explore the character of pregnant subjectivity with greater passion for the condition and with greater interest in how it might be manifested in language. This was the beginning of a feminist conceptualization of a speaking role for pregnant women themselves.

The pregnant subject's speech was highly problematic. For Kristeva, meditating on the subject in "Motherhood According to Giovanni Bellini" (1975), the voice of the pregnant woman was present and specific, but it was also virtually inaccessible. In Kristeva's understanding, as in her memory of her own experience of pregnancy, the pregnant woman as a subject was deeply and primally split within herself.

> Cells fuse, split, and proliferate: volumes grow, tissues stretch, and body fluids change rhythm, speeding up or slowing down. Within the body, growing as a graft, indomitable, there is another. And no one is present, within that simultaneously dual and alien space, to signify what is going on. "It happens, but I'm not there." "I cannot realize it, but it goes on." Motherhood's impossible syllogism.[12]

By virtue of the growing fetus, Kristeva's pregnant woman enters what Kristeva termed an *"enceinte,"* a separate psychological space, a walled-in enclosure or a beltway on the very border of language. This liminal space functions as an instinctual preserve at the supposed threshold where nature joins culture. An "I" is present, but only in so far as it recognizes its own erasure: "'It happens, but I'm not there.'" This "I" has no control over what is happening within her body, which fuses, splits, proliferates, grows, stretches, changes rhythm, speeds up and slows down presumably without her active participation. She knows only that "it goes on."

However, out of this self-division, as Susan Stewart interprets Kristeva in her book, *On Longing*—while pointing out that one of the meanings of the word *longing* is "the fanciful cravings incident to women during pregnancy"—the "subject is generated, both created and separated from what it is not." Such separa-

tion from self is literally pregnant with the possibility of meaning. Unlike Beauvoir and Firestone, for Kristeva, Stewart writes, the "initial separation/joining
has a reproductive capacity that is the basis for the reproductive capacity of all
signifiers." In other words, in that "place of margin between the biological 'reality' of splitting cells and the cultural 'reality' of the beginning of the symbolic,"
not only pregnant speech, but all speech is born.[13]

Nevertheless, full-fledged political speech remains inconceivable for Kristeva's
desiring pregnant subject, for what she speaks is a private language. Kristeva was
rare among mid-twentieth-century psychoanalysts for the time and thought she
spent on the subjectivity of pregnancy. Adrienne Rich was almost unique among
the feminist poets and political theorists of her generation for doing the same. In
Of Woman Born (1976), Rich also described pregnancy as an experience of doubleness, but differently. Where Kristeva was moved to see in the pregnant figure
reflections of symbolic and universal motherhood, revealing a romantic bent in
her evocations of the pregnant "I," Rich was a realist, and a pragmatist. "The
child that I carry for nine months can be defined *neither* as me or as not-me," she
wrote, cutting through Kristeva's equivocations. "Far from existing in the mode
of 'inner space,' women are powerfully and vulnerably attuned both to 'inner'
and 'outer' because for us the two are continuous, not polar."[14] Rich's analysis of
pregnant subjectivity emphasized the connections rather than the separation of
the polarities that coexist within a pregnant woman, and sought the political
rather than the psychoanalytic implications of her bodily condition. Pregnant
speech is generated and claimed, for Rich, through the enunciation of the place
and position of pregnancy, not their renunciation.

Addressing the social dimensions of reproduction, Rich assigned a quite different interpretation to the pregnant subject's enclosure and apparent lack of
voice than did Kristeva. According to Rich, what it is that "happens" or "goes on"
in pregnancy that guarantees that the pregnant woman "cannot realize it" is not
a symbolic aphasia at all, but the silently insidious removal of the woman from
authority over her own body:

> As the means of reproduction without which cities and colonies could not
> expand, without which a family would die out and its prosperity pass into
> the hands of strangers, she has found herself at the center of purposes not
> hers, which she has often incorporated and made her own. The woman in
> labor might perceive herself as bringing forth a new soldier to fight for the
> tribe or nation-state, a new head of the rising yeoman or bourgeois family,
> a new priest or rabbi for her father's faith, or a new mother to take up the
> renewal of life. Given this patriarchal purpose she could obliterate herself
> in fertility as her body swelled year after year.[15]

Taken together, in the 1970s Kristeva and Rich mapped for the first time a pregnant subject whose duality forms the basis for a recombination of concepts previously thought to be binary opposites: self and other, inner and outer, private and public, silence and speech, past and future, physical and spiritual. They also clarified what are still the boundaries of contemporary thought about pregnant subjectivity. On one extreme, the pregnant woman appears in a meditative, half-conscious state of imminence. Her separate selfhood is precarious, and her speech needs translation. On the other, pregnant subjectivity appears as a field for the woman's active and deliberate world making, if not always her successful control, and her ability to signify requires both molding and restraint.

The Mirror Stage

It is instructive to note that both Kristeva and Rich were studying visual representations of maternity when they began to theorize pregnant subjectivity. Kristeva was looking at the paintings of Giovanni Bellini, and Rich, as we shall see, at her own family photographs. For each, visual representations provided a crucial distance that helped them to articulate and reorient their own perspective toward pregnancy. As another French psychoanalyst, Jacques Lacan, has proposed in "The Mirror Stage as Formative of the Function of the I," the reification and reflection inherent in such visual images is a crucial stage in the child's initial creation of an image of the self.[16]

One can postulate that the pregnant woman, whose body image and ego ideal are undergoing such radical change, enters a second such "mirror stage." It is necessary only to recognize how visual representations strengthened both Kristeva's and Rich's interrogations in order to see the value of the insight that can be created by such images. For instance, what Kristeva comes to understand in looking at Bellini looking at maternity is that womanhood under patriarchy is portrayed like pregnancy, as doing without knowing, and that the woman herself does not determine the meaning of the gaze that so portrays her. The gaze of the pregnant woman at the image of the pregnant woman especially recognizes *misrepresentation*.

Adrienne Rich recalled becoming visible as a pregnant woman as an ambiguous experience. Sometimes it was very pleasant:

> As soon as I was visibly and clearly pregnant, I felt, for the first time in my adolescent and adult life, not-guilty. The atmosphere of approval in which I was bathed—even by strangers in the street—was like an aura I carried with me, in which doubts, fears, misgivings, met with absolute denial. *This is what women have always done.*[17]

At other times it could be amazingly painful:

During my own first pregnancy, I was invited to give a poetry reading at an old and famous boys' preparatory school in New England. When the master responsible for inviting me realized that I was seven months pregnant he canceled the invitation, saying that the fact of my pregnancy would make it impossible for the boys to listen to my poetry. This was in 1955.[18]

It was only when Rich learned to deflect the gaze with her own look back that she could reassign the meaning of those distorted reflections. But once again, to confront the hostile gaze was very difficult:

I avoided this journey back into the years of pregnancy, childbearing and the dependent lives of my children, because it meant going back into pain and anger that I would have preferred to think of as long since resolved and put away.[19]

Finally, Rich writes, she found "other views" that could counter the closed circuit of cultural stereotypes that encircled the childbearing woman. Some of the most valuable were photographs, in which she saw critical resources for the reconstruction of buried histories:

For many years I shrank from looking back on the first decade of my children's lives. In snapshots of the period, I see a smiling young woman, in maternity clothes or bent over a half-naked baby; gradually she stops smiling, wears a distant, half-melancholy look, as if she were listening for something.[20]

What Rich saw in those photographs were images of a past self who was listening for something or someone, hoping for help. Understanding came later. By means of the photographs the sense of selfhood that had been lost at the time became recoverable to language. That is, instead of being split by an active/passive polarity formed along the axis of gender, where "pleasure in looking has been split between active/male and passive/female," to use Laura Mulvey's formulation, Rich's spectator is primarily split as an historical subject, divided between a woman who once was and a woman who now is.[21] The one is alienated from her own body, seeking though not finding an avenue of escape. The mute appeal she records exists in the present time of the photograph. The other is her rescuer, who later, upon recognizing her, is helpless to change what once was but is pleased and empowered to speak words that liberate her into her (own) future.

Photographs of her own maternity clearly engage Rich in a kind of seeing that circulates from past to present, and thereby bears an active relation to the pleasure of the gaze. The subject position of such a female spectator is double, both subject and object, twinned over time through the medium of photography.

Out of Sight, Out of Mind

When the second wave of feminist thinking and writing began in the late 1960s, not pregnancy but childcare was at the center of many debates. Social issues such as the conflict between motherhood and work were addressed both theoretically, in books such as Tillie Olsen's *Silences* (1965), and practically, in the demand for daycare and shared responsibility for childrearing, as in Dorothy Dinnerstein's *The Mermaid and the Minatour* (1976). By the late 1970s, however, a shift of emphasis occurred. With some major exceptions, especially in the work of Angela Davis, Ann Oakley, Mary O'Brien, and Mary Kelley, the politics of women's fertility largely gave way to a theoretical discussion of the female body, focused on questions of sexuality, women's desire, and the constitution of femininity within the confines of the sex/gender system. In the decade that followed, many books and essays were published on the gendered body that made virtually no mention of pregnancy or childbirth.

But continuing to isolate discussion of the image from the social reality of pregnancy, especially as gender roles were being reconstituted, proved debilitating and impossible to sustain. By the end of the 1980s, in pioneering anthologies such as Gena Corea's *Man-Made Women: How New Reproductive Technologies Affect Women* (1985) and Michelle Stanworth's *Reproductive Technologies: Gender, Motherhood and Medicine* (1987), and in monographs such as Emily Martin's *The Woman in the Body: A Cultural Analysis of Reproduction* (1987), Zillah Eisenstein's *The Female Body and the Law* (1988), and Barbara Katz Rothman's *Recreating Motherhood: Ideology and Technology in a Patriarchal Society* (1989), there was an attempt to reopen and reassess the relation of contemporary gender theory to changing reproductive practices.

For the most part, however, these writers did not linger upon the visual representation of the pregnant woman, as had the earlier Kristeva and Rich. Despite the effort of academic writers to make reproduction a focus of feminist theory, by and large images were left to authors outside the academy, such as the collective who presented successive editions of *Our Bodies, Ourselves*, or to activists in the home birth movement, for whom photographs were publicity. Indeed, it was during this period that we began work on *Pregnant Pictures*, convinced that there was no place in the academy for images of pregnancy as a research topic.

THE IMAGE WARS

In the culture wars of the 1980s and 1990s, ignoring images rapidly ceased to be a possibility. The 1980s saw an increasingly successful conservative attack on the right to abortion that had been secured by the 1973 *Roe v. Wade* Supreme Court decision. From the Hyde Amendment of 1980, denying Medicare funding for abortions except where the pregnancy endangered the life of the mother or where the woman was pregnant as a result of promptly reported incest or rape, to the 1992 Supreme Court decision in *Planned Parenthood of Southeastern Pennsylvania v. Casey*, which upheld laws imposing consent requirements, a twenty-four-hour waiting period and parental consent for those seeking abortion, and reporting and record-keeping requirements for abortion providers, reproductive freedoms were continually chipped away. Because the *Roe v. Wade* decision had legalized women's right to abortion on the grounds of a constitutional guarantee of privacy, images of what was "going on" inside the private space of the pregnant woman's body that she "cannot realize," to use Kristeva's formulation, suddenly became a matter of public concern as various groups all claimed the power to interpret it. Early to respond were historians of the struggle for the right to abortion, such as Kristin Luker, in *Abortion and the Politics of Motherhood* (1984), Rosalind Petchesky, in *Abortion and Women's Choice: The State, Sexuality, and Reproductive Freedom* (1984), and Faye Ginsberg, *Contested Lives: The Abortion Debate in an American Community* (1989). But they did not yet have a distinct notion of the relation of fetal images to the creation of a semimystical fetal personhood whose aura of sanctity was conjoined with the sanctity of life itself.

At the same time, new image-making technologies such as sonography and real-time video displayed the contents of women's reproductive organs to a broad audience. The increasing focus and resolution of ultrasound visualization was making the image of the fetus both comprehensible and commonplace, while seeming to remove the mother's necessary presence from the depictions.

The 1985 production of the film *The Silent Scream*, in which Dr. Bernard Nathanson used fetal images very successfully as supposedly objective manifestations of the life that was tortured and murdered in abortion, changed the terms of discourse. The idea for the film was born, apparently, after an article was published in the *New England Journal of Medicine* proposing that maternal bonding with early ultrasound images might result in fewer abortions.[22] *The Silent Scream* was widely aired on network television, implicating the media in the promotion of fetal imagery. Countering the use of fetal images in the film and in the anti-abortion posters that followed, depicting mangled fetuses as innocent murder victims, meant in part deconstructing the visual status of the fetal subject. In their film made in response, for instance, Planned Parenthood critiqued Nathanson's images of the pregnant woman as a childlike person in whom the right to reproductive freedom could not be properly invested.[23]

It became necessary to resuscitate the social visibility of the pregnant woman as a counterpoint to the increasing social visibility of the fetus or stand in danger of losing the fight for reproductive freedom. "During the 1960s and 1970s, an enormous amount of ink was spilled and vocal cords frayed simply to introduce the idea that women are people, that we have done a pretty good job over the years reproducing children under less than favorable circumstances, and that we ought to be accorded the liberty to determine when or whether we want to be mothers," note anthropologist Lynn Morgan and philosopher Meredith Michaels in the introduction to their book, *Fetal Subjects, Feminist Positions* (1999). But since then, they continue, "the social organization of reproduction in the United States has unfolded in a way that routinely erases women from the picture and rationalizes the presence of fetuses." It is no wonder that feminists have cautioned against an excessive focus on the fetus. As fetuses in their "maternal environments" become ubiquitous, women seem to vanish.[24] Phrases like "routinely erases women from the picture" and "women seem to vanish" indicate that a return to the visual is a necessary ground of contestation.

Fetal Photographs

Rosalind Petchesky's 1987 essay, "Fetal Images: The Power of Visual Culture in the Politics of Reproduction" gave the theoretical foundation for this return of images of pregnant women to feminist texts. It was published only two years after *Abortion and Women's Choice*, which hadn't even mentioned them. There was, as well, a new twist. In Petchesky's essay, unlike in Kristeva's or Rich's writings, it was actually pictures of the fetus, not the pregnant woman, that were central. Petchesky's argument that "from their beginning, such photographs have represented the foetus as primary and autonomous, the woman as absent or peripheral" identified the *absence* of the pregnant figure from that scene as a problem, not, as in Beauvoir or Firestone, as a potential solution.[25] Interestingly, Petchesky's move to reinstate pregnant subjectivity, like Kristeva's and Rich's efforts before her, described a scene of looking at images. But rather than looking at paintings or the family album, Petchesky's pregnant women were readers of ultrasound images. Their interpretations of these images could not be taken for granted, but revealed their desires and their capacity for choice.

Conservative anti-abortion ideologues who wanted to require that every woman seeking to end a pregnancy be shown a sonogram of her fetus first and be guided in its interpretation, on the grounds that she would then be unable to go through with the procedure, did not fare well in Petchesky's analysis. Neither did radical feminists who agitated against women's alleged victimization by the "ancient masculinist impulse to 'confine and limit and curb the creativity and potentially polluting power of female procreation.'"[26] Instead, Petchesky demonstrated that pregnant women will exhibit any number of a wide array of different responses to seeing sonograms of their fetuses, depending upon social differences such as race, class and sexual preference as well as biological factors such as age, physical condition and family fertility history. They might instantly bond with the image as making the fetus "more our baby"; they might resist the "moral abstraction that they are being made to view;" they might welcome such technologies of visualization as part of a high status, high-tech effort that would help them produce 'the perfect baby.'"[27]

Above all, Petchesky argued, to observe pregnant women watching ultrasound scans, and to listen to them describe the fetal images that they saw, makes it impossible to maintain that pregnant women are simply passive victims of reproductive technologies, or that they are easily led by visualizations to relinquish what they understand as their own rights of interpretation. Instead, what comes through is their differences, their social and political positions—exactly the necessary base upon which to build a movement to protect their rights.

Petchesky's now classic analysis of the interpretation of fetal images became the pivot for redirecting feminist attention in the 1990s back toward the pregnant woman. It initiated the remarkably varied writings that, throughout the 1990s, have deconstructed visual images of the fetus in relation to the social construction of the pregnant woman. Books and articles such as Sarah Franklin's "Fetal Fascinations: New Dimensions to the Medical-Scientific Construction of Fetal Personhood" (1991), Carol Stabile's "Shooting the Mother: Fetal Photography and the Politics of Disappearance" (1992), E. Ann Kaplan's "Look Who's Talking Indeed: Fetal Images in Recent North American Visual Culture" (1994), Barbara Duden's *Disembodying Woman: Perspectives on Pregnancy and the Unborn* (1993), Lauren Berlant's "America, 'Fat,' the Fetus" (1994), Susan Squire's *Babies in Bottles: Twentieth Century Visions of Reproductive Technology* (1994), Karen Newman's *Fetal Positions: Individualism, Science,Visuality* (1996), Dion Farquhar's *The Other Machine: Discourse and Reproductive Technologies* (1996), Valerie Hartouni's *Cultural Conceptions: On Reproductive Technologies and the Remaking of Life* (1997), and Lynn Morgan and Meredith Michaels' *Fetal Subjects/Feminist Positions* (1999), all elucidate and defend the rights of the pregnant subject. Images of maternity once more are central to these analyses because of what they obscure rather than what they reveal.

PREGNANT SEXUALITY

This new deliberate gaze at pregnant women is complicated in many ways by the sexual associations of pregnancy. The pregnant belly customarily invokes heterosexual intercourse, whether or not such activity has actually occurred. But pregnancy also invokes female sexuality more broadly. Even though, as feminist philosopher Luce Irigiray has pointed out, female sexuality is usually figured as hidden and internal, pregnancy is a time when its existence becomes evident, and nearly impossible to conceal.[28]

However, the sexual implications of the pregnant figure are far more extensive than even its evocation of heterosexual intercourse. Reproduction itself is a sexual function, and childbearing is an aspect of female sexuality that is both powerful in itself and different from the male norm. While experiences of childbearing are diverse, pregnancy can have a significant erotic dimension for both men and women. As Susie Bright recalls in *Susie Bright's Sexual Reality: A Virtual Sex World Reader*, when she was pregnant she "began to wonder if anyone knew what went on in women's sexual lives during pregnancy. The most definite statement the books managed was: Sometimes she's hot, sometimes she's not. This wouldn't be the first time that traditional medicine had nothing to contribute to an understanding of female sexuality. . . . Your average Mary's physical transformation is quite different from an immaculate conception."[29] Pregnant sexuality is one of those secrets that are hidden in plain sight.

Then, although it is distinctively female, what is going on within the pregnant body defies conventional understandings of gender as well as sex. Contained within a pregnant woman's body are both the male-gendered sperm and the female-gendered ovum, as well as an embryo or embryos of either or both sexes. The pregnant woman's female body is a body that "holds" or "transmits" an ambiguous gender, incorporating these male and female elements. Pregnancy is in this sense a liminal state, confusing customary social boundaries. In part because of this "gender trouble," to use Judith Butler's critical term, images of the pregnant woman invoke a heterogeneous, multiplied sense of personhood that does not fit the usual understanding of a single-sexed subject.

Difficulties in representing pregnant women also reflect the fact that Western cultures have traditionally tried to separate the maternal from the sexual in women's roles, and in women's lives. As Susie Bright declares, it is an "awesome feat of American puritanism to convince us that sex and pregnancy do not mix. It's the ultimate virgin/whore distinction. For those nine months, please don't mention how we got this way. We're Mary now."[30] This drive to fragment female sexuality is so pervasive and deeply rooted that it seems natural.

But in an essay entitled "Breasted Experience: The Look and the Feeling," political philosopher Iris Marion Young makes a number of useful observations about how this split serves the interests of a patriarchal order. "Patriarchy," writes Young,

is founded on the border between motherhood and sexuality. Woman is both, essentially—the repository of the body, the flesh that he desires, owns and masters, tames and controls; and the nurturing source of his life and ego. Both are necessary functions, bolstering the male ego, which cannot be served if they are together, hence the border, their reification into the hierarchical opposition of good/bad, pure/impure.[31]

Young argues that separating the functions of motherhood from those of sexual availability maintains male power over both: "The separation often splits mothers; it is in our bodies that the sacrifice that creates and sustains patriarchy is reenacted repeatedly. Freedom for women involves dissolving this separation."[32] But clearly this separation is continually reproduced. We can see this happening, she writes, in the way that our culture fetishizes images of breasts, and detaches their "look" from the experience of having a body that has breasts.

In another essay, "Pregnant Embodiment: Subjectivity and Alienation," Young also points out that the pregnant body does not correspond to most currently accepted theories of "the body." Being a "container" as well as "herself," the pregnant woman "reveals a paradigm of bodily experience in which the transparent unity of self dissolves and the body attends positively to itself at the same time that it enacts its projects."[33] But far from Kristeva's pregnant woman who cannot "know," Young's account of pregnancy describes a physical, sexual, social knowingness that stretches the boundaries not only of a woman's body but of our social thought about possessive individualism, about the deceptively "natural" seeming unity of the body in general, and about female sexuality. The split subject of pregnancy challenges patriarchal paradigms for male consumption of female sexuality by means of the gaze.

Pregnant subjectivity, then, overturns the conventions upon which the patriarchal representation of women rests. The pregnant woman inhabits a body that both is and is not "hers." Her sense of self does not fit the usual understanding of a speaking subject. She can emit a magnified aura of eroticism along with increased narcissistic pleasure in her own body. Because of this deviant "fluidity," as Luce Irigiray terms it, while the sexuality of pregnancy does not generally go unnoticed, its specific characteristics often go unexpressed.

REPRODUCTIVE POLITICS

The relative absence of images of pregnant women in the public canons of U.S. photography is not solely a function of conflict over the difficulty of representing female sexuality, however, since it is counterbalanced by the overwhelming numbers of images of other kinds of women's bodies, highly sexualized and available for voyeuristic consumption. It has more to do with the difficulty of positioning pregnancy itself. One could say that pregnant women are spared this ongoing objectification, and that being kept out of images enables them to experience pregnancy as a more private event. Many a pregnant woman already feels enough like a spectacle and would just as soon not be further featured in the feminine visual position of to-be-looked-at-ness.

But as feminism has taught us, the personal is political, and pregnancy is not simply a private event. The development in the 1960s of highly effective (although sometimes hazardous) methods of birth control suitable for mass utilization, and the spectacular growth in medical research over the past decades in fields such as reproductive technologies, fetal surgery and genetics has resulted in a previously unimaginable degree of medical management of reproduction. Where once prenatal care was the responsibility of midwives and general practitioners, it is now often in the hands of several increasingly differentiated medical subspecialists, who are in turn supervised by giant corporate insurance programs and supplied by multinational corporations that produce and sell biomedical materials, drugs and equipment. Private industries that profit from fertility management have also arisen.

In addition, intense public debate about new reproductive practices, maternal health, maternity leave and child-care provisions, teenage pregnancies, gay and lesbian and single parent families, forced sterilization, birth control technology and access, the care of babies born with AIDS or drug addiction, surrogate parenting, legislation governing child custody cases in which the determination of parenthood is abstract, and the ethics of abortion have all made pregnancy highly visible and contentious as a public policy issue.

These changes in the social practices of reproduction have not, however, frequently entered into the photographic repertoire with anything like the wide range of social relations that they actually involve. Absence here serves a variety of political and economic agendas. We have seen cheering images of Louise Brown, the first "test tube baby," but the more ambiguous physical aspects of such a modern pregnancy—for instance, frightening medical procedures—are seldom pictured. States of fatigue, stress, conflict, isolation, poverty, disease and alcohol and chemical toxicity, all of which can and do accompany contemporary experiences of pregnancy, are rarely represented visually in the public space. Although more than half the people now employed in the United States are women, and childbearing women of all classes increasingly elect to stay on the job throughout their pregnancies, we virtually never see photographs of pregnant women actually at work outside the home.

Furthermore, science is making the formerly fantastical figure of the cyborg, to use Donna Haraway's term, an actuality.[34] As Judith Halberstam and Ira Livingston explain, the recombinant possibilities of sex and gender that have been opened up by assisted reproduction and cloning have truly put us into the era of "posthuman bodies." Egg harvesting, for instance, is now fully included in these new processes of "extension, attenuation, miniaturization, and crosswired interdependence of the networks that implicate the body."[35] But a new ethics to match the potential of entirely new possibilities for use and control of human fertility is seldom explored in public representations.

The lack of a widely available, fully expressive repertoire of photographic images of pregnancy thus accompanies and supports a troublesome silence on topics that carry vital implications for both individual women and for society at large. Shielding pregnant women's bodies from view can conceal attempts to control women's role in human reproduction as the science of pregnancy progresses. But the way those visual images of individual pregnant women do appear also often serves as a screen or foil for changes in social policies and punitive cultural attitudes toward women's bodies and lives. The pregnant woman as an individual needs to look at representations of her state in order to better "see" herself; but images of pregnancy also reveal the state of society in general.

"Images by themselves lack 'objective' meanings," Petchesky wrote in the conclusion to "Foetal Images." Meanings come from the "interlocking fields of context, communication, application and reception." She continues,

> Can feminism reconstruct a joyful sense of childbearing and maternity without capitulating to ideologies that reduce women to a maternal essence? Can we talk about morality in reproductive decision-making without invoking the spectre of maternal duty? On some level, the struggle to demystify foetal images is fraught with danger, since it involves re-embodying the foetus, thus representing women as (wanting-to-be or not-wanting-to-be) pregnant persons. One way out of this danger is to image the pregnant woman, not as an abstraction, but within her total framework of relationships, economic and health needs and desires.[36]

For many, including ourselves, pregnant pictures hold the promise of this way out.

2) THE LABORS OF ART

There is probably no subject that cannot be beautified;
moreover, there is no way to suppress the tendency inherent
in all photographs to accord value to their subjects.

—Susan Sontag

The photo of the pregnant belly comes close to being
repulsive.

—Roi Partridge to Imogen Cunningham, September 1, 1964

MODERNIST PREGNANCY

Representations of pregnant women—painted, drawn, carved and molded—
have long existed. Art photographs of pregnancy, however, did not appear until
the early twentieth century when the advent of photographic modernism ush-
ered in an aesthetic climate that began to make them thinkable. Their numbers
remained very limited, however, and the scope of their appeal small until the last
quarter of the century.

Photographic modernism emerged at a time when faith in widespread, technologically assisted cultural development made it increasingly acceptable to
think of photography as art. Modernism in photography was premised in part
on the idea that an exalted subject was no longer essential for a photograph of it
to be a work of art; photographic art could be made from anything by virtue of
the individual photographer's strength of vision. As Susan Sontag has noted,
"The most enduring triumph of photography has been its aptitude for discovering beauty in the humble, the inane, the decrepit. At the very least, the real has a
pathos. And that pathos is—beauty."[1] Alfred Stieglitz's concept of "equivalence"
and Cartier-Bresson's term "decisive moment"—two theoretical models that
gained particular credence within the range of modernist practice—both
assume that profound visual statements can emerge from the most ordinary or
unexpected subject matter.

The case of pregnancy shows, however, that modernist art photographs were
not easily made from any subject matter, and that form does not, in fact, function
this independently of content. Initially hailed as an instrument for democratiza-

Manuel Alvarez Bravo, "Maternidad," 1948

tion, photography, it turns out, represents and reinforces the shifting social order through its practitioners' choice of subjects from which to make art as well as their methods of representation. The content of a modernist art photograph must be culturally acceptable for the image to be seen as art.

An amusing study conducted by French sociologist Pierre Bourdieu suggests how fully cultural notions of taste, concealed in a universalizing discourse about "art," supported the avoidance of a modernist gaze at pregnancy.[2] Bourdieu set out in 1963 to discover how the socially constructed norms of middle-class taste worked to support modernist photography's claim to the status of fine art. Among the questions Bourdieu asked a group of 692 subjects in Paris and Lille was what they thought of the idea of a photograph of a pregnant woman. The example he used was a discreet image by Manuel Alvarez Bravo, the artistic status of which had been assured by its inclusion in Edward Steichen's 1955 *Family of Man* exhibition at the Museum of Modern Art. The great majority of Bourdieu's respondents judged that an image of a pregnant woman could not be beautiful either as an abstract idea or in Bravo's actual photograph.

Moreover, they felt that it would be extremely undesirable to hang such an object on the living room wall and call it "art." They counted photographs of "a woman breast-feeding," "a folkdance," "a weaver at work," "a still life," "a first communion," "a snake," "a rope" and "a metal frame" all more desirable to look at than the pregnant woman. The appeal of Alvarez Bravo's photograph of the pregnant woman did score higher—though only marginally—than the appeal of "cabbages," "a railway cemetery," "a butcher's stall," "a quarrel between tramps," "a wounded man" and "a car accident."

It was impossible for Bourdieu's respondents to transcend the taboo of the pregnant subject. As one of them said, "A photograph of a pregnant woman is fine as far as I am concerned, but no one else is going to like it." Another wanted to know "Whom would you show it to?" Bourdieu reported that when the subjects of his study were shown the photograph of a pregnant woman, the reaction was almost always the same: "The things they go out looking for! . . . The things they photograph! . . . Taking things like that, for heaven's sake!"[3]

While Bourdieu's study explored the responses of a particular and limited set of French viewers to photographs of pregnancy, his subjects gave rarely articulated expression to a kind of discomfort in viewing photographs of pregnancy that is much more widespread. It took a long time for modernist photography to find ways to negotiate this cultural taboo and to include pregnancy within the boundaries of what viewers would deem acceptable or even desirable subject matter for art.

THE SCOPIC STANCE

Art photographs in the modernist tradition are made and viewed within what can be called a *scopic framework*. This term refers to an entire system of relationships between representation and viewing that privileges optical over other kinds of experience while at the same time infusing the optical with ideology. Photographs that use a scopic framework—primarily those that circulate in the dominant modalities of art, journalism and advertising—employ stances for viewing that are closely aligned with power relations in the society.

Scopic photographs offer their viewers a pleasurable sense of visual mastery in relation to the subject matter depicted in the photograph. They establish the sense of a privileged position, a ringside seat that provides the feeling of acquiring knowledge from a position of safety. Most often in a scopic system, viewers with a relatively established social status contemplate images of those in more turbulent circumstances, conveniently contained within the boundaries of the photographic frame.

This sense of visual mastery can both reinforce and undermine the actual social positions of photographer, subject and viewer. By establishing a normative distance for viewing, the scopic relation draws the viewer into a voyeuristic position vis-à-vis the scene in the photographic frame, which may in the case of pregnancy be especially awkward. Susan Sontag invokes the powerful shifts scopic viewing sets up by highlighting the fact that it rearranges social relationships. "Like a pair of binoculars with no right or wrong end," she writes, "the camera makes exotic things near, intimate; and familiar things small, abstract, strange, much farther away."[4] Pregnant women, being both exotic and familiar, strange and intimate, may be particularly difficult subjects for the modernist binoculars to fix in focus.

Scopophilia

The term "scopic" also refers to *scopophilia*, or pleasure in looking. This pleasure is understood to have an erotic dimension. But where is the visual pleasure in a pregnant picture? Feminist film theory provides a framework that is helpful for analyzing the erotics of the gaze in modernist photography. Laura Mulvey's well-known essay "Visual Pleasure and Narrative Cinema" (1973) lays out a gendered model of the viewer's gaze, in which the position of viewer—open in different ways both to male and female viewers—is understood to be a masculine position.[5] That is, when images of women are offered to viewers of classical Hollywood cinema, they are designed to give pleasure in relation to the viewer's ability to appropriate them voyeuristically. Presumably this erotic, voyeuristic component of the filmic gaze would operate for photographs of pregnant women as well.

In the years since Mulvey's formative ideas were first explored, the model has become less strictly gendered and more sexually complex. Yet problems in extending the visual pleasures of the masculine scopic gaze to photographs of pregnant women are not solved by deconstructing gender. The notion that erotic, voyeuristic possession is a key mechanism for showing and viewing photographs of women within a scopic visual economy remains fundamental. But it is difficult to structure the pleasure of viewing around voyeuristic erotic appropriation in this instance. While the sexualized imaging of women is well developed in the scopic economy, and provides an emblematic example of its working structures, pregnant women as photographic subjects seem to block the scopic gaze.

Maternal sexuality, embodied by the pregnant woman, does not lend itself easily to appropriation. Instead, a vigorous patriarchal mandate keeps maternity and sexuality separate. There is, as Bourdieu demonstrated, a deep discomfort with applying the gaze, with its implied voyeuristic eroticism, to the figure of the pregnant woman.

During the 1960s, painter Alice Neel made an intensely original series of paintings of pregnant women in which she explored what it means to represent the pregnant body visually. Art historian Pamela Allara argues that Neel's work on pregnant women constitutes a rare analysis of the ways in which maternal sexuality interferes with the viewer's gaze at the pregnant figure. For Allara, Neel's 1964 painting "Pregnant Maria" especially illuminates Neel's discovery that:

> No fantasies of possession are possible when her very condition indicates a prior claim to this property. Because her sexual history is inscribed on her body, the male gaze cannot penetrate her. Maria presents her body to be surveyed, but with the erotic gaze blocked, *her* gaze and its desire dominate.[6]

Allara here postulates that the pregnant body in Neel's painting actually produces a reversal of the gaze, accomplished by blocking and deflecting its path. Maria's pregnant belly implies an already-spoken-for sexuality that underlines the contradiction of using a maternal figure to provide the public with the voyeuristic mastery of erotic viewing. At the same time, the pregnant Maria's gaze—its own active desiring impossible to ignore—looks back and dominates.

Scopophobia

Photographer Gerard Malanga's 1985 image "Esther, 7 months," along with
the text that he wrote to accompany it, suggests that this role reversal may be a
powerful factor in pregnancy's upsetting of art photography's scopic stance. Far
from being able to look at anything and make it into art, the photographer who
seeks heroic visual mastery over the pregnant woman may experience great
difficulty in securing the necessary sense of erotic conquest. Of "Esther, 7
months," Malanga writes,

> In all the instances the young girls who've been to my studio never consid-
> ered the situation of being photographed nude, so when Esther revealed
> her pregnancy before the photo-session began, there was no way that I
> could seduce her, as previous with other models, into undressing through
> the continuity of photographing her. I was no longer the challenger but
> the one being challenged. The roles were reversed. I became the subject of
> her gaze. She became the voyeur of my participation with her.[7]

Malanga's statement reveals a concept of the photographer's "gaze" as a mode
of seeing closely linked to sexual possession: "seduction" ambiguously connotes
both actual and voyeuristic sexual engagement. But Malanga also sees the pregnant woman as both untouchable and unmanageable within this framework. By
virtue of declaring herself pregnant, Esther is no longer a "young girl" but has
entered a completely different sexual category.

Malanga responds photographically by overlaying his pregnant subject with
the rectangular shape of a window, complete with the horizontal bars of venet-
ian blinds. The window shape is precisely layered over the reproductive area of
her body, slicing off the most pregnant part of her belly. This imposition of
Cartesian rationality serves as an attempt to bring the unruly and challenging
pregnant body into line. The imposed rectangle of light bears the form of a window, but it is a window that is not transparent. Even as someone deeply involved
with the erotics of the gaze, Malanga evidently found himself unable to master
the pregnant subject.

MODERNIST VENUES

There have been at least four important efforts to include photographs of pregnant women within the modernist art canon. First, in the 1930s, photographers
affiliated with the Farm Security Administration (FSA), such as Marion Post Wolcott and Russell Lee, deliberately included pregnant women in their documen-

Gerard Malanga, "Esther, 7 Months," 1985

Tina Modotti, "Mother
and Child: Tehuantepec,
Oaxaca, Mexico," c.1929

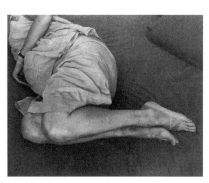

Dorothea Lange,
"Winter, California,"
1955

tary images of rural families. Their purpose was to show the subjects as members of ordinary American families—neither defective nor degenerate—and thereby to increase the public's willingness to support the social service programs of the Roosevelt government. "We want to show them that you're a human being, a nice human being, but you're having troubles," Russell Lee explained in 1937 to a Minnesota woman whom he wished to photograph.[8] Within this mode of documentary practice, modernist photographs of pregnant women gained a social context that made them acceptable to gaze at.

Second, there is work by individual artists responding to the political and aesthetic issues of the time. While Tina Modotti made photographs of pregnant women in Mexico as early as the 1920s, a number of U.S. artists began openly to make and publish occasional photographs of pregnant women in the 1940s. This isolated work, much of it complex interpretations of pregnancy, includes images by pioneering women photographers such as Barbara Morgan, Imogen Cunningham, and Dorothea Lange, as well as by men such as Harry Callahan. Largely unheralded at the time, these were in fact landmark photographs, for they were the first successfully to include pregnancy in the modernist's scopic contemplation of women's bodies.

Edward Steichen's widely traveled 1955 exhibition *The Family of Man*, together with its ensuing book, provided a third, institutional, context in which art photographs of pregnancy could be gathered together for the first time.[9] Steichen formed the largest such collection ever seen by the general public. Despite its

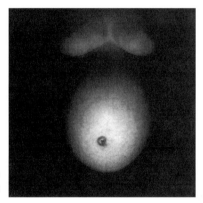

Harry Callahan, "Eleanor," 1949

Hideo Haga, "A Pregnant Japanese Woman Hurrying on Her Way," 1952

universalizing framework, the photographs Steichen selected for his exhibition went beyond idealization and romanticization to picture a surprising range of experiences. One notable photograph by Japanese photographer Hideo Haga, for instance, shows a pregnant woman hurrying amid the crush of urban pedestrians. This image is an extremely rare example of pregnancy depicted in a public, active, setting. However, the photographs in *The Family of Man* remained ghettoized within Steichen's concept of picturing the human life cycle. Later projects that operated within a similar framework, such as *The Family of Woman*, published in 1979, continued to provide a setting for the publication of photographs of pregnancy that otherwise would not have found a public venue.[10] But they also continued to ghettoize the images.

A fourth effort to open modernist art photography to the representation of pregnancy began in the late 1960s and early 1970s in conjunction with the second wave of the women's movement. Women (mostly) artists began to produce a significant quantity of personal work dealing with pregnancy, including self-portraiture and extended series' of portraits of pregnant women. In the late 1980s and 1990s the content of some of this work became overtly political. Only a few

Helen Levitt, "New York," c.1942

of these works have been exhibited or published previous to their appearance in this book.

PREGNANCY AND SOCIAL CLASS

All four of these attempts to represent pregnancy within photographic modernism differentiate their visual treatment of pregnant women according to social class. When a pregnancy is understood to be taking place within a marriage and in an economically self-sufficient family, the pregnant woman is carefully depicted as protected, isolated, static and idealized. When a pregnancy is not socially sanctioned in these ways, the photographs place the woman within telling life circumstances, offering a social narrative.

As a result, middle-class pregnant women are most often pictured alone, apart from their larger material and social contexts, usually in a private domestic interior or a secluded setting. Low-income pregnant women are most often portrayed as public spectacles whose domestic arrangements can be fully exposed. While middle-class women almost always assume poses that deliberately display the form of their bodies without revealing personal history, photographs of poor women often render their personal space more vulnerable. They are very rarely represented as withdrawn in private reverie, but instead are almost always pictured with other people in a social, often public, space, such as the street. Placed among others, poor pregnant women can be visually connected to social problems.

Photographs of economically disadvantaged women are also more apt to allow some of the more difficult physical aspects of pregnancy to enter the picture. Class is the basis for a critical dividing line, with strictly idealized, isolated pregnancy on the side of the middle class, and on the other side, pregnancy represented as a multifaceted experience with potential negative consequences for women from lower-income groups.

Helen Levitt's 1942 photograph of two young women on a New York City sidewalk is a good example of this convention. It is a formally complex photograph in which the young woman who is pregnant is only one part of a wider social situation. In this photograph one woman is visibly pregnant while the other carries two bottles of milk. The image portrays the pregnancy as at least in part an uncomfortable burden. The pregnant woman appears to be looking enviously on as the other, a slender figure, walks by on her errand, which will allow her, eventually, to put down the milk. The pregnant woman does not look pampered or sheltered or particularly joyous. Instead she is awkward and distracted, a figure who must make her heavy way along the public street. Levitt's image suggests the weight of growing up female and becoming a mother without the benefit of privilege or privacy. Another Levitt image shows the figure of a preg-

Helen Levitt, "New York," c.1939

nant woman as drawn by children in chalk on a brick wall. In becoming a piece of graffiti, the pregnant woman merges entirely with the streetscape. Her figure is transparent, her inside fully exposed to public view.

Middle-Class Patterns

While photographs of pregnant women who are economically disadvantaged make repetitive use of the visual strategies developed in the documentary traditions of environmental portraiture, photographs of middle-class pregnant women—which form the vast majority of art photographs of pregnancy—also exhibit recurring visual themes that bear examination. Portrayed as outside any specific social relations, the middle-class subjects represent a general, idealized concept of pregnancy rather than an individual's specific experience. In the images of these women, pregnancy is celebrated as a private universe of personal fulfillment, premised on the luxury of withdrawal from everyday concerns. Yet these seemingly universal images are in fact specifically grounded in a class-based ideal of pregnancy, that of secure, joyous domesticity.

In one carefully posed picture after another a great effort is made to represent externally through visual metaphor, rather than literally as in the chalk graffito, the inner workings of the pregnant body. This metaphoric referencing of internal events takes several forms. The woman may appear to occupy a womblike space, which can be indicated by an oval-shaped frame, by the presence of water, or by a dark, formless background. Bob Saltzman's sensuous photograph of two pregnant women floating in water, for example, places its subjects in the visual equivalent of a womb-space. With this interpretation, pregnancy is acknowledged symbolically as a rite of passage. The pregnant women pictured in a womb-space act as stand-ins for the babies within them. They also stage their

Bob Saltzman, untitled, n.d.

Tammy Cromer-
Campbell, "Breech,"
1993

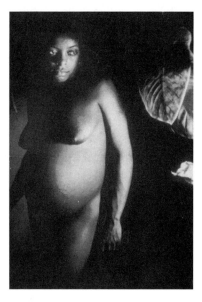

Shawn Walker, untitled, n.d.

Paul Himmel, from *The Family of Man*, 1955

own invisible social gestation period—the one they undergo before being reborn as a mother. Another example is Tammy Cromer-Campbell's studio photograph "Breech," which pictures a pregnant woman enacting a difficult, entangled delivery of herself.

In addition, the middle-class pregnant woman often sits or stands next to a window, gazing out as if lost in thought. The window, for which a doorway is sometimes substituted, suggests a threshold or boundary between inside and outside, known and unknown, the private domestic space that surrounds the woman and the world outside. Here again, the protected private space around the woman takes on the qualities of a womb; it is a sheltered surrounding with a point of entry / exit leading to the larger, more public world outside. In these pictures not only may the boundaries be ambiguous within the woman's body, as between woman and fetus, but also between the woman and the world around her. It is usually presumed that her worldly withdrawal is desirable, but Shawn Walker's photograph gives the theme an interesting twist by articulating the shadowy space of the room in a way that seems as threatening as it does protective.

Often the middle-class pregnant woman is represented as childlike, vulnerable, lost in a dream world, such as in Paul Himmel's archetypal 1955 photograph which was published in *The Family of Man*. Though not inhabiting a womb-space, the pregnant woman enacts a reflective inner state, covering up her adult sexuality and standing in for the innocent life within her.

The middle-class pregnant woman, generally pictured as a solitary person, is not infrequently accompanied by potted plants and domestic animals, as in Elliott Erwitt's image, which is an excellent example of this convention. Such references to domesticated nature may be read as attempts to contain the powerful natural forces, not always benign, actually involved in pregnancy.

The strict stylization and striking absence of negative implications in the middle-class repertoire indicate deliberate avoidance of potentially uncomfortable and frightening aspects of pregnancy. Images that convey apprehension are highly unusual. Although pregnancy is often accompanied by physical discomfort, this is seldom alluded to in photographs of middle-class women. Rather, they make repeated attempts to suppress the difficult, contain the unmanageable, and represent the invisible in symbols.

Elliot Erwitt, from *The Family of Man,* 1955

Imogen Cunningham, "Behind the Screen," 1957

Some Exceptions

Most photographs that employ these middle-class themes carefully avoid challenging their narrow concepts of pregnancy, but there are some important exceptions. Imogen Cunningham's photograph entitled "Behind the Screen" (1959) provides a substantial further exploration of the position constructed for the middle-class pregnant subject. It particularly explores her relation to concepts of nature and culture. Placed outdoors in a safe, sunlit wooded area, the folding screen behind which the nude pregnant woman stands can be seen as symbolizing geometrical order and rationality. The woman is placed against the far edge, where the rectangular frame of the screen is all that separates her from the dark, formless void of the forest. The woman stands half in light, half in shadow. The rectilinear frame of the screen acts as a defining element, pulling the pregnant figure just barely into the realm of culture; while keeping her isolated, visually in a box that divides her exactly at the point of her genitals. The material of the screen, stretched on the frame, puts the figure at a distance; we see her through a veil, a cultural overlay that renders her body hazy. Cunningham's photograph uses the lyrical, romantic mode of picturing middle-class pregnancy, while also commenting astutely on the marginal, isolated, liminal social place of the middle-class pregnant woman.

Arthur Rothstein in "Sharecropper's Wife" (1935) and Barbara Morgan in "Pregnant" (1943) also both appear to follow class-based rules for picturing pregnancy. However, Rothstein's dramatic, low-angled photograph of a rural pregnant woman and young child invites comparison with Morgan's equally dramatic image of a woman's pregnant nude torso, precisely because, taken together, the abstract nude torso and the social document allow us to perceive the politics behind these formal conventions.

Rothstein's image has appeared in a number of histories of the '30s. Critics have tagged it as an instance of "documentary photography" and evaluated it as a more or less successful expository effort to draw attention to the general conditions of rural poverty during the Great Depression. It needs, however, also to be seen as a particular way of depicting pregnancy within an overarching discourse about reproduction.

Morgan's arresting, primal pregnant nude, on the other hand, has been designated as "art" in a more self-consciously aesthetic sense, and it foreshadows her later work with formal strategies for photographing the bodily expressions of the Martha Graham dancers. It has not been seen as a specific way of depicting an ideology of reproduction, either. Although a pregnant woman is its obvious subject, her body seems to hold chiefly a formal interest for the photographer. No historical narrative about reproduction has been connected with the way that Morgan made the image.

In fact, Rothstein's manner of shooting has a great deal to do with the politics of formalism as well as welfare. The low, oblique shot that, in this image, segments the pregnant body and places the belly at the center of attention, was one that many documentary photographers favored during the '30s. It is known as the "heroic angle" because it positions viewers so that they must look up at the subject. Rothstein's famous "steer skull" photographs, his "Plow that Broke the Plains," and many of his photographs of farmers and farm machinery also attempt to lend an additional dynamism to a plain tale by telling it from this unexpected angle. But in "Sharecropper's Wife" the effects of such a shot are calculated for a different aim. The angle lends an abstraction to the image that subtly objectifies the woman, whose body is oddly unbalanced by the point of view. In her apparent discomfort, the photograph represents her as a responsible member of the "deserving poor."

The need to defuse the American public's widespread anger toward, fear of, and disdain for the fertility of the poor runs deep in many FSA photographs. As a propaganda arm of the Roosevelt government, the FSA mission was to help put its social programs in place and assure taxpayer compliance. The FSA could not afford to suggest that the poor were thoughtlessly reproducing themselves on public welfare. Concern about how many of the woman's children would appear in her photograph prompted Dorothea Lange to alter the composition of "Migrant Mother" to show fewer children. Rothstein's photograph as well originally had at least one additional child at the left side of the frame before it was cropped. "Teach the underprivileged to have fewer children and less misery," snapped one visitor to the FSA exhibit at The International Photographic Salon, mounted at New York's Grand Central Palace in 1938.[11] So the defamiliarizing angle of Rothstein's "Sharecropper's Wife" makes the woman's poverty rather than her pregnancy appear to be the problem. If a poor woman were going to be pictured pregnant during the Depression, it was best to make her look noble but anxious.

Barbara Morgan, on the other hand, made her image as a middle-class woman artist working in the pronatalist late 1940s. She was not working for the government, and there is no indication that the pregnancy that is pictured is a social problem. It seems instead that the near-term pregnancy she depicts is the straightforward, unproblematic fulfillment of a natural drive. The white middle-class woman who possessed that drive was the contemporary equivalent of a fertility goddess. Simply by gestating, she was doing her job. In Morgan's photograph, all is balance and symmetry. The formal choices Morgan makes—setting her subject alone into the frame and placing her against a darkened background—indicate that the pregnant woman need be concerned only with her own ripe body and the protection it affords the pleasantly burgeoning life within.

But this in fact was not, just as Rothstein's was not, only a personal perspective on a private condition. After the war, when Morgan made this photograph, it was widely held to be in the national interest to encourage such women to produce babies, just as it was said to be in the national interest during the Depression to discourage the poor from "breeding." Morgan's overtly "artistic" representa-

Arthur Rothstein, "Sharecropper's Wife, Arkansas," 1935

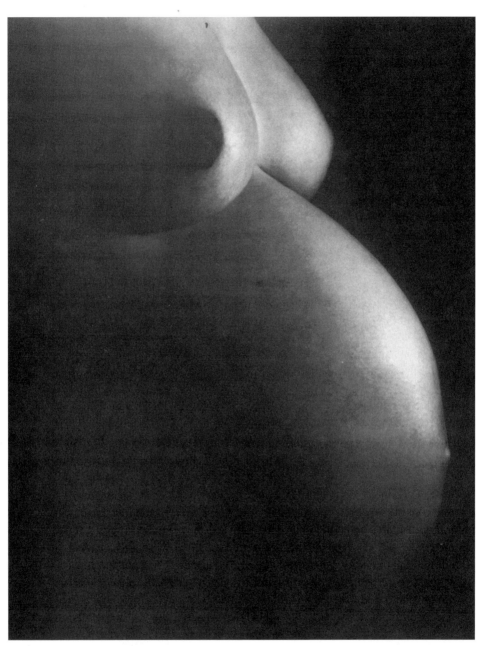

Barbara Morgan, "Pregnant," 1942

tion of a pregnant woman, like Rothstein's "documentary" representation, is complicit with the constructions of gender and class that are hidden within the modernist view of pregnancy.

Outside the United States

It is only beyond the borders of the United States that the relation of modernism to class in the depiction of pregnancy has been explicitly portrayed. Neither Arthur Rothstein, working for the Roosevelt administration, nor Barbara Morgan, working as an individual artist, produced as far-reaching an analysis of the social formations of pregnancy as did the German artist John Heartfield, working as part of the resistance against the rise of fascism in Europe during roughly the same period. Comparison of their work with Heartfield's exposes the ideological limits of photographic modernism in the United States in relation to the politics of the family. Privatized notions of reproduction, reflected in Morgan's vision, and the liberal solution of distributing governmental loans to displaced families, supported by Rothstein, do not directly address the fundamental connections among nationalism, capitalism, pronatalism and militarization that defined modernity for European radicals in the 1930s and 1940s. American photographers' avoidance of these relationships is striking, even though, as Heartfield demonstrates, the necessary evidence does not lie far below the surface.

In Heartfield's 1930 photomontage, published in the German communist journal *AIZ*, a disheveled and uncomfortable working-class mother wears an ill-fitting dress and an anxious expression as she sits squarely and heavily facing the camera. Unlike the "Sharecropper's Wife," however, this pregnant woman keeps no child by her side. Instead, Heartfield has pasted an image of the body of a dead German soldier behind her head, rendering the conceptual space between the two figures temporally indeterminate and sinister, like a nightmare. The torso of the Heartfield pregnant woman, although fully clothed, is the same primordial, ripe figuration of pregnancy as Barbara Morgan's photograph. But the photomontage emphasizes the social relationships rather than the biological drives responsible for her state.

Heartfield's caption, printed along the lower edge of the image, translates as: "You mothers, let your children live." His original photomontage bore a longer, more pointed caption, which was lost in publication. It read, "Those who are forced to deliver human material, take heart! The state needs the unemployed and soldiers!"[12] The plea refers ironically to the gender politics of the fascist movement, which explicitly encouraged German women to stay at home and bear children to swell the ranks of the Aryan race and, of course, eventually to

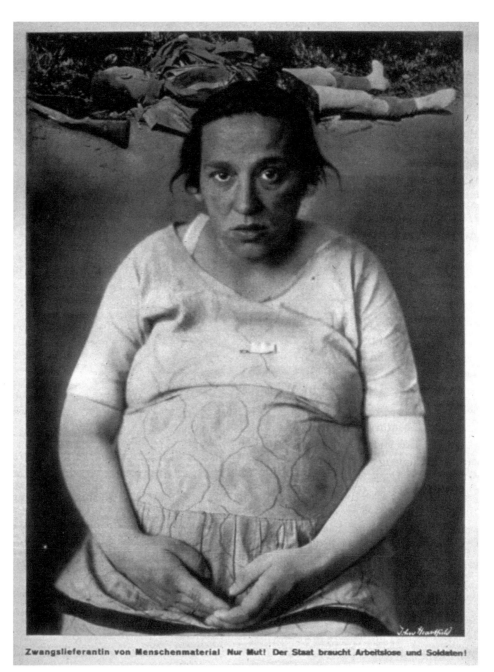

Zwangslieferantin von Menschenmaterial Nur Mut! Der Staat braucht Arbeitslose und Soldaten!

John Heartfield, photomontage, 1930

serve as cannon fodder in the German army. The young soldier lying dead behind the pregnant woman was some woman's child.

Both captions also refer, without irony, to the class-based antiwar agitation of the German Communist Party with which Heartfield was at this point allied. Heartfield's image seeks to expose the brutal and violent exploitation of "family values" by militarist interests. In Heartfield's image the contradictions of the pregnant subject are no longer shown as purely psychological, or contained within a private, marginalized family drama, but are placed at the center of communal political life.

MODERNIST ART PHOTOGRAPHS AND SEXUALITY

Modernist art photographs in the United States work hard to suppress consciousness of the ways in which the social realm defines and delimits motherhood. But at times they also do manage to elucidate aspects of the sexuality of the pregnant woman, still considered challenging and unmanageable in our culture. Beginning in the 1960s, a small number of artists began to make images that succeed in containing references to both motherhood and sexuality. They accomplish this by presenting but strictly separating the two within each image. That is, in each of these photographs of pregnant women the artist struggles to keep maternity and sexuality visually distinct. It is this separation that allows the artist to be able to represent both together.

Ruth Bernhard's "Seed" (1971), a formal portrait of a seated pregnant woman, alludes directly to the sexuality of the pregnant woman. Harkening back to the nineteenth-century's formal photographic portraits, it portrays the woman as Madonna-like, and places her within an egg-shaped, womb-like oval frame. The woman's flowing clothing accentuates her enlarged breasts, her belly and the division between her legs, while at the same time it suggests her modesty. This modesty is characteristic of many art photographs of pregnant women, that seek to emphasize the contours of the body while desexualizing them.

Nevertheless, the viewer is drawn to the small rectangular box of earth with a large avocado seed planted in it. The woman holds this object, which refers to the shape of the labia, in her lap positioned over her genitals. A single sprout has split the seed into two halves and now grows straight up in front of the woman's belly. The seed and sprout carry multiple associations to both male and female genitalia. The way the woman encloses the box with her hands and presses it to her body raises the possibility of self-insemination. Thus we have an image of the complicated, multiply gendered and simultaneously self-contained sexuality of a pregnant woman. The box is a frame within a frame, an external representation on several levels of what is going on inside the woman's draped body. The

Ruth Bernhard, "Seed," 1971

sexual content of the Bernhard photograph serves as a subtext within the overall frame of the pregnant woman as Madonna. Since its explicit sexual allusions make this subtext too threatening to function as an overt commentary, it is tightly confined within the image of the rectangular box.

Whereas the Bernhard photograph remains within the tradition of idealizing middle-class pregnancy, Jack Welpott's 1968 photograph of a costumed pregnant woman who stands with arms akimbo and looks down on the viewer performs a more overt inversion of representational conventions. Choosing the carnivalesque as his frame of reference, Welpott here refers to female archetypes that are quite different from the Madonna—the burlesque dancer, the circus performer, the evil seductress, and the monstrous mother. He represents the woman as a powerful self-parodying agent who appears to flaunt her pregnancy as an emblem of female sexuality. By virtue of her commanding stance she also seems to dominate the viewer who, as Malanga put is, is "the one being challenged."

But the costume of the woman creates an important visual distinction. Her brassiere and skirt, above and below her swollen midsection, function boldly to dramatize and protect her breasts and genital area. Between these paired articles of clothing protrudes her enormous pregnant belly. It is covered only with a delicate white veil, something more commonly associated with brides and vir-

Jack Welpott, "Anna (1),"
1964

Bob Saltzman,
untitled, 1989

ginity than with pregnancy. In its overt representation of sexual agency in a pregnant woman, this photograph is highly unusual. It portrays her as a fantastic,
possibly malevolent, priestess of reproduction. Yet at the same time, it visually
separates the pregnant belly and veils it, perhaps ironically, with references to sexual purity.

Bob Saltzman's 1989 photograph also conjoins purity, sexuality and power but
in a very different way, using a delicate white rose as an emblem of the flowering
of female sexuality. While the flower is inviting, the woman's monumental figure
and her hand on her belly indicate that she, not the viewer, is possessor of its
fruit. Bruce Davidson's photograph, published in 1970 in his book *East One Hun-
dredth Street*, uses a familiar trope of exoticism on an unfamiliar subject, offering
up the pregnant figure as a passive odalisque, ripe for the male gaze. Perhaps
because the woman is black and pictured in poor, crumbling surroundings, class-
and race-based conventions allow her to be more openly objectified. Unlike in
Malanga's studio, the balance of power tilts in favor of the photographer. The
usual separation of maternity and sexuality is diminished in this image. The customary contradictions fail to reassert themselves. Marion Belanger's photograph
of a black pregnant woman, on the other hand, refuses the very assumptions that
would bring pregnant sexuality to this kind of exposure. Cropped and framed

Bruce Davidson, from
East 100th Street, 1970

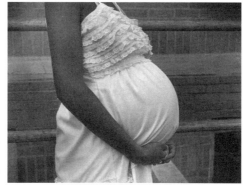

Marion Hoben
Belanger, "Due Date,"
1987

against a gritty urban background, it presents the woman's body as a protected, cherished oasis in the cityscape, although it also renders her anonymous.

Pregnancy Unruled

Art images very occasionally represent frightening and grotesque aspects of pregnancy, or the defilement or degradation of the pregnant body. This work breaks many of the visual taboos that surround the depiction of pregnancy and extends itself beyond the platitudes that would convey the "safety" of middle-class pregnancy and the successful containment and social control of the poor. Photographs such as those by Jack Welpott and Joel-Peter Witkin violate the image of pregnancy for shock value, and reach for powerful subliminal meanings from the threatening side of procreation. The pregnant figure is portrayed in a photograph by Welpott as a victim of vandalism, although the markings overlaid on her body are clearly carried on a window that has been placed in front of her.

Jack Welpott, "Anna (2),"
1964

This image defies most accepted ways of portraying a pregnant woman, and is simultaneously frightening and grimly comic. Joel-Peter Witkin's disconcerting image entitled "ID Photographs from Purgatory: Two Women with Stomach Irritations" is an edgy depiction of a ritual for which the rules and rationale remain unclear. Witkin himself describes this image cryptically as articulating the theme of "our spiritual and physical lostness."[13] Like another of his images, "The Wife of Cain," it links pregnancy with religious concepts of good and evil, referencing the mythic power, the sexuality, and the dread of female embodiment.

MODERNISM TO POSTMODERNISM

Beginning in the 1970s, with the support and encouragement of the feminist art movement, the number of art photographers who chose pregnancy as a subject increased, although the increase in volume of photographs of pregnancy was only partially reflected in public exhibitions and publications. By the 1980s this movement led to a much richer and more diverse representation of pregnant subjectivity, which also began to join the individual concerns with the social frame.

The women's art movement, an outgrowth of the "second wave" of feminism in the United States, was a crucial force enabling this increase in photographs of pregnancy. The feminist claim that the personal is political legitimated and encouraged the use of women's everyday experiences in the making of art, contributing to both the expansion and the breakdown of a modernist formalist aesthetic.

In the 1970s, the social context for producing and consuming art photography, as for the women's art movement in general, was predominantly white and middle class, although race or class were seldom acknowledged as issues. Instead, young photographers who emerged in this period, the first generation trained in the newly established photography programs of colleges and universities, were encouraged to develop an ahistorical "personal vision." In the early '70s, however, pregnancy was still the wrong kind of "personal experience" to photograph. It emerged as a possible theme for personal work only in the late 1970s, coincident with the baby boom among educated professional women. This work was rarely shown in public venues.

The photographs of pregnancy that artists made in this period expand upon and alter the modernist themes we have been discussing. The first major portfolios of photographs of pregnant women, produced by such photographers as Joanne Leonard, Ann Chwatsky, Maggie Hopp, Martha Everson, Carla Shapiro,

Joel-Peter Witkin, "I.D. Photograph from Purgatory: Two Women with Stomach Irritations," New Mexico, 1982

Joel-Peter Witkin, "The Wife of Cain," New Mexico, 1981/1982

Sheila Mclaughlin, S. Schwartzman, Paul B. Goode, Nancy Stuart and Willie Ann Wright appeared this time. In many cases, the impulse to work with pregnancy as a subject came from the artist's own experience and strong feelings or conflicts about childbearing. Drawing on the traditions of environmental and/or staged studio portraiture, these projects invited an extended exploration of the pregnant woman as subject. Combining the middle-class pose of the solitary pregnant woman with the possibilities of setting up a scene, they used the "directorial" mode to articulate the psychological complexities of pregnancy. A number of photographers used environmental and staged idioms to work with pregnant self-portraiture as well.

During the same period a smaller group of photographers expanded the social documentary tradition to represent the diversity of experiences of pregnancy. Ambitious photo-essay projects with an overt social consciousness, by Cathy Cade, Polly Brown and Kira Corser, were important contributions to the fuller representation of the social realities of pregnancy that had not—and still have not —received the kind of public attention they deserve. Both approaches to picturing pregnancy have rich potential.

Second-Wave Strategies of Portrayal

Joanne Leonard's longstanding interest in pregnancy has had a more public profile than most. It is instructive to compare photographs taken from two of her series, one a group of portraits of pregnant women and one a personal set of collages that followed her own experience of miscarriage. While the first image, published in *The Family of Woman* in 1979, enshrines pregnancy as a radiant transformation of the everyday, the later image, entitled "Rupture," provides a visual testimony of physical problems in pregnancy. Leonard's incorporation, through collage, of a disturbing medical illustration of a ruptured uterus departs from the conventional emphasis on positive imaging, which is generally the first phase of

Joanne Leonard,
"Sonia," 1966

Joanne Leonard,
"Rupture," 1973

Jim Klukkert, "Nina and
Zack," 1983

bringing into view any social group whose image has historically been suppressed. Leonard crossed an important boundary with this series, daring to present material common to many women's lives but still seldom addressed openly.

Jim Klukkert crossed a different stylistic boundary in his extensive documentation of the event of pregnancy within his own family. Klukkert used a wide-angle lens and a "shoot from the hip" style more frequently employed in street photography in order to depict pregnancy in the ongoing context of his daily life.

Willie Anne Wright,
"Before Juliana," 1989

Although his photographs do include elements of posing, they also possess a spontaneous dynamism that is synchronous with the often chaotic energy of family life.

Two other series of photographs of pregnancy from the 1980s are of particular formal interest. Willie Anne Wright's staged portraits of pregnant women in sensuously lush settings refer to pregnancy specifically in the way they are made. Wright uses a pinhole camera constructed out of a large box that is about the size of a fully pregnant belly. Because the exposure time is considerable, each photograph undergoes a relatively lengthy "gestation." Her photograph of a pregnant woman in a tent made out of screen mesh picks up the familiar theme of a protected womb-space within the photograph, but in this case it is one through which the figure can still be seen.

The formal structure of S. Schwartzman's remarkable series of stereographs also mimics aspects of pregnancy. Without a special viewer, they appear as a pair of nearly identical images, referring to the doubled being of a pregnant woman who carries a child. Viewed with a stereo viewer, they appear physically three-dimensional, the roundness of the pregnant belly made even more prominent by this technique of observation. One image wittily alludes to several central themes in the middle-class iconography of pregnancy. The woman pictured holds on her lap an oval mirror, reflecting her head upside down at the level of her genitals and making her seem to be giving birth to herself. She is not only apparently being birthed, but she is also observing the passage from within the reflection, with a bemused expression. Pregnancy is pictured here as an endlessly self-referential condition that gives birth to a new consciousness of pregnancy *ad infinitum*. In another Schwartzman image, the subject, pregnant but not yet visi-

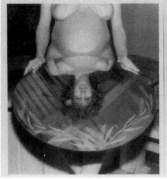

S. Schwartzman, from
the *Pregnancy Series*,
January 22, 1982

S. Schwartzman, "First
Month of Pregnancy,"
from the *Pregnancy
Series*, June 21, 1981

bly so, appears to be pushing against the outer boundaries of her own symbolic
womb, with its entrance / exit far behind her.

SELF-PORTRAITURE AND VISUAL DOUBLING

When Diane Arbus made, in 1945, a lyrical self-portrait in which she regarded her
pregnant figure quizzically in a mirror, her idea was unusual. It was not until
the 1970s that photographers commonly thought of making pregnant self-
portraits. Many of these employ strategies of *visual doubling* to refer to pregnant
self-consciousness. Visual doubling is the placement within the frame of an additional figure as a kind of echo that relates to the subject without exactly mirroring it. There is sufficient visual commonality for the two elements to be connected, and, at the same time, enough difference for them to provide a suggestive
commentary on one another. The differences between the two elements encourage comparison, and the consequent construction of meaning.

A number of portraits and self-portraits succeed in conveying the ambiguities of the pregnant woman's sense of self by using visual doubling quite literally. For instance, Joan Harrison's introspective double self-portrait enacts the subjective sense of having a split identity. In an image that is otherwise based on the conventional middle-class motif of a pregnant woman gazing out a window into the great unknown, Harrison pictures a gaze that is both inward and outward looking.

Nancy Roberts' self-portrait of her pregnant belly, breasts and arms, with a slide of herself as a young child projected onto the center of her belly, is also an obviously constructed image that evokes the ambiguity and confusion of boundaries during pregnancy. Both literally and symbolically, her belly becomes a projection screen, implying the unknowability of its contents except by projected imagination. The image of herself as a child floating in an inner tube in the ocean refers not only to the child within her who floats in oceanic amniotic fluid but also to her own coming into the world. Roberts here evokes the fluidity of boundaries between mother and child, and the difficulty of distinguishing between internal and external. Two images of Roberts, fused into one, represent the continuity of time and life, and the image of Roberts as a child overlays the location of her own as yet invisible child. Two additional works from Roberts'

Joan Harrison,
"Ambivalence, June 2,
1997"

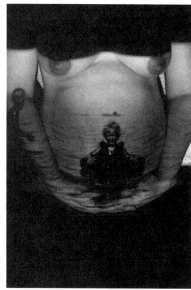

Nancy Roberts,
"Self-Portrait," 1990

Nancy Roberts,
untitled, 1989

Nancy Roberts,
"Naming Sydney," 1993

series explore a pregnant woman's efforts to imagine and relate to what is going
on inside of her through reference to other systems of representation, such as
diagram and text.

Judith Black's studies of herself and her children over an extended time period
include a pregnant self-portrait "Self-portrait (with Laura) May 25, 1968" and a
1997 portrait of her daughter Laura pregnant entitled, "Laura (Father's Day, Her
Birthday Early, Mine Late, 17½ Weeks) (For Lucas who was born too early), June
15, 1997." Both pictures use visual elements to segment the body. In the 1968 pho-

Judith Black, "Self-Portrait (with Laura)," May 25, 1968

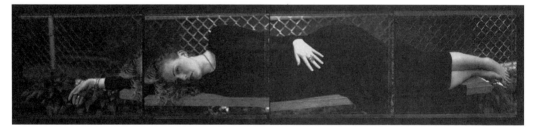

Judith Black, "Laura (Father's Day, Her Birthday Early, Mine Late, 17 1/2 Weeks) (For Lucas who was born too early)," June 15, 1997

tograph, the edges of a mirror slice breast and belly, and the figure appears tense and uncomfortable, her mouth covered by her arm in the act of photographing. In the 1997 photograph, on the other hand, the figure reclines languidly in a public space. The divisions between frames serve to elongate her elegant pose. While they are not precisely doubles, the pairing of these images over time provides an historical perspective on the body-knowledge of pregnancy.

Bea Nettles' photographs from her own two pregnancies are also worth comparing as a pair of images made over time. The photograph from her first pregnancy, "Three Bluebirds," published in *Flamingo in the Dark* (1978), is a sensuous, dreamlike and affirmative image, but the photograph from her second pregnancy, "Pregnant," published in *Complexities* (1992) is more conflicted. It includes not one but three separate although connected self-portraits. Two nude pregnant torsos, shimmering in soft focus against a dark background, are contrasted with

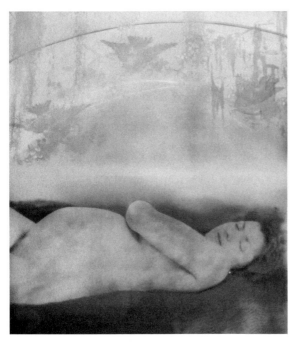

Bea Nettles, "Three Bluebirds" from *Flamingo in the Dark*, 1978

Bea Nettles, "Pregnant," from *Complexities*, 1992

a smaller photograph of herself hurriedly downing a cup of coffee. The triptych portrays conflicting and coexisting modes: the pregnant woman is unselfconscious luminous body, content simply to be, *and* acculturated striver, anxious to make an impact in the world.

Sometimes the doubles are doubled, as in Jessica Boyatt's uncanny arrangement of two pairs of pregnant sisters that highlights family resemblances. And sometimes the doubles are not even human. Ann Chwatsky's photograph calls

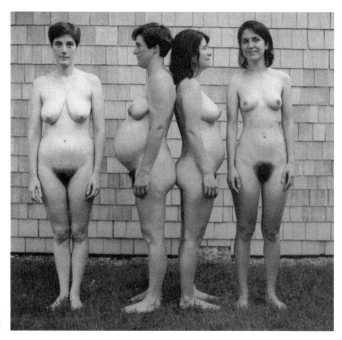

Jessica Boyatt,
"Pregnant Sisters," 1994

Ann Chwatsky, from the
Pregnancy Series, n.d.

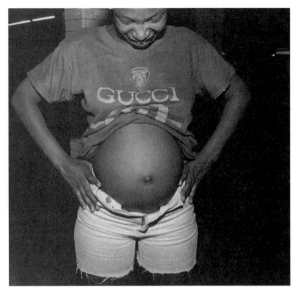

Monte H. Gerlach,
"Susan," 1979

Lydia Ann Douglas, "I'm 5 Months
Pregnant," June 5, 1987

Nancy M. Stuart,
"Twins," from *Life
Begins at Forty*, 1991

attention to a visual echo between a voluptuous pregnant woman and the
curved, formal chair upon which she sits. It refers to the simultaneous comfort
and awkwardness furnished by the middle-class conventions of pregnancy.

PREGNANCY AS SPECTACLE

Sometimes, also, the doubling strategies serve to split the pregnant subject herself
into observer and observed. This can be done literally with mirrors, as in Monte
Gerlach's portrait of a dismayed woman regarding her image, or it can happen

more conceptually as in Lydia Ann Douglas' and Nancy Stuart's pictures of pregnant women as observers of the condition of their own bellies. To picture the pregnant woman as active witness of the spectacle she creates helps to counteract the claustrophobic way that a pregnant woman is usually doubled in onto herself. Establishing an ironic relation toward her body opens a reflective distance.

In Sylvia Plachy's humorously theatrical photograph of a pregnant woman exhibiting her belly in an elevator, the subject's facial expression appears to be mirroring that of a shocked viewer. She is using the womblike space of the elevator as a dramatic public stage, both creating a spectacle of herself and reacting

Sylvia Plachy, "Yo,"
February 1992

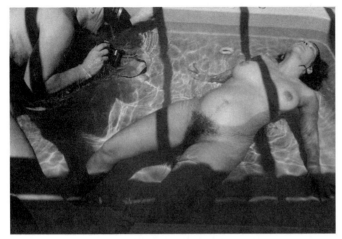

Joan Rosenstein,
"Obsession II," 1988

Judy Dater, "The
Voyeur," 1968

to it by simulating the look of a spectator. The photograph references both overt
and covert scenarios of exposure including that of the panopticon, signified by
the looming presence of a surveillance camera in the corner of the elevator.

By contrast, Joan Rosenstein portrays the pregnant woman as a singularly passive object of an aggressive male gaze. Judy Dater's "Voyeur" alludes to the possibility of "womb envy" implied by the male gaze. Both Rosenstein and Dater present the pregnant subject as a fascinating spectacle for others and play down her

capacity to observe and know for herself. The explicit figure of a voyeur in both photographs is one way to counteract the tendency of the pregnant woman to deflect the viewer's scopic gaze, since someone else is also visibly spying on her.

Bodily Power, Humor and the Grotesque

In *The Female Grotesque*, Mary Russo defines the grotesque body as simultaneously "open, protruding, irregular, secreting, multiple and changing."[14] Such an array of qualities easily relates to the rapid growth and striking protuberances of the pregnant body. Humor provides a way for the woman herself to put the grotesqueness of pregnancy into perspective.

Cheryl Younger's playful riff on heaviness, fruitfulness and the conventions that associate the pregnant woman with nature satirizes the grotesque. She poses in front of a pile of watermelons, the stripes of her dress over her big belly matching those of the melons.[15] The picture uses doubleness in a way often found in family snapshots of pregnant women, to draw an explicit connection between the environment and the pregnant figure. Younger writes, "Great warmth, laughter, and pleasure welled up in me as I drove into the Coral Fruit Market that day. Here was something I could relate to after months of feeling awkward and pubescent."[16] By representing her body as an oversized fruit, Younger found a way to articulate both her subjective sense of physical awkwardness and her delight in portraying that feeling.

Cheryl Gwen Younger,
"Watermelons and Me,"
June 1997

Karl Baden, "Liz,
Weare, N.H., 5/28/94;
Birth Minus 23 Days,"
1994

Frank Ward, "Vivian,"
1984

Karl Baden relies upon a similar sense of humor when he visually links his wife's pregnant belly to a phallic-looking gas tank. Constructing an imaginary affinity between large rounded containers, the picture also invites contemplation of the traditional male role in conception, of the common childhood fantasy of impregnation through the navel, and of the phallic character of the pregnant belly itself.

Younger's and Baden's photographs share the commonplace impression of pregnancy as a heavy, static bodily state. Frank Ward's photograph of his pregnant wife leaping across the room surprises by inverting this expected sense of

Bryn Campbell, from
The Family of Woman,
1979

how a pregnant body behaves. Ward draws on the commonplace middle-class iconography of a nude pregnant woman posing in a domestic space that includes a window, doorway, and potted plants. But his is an image of magical weight-lessness. The smile on the subject's face makes it also one of clowning. It appears that the subject is almost as surprised as the viewer to find herself airborne. Indeed, when pregnant subjects are represented as having bodily power, they generally are made to appear absurd and consequently less threatening. In a diff-erent way from Younger's self-portrait as a watermelon woman and Baden's anthropomorphic tank, Ward invokes the grotesque, but his picture also hints at the marvelous.

Much more earthbound, the woman in Bryn Campbell's photograph looks equally cheerful surrounded by the fruits of her fertility. Her living room, swarming with small bodies, is not the tranquil domestic space of middle-class pregnancy. Like Younger's self-accepting reference to the awkwardness of her own body, Campbell's image comically overstates the social nightmare of a woman with too many mouths to feed. Viewers can laugh at the spectacle of reproduction run amok, yet the sight of so many seemingly well-cared-for chil-dren in that crowded space may cause them also to question class-based stereo-types.

Some photographs document performances in which pregnancy is staged for comic effect. The fine-art traditions of Western painting and sculpture, which have rarely portrayed the pregnant figure, can be sources of this humor. Cindy

Cindy Sherman,
"Untitled," 1989

Martha Everson, "Ladies of the Spring," n.d.

Sherman's formal, framed "History Portrait" of a pregnant woman who is nude except for an elaborate Medusa-like headdress and a lacy fabric draped over a plastic prosthetic belly, cuts an absurd figure, raising the question of why the dignified women in so many formal portraits are never visibly pregnant. Martha Everson's five pregnant women posing in the park, on the other hand, are themselves ironic in their intensely graceful statuesque stances. Their five living bodies appear frozen, like marble, in time; they seem at once both eternal and anecdotal, like

pregnancy in general. These photographers use the potential humor of the pregnant figure to expand the fine-art traditions and critique their absences.

Not So Funny: Bodily Power and the Grotesque Revisited

A few photographs from this period construct attitudes toward the pregnant
woman's bodily power without particularly making a joke of them. These
images use the unexpected, upon which humor is based, but they reorient the
humor away from the pregnant woman's bodily grotesqueness. If, as Freud
writes, jokes are ultimately made at the expense of a woman, these photographs
attempt to rewrite the formula. They consider the physical awkwardness of
pregnancy enough of a cosmic chuckle for the woman to deal with in itself without needing to emphasize its absurdity further. Sally Mann's photograph "Jenny
and Her Mother," for instance, allows the pregnant woman to portray her bodily
discomfort in a way that is both melodramatic and poignant. The needy embrace
of her teenage daughter, who appears as both child and possible future mother
herself, overshadows potential self-deprecating humor.

Carla Shapiro's picture, shot from below, of a woman's manicured hands

Sally Mann, "Jenny and Her Mother,"
Lexington, Virginia, 1984

Carla Shapiro,
untitled, n.d.

Sheila McLaughlin,
untitled, n.d.

clasped over her pregnant belly, transforms the woman's long, sharp-looking, painted fingernails from emblems of femininity into seriously dangerous weapons of defense. Sheila McLaughlin's photograph, part of an extensive series on pregnancy, which includes interviews, depicts a pregnant woman sitting in a homelike environment, but wearing a uniform and holding a rifle with bayonet. That she works as a security guard, a fact that is revealed in the interviews, does not diminish the shock value of the image. Both of these pictures portray the pregnant woman as equipped to take extreme measures, resituating grotesqueness in the compulsions of a violent society.

PREGNANCY AS NARRATIVE

A number of artists have attempted to articulate the process of gestation over time, rather than trying to sum up some aspect of it in individual pictures. This has led to some highly inventive ways to represent the evolution of pregnancy. Chuck Swedlund and Karl Baden, for instance, both made flipbooks of their wives changing form. They used sequences of schematic photographs, viewed

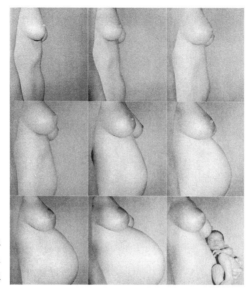

Karl Baden, from
*Gestation Animation: A
Labor Manual*, 1994

Gail S. Rebhan,
panel from "280 Days,"
1984

in rapid succession, to suggest the passing of time and bodily shapes. Baden has also used his flipbook as the basis of a grid. Gail Rebhan chronicled each and every day of her first pregnancy, photographing herself in the same stance each time, looking into the mirror of her clothes closet. She then printed a matrix of images for each month, in which the viewer can read subtle changes and a self-conscious attempt to impose formal order on an unruly situation. Linda Brooks' single, dramatic photograph implied an entire "nesting" narrative of preparation for the arrival of her baby.

In these images, the process of change seems welcome. But in Patti Ambrogi's grid of images of her twin daughters playing in the park in golden, late afternoon light, the more idyllic pictures are overlaid with a disturbing narrative text about drug-addicted mothers and babies with AIDS. By juxtaposing these dream and nightmare images, Ambrogi is able eloquently to switch the focus from changing bodily shapes to the necessity of changing the viewer's ideas about their meaning.

THE PREGNANT WOMAN AS POSTMODERN SOCIAL SUBJECT

In the 1980s, the culturally privileged definition of the family, long contested, finally grew broad enough to begin to acknowledge the fact of single-parent

Five months pregnant
After acknowledging some anticipation of the birth, I thought about
how having a baby will make everything I do, different

Linda Brooks, "Five Months Pregnant," 1983–84

Patti Ambrogi, "Good Luck," 1992

families, and gay and lesbian parents. Public debate over surrogate motherhood, transracial adoption, and health insurance for domestic partners also challenged family boundaries and stereotypes. Increasing recognition that the "Kodak" model of the middle-class nuclear family did not represent most Americans' family experience informed a number of photographic projects that attempted to revise the image of pregnancy in the interest of social change.

Gay and lesbian parenting, to take one prominent area of struggle, has provided an intensively contested ideological challenge to the myth of the heteronormative nuclear family. Philosopher Iris Young writes that lesbian mothering "may be the ultimate affront to patriarchy."[17] Yet lesbian mothers are not something new; they have always existed, although not always so openly. Photographic projects documenting the lives of lesbian-parent families, designed for viewing within the lesbian community, date at least from the 1970s. These images became somewhat more widely visible in the 1990s, and their makers have had to work through the conditions of their wider visibility.

Cathy Cade was one of the first to have photographed lesbian mothers over a period of years, publicly presenting her photographs in a self-published book entitled *A Lesbian Family Album* (1987). A lesbian mother herself, Cade worked as an insider, articulating the experiences of lesbian-parent families in her own community. Cade uses close, intimate framing to create images of the individu-

Cathy Cade, "Jyl and Family Cuddle," n.d.

Cathy Cade, "Worried," n.d.

ality and sensuality of her subjects. She also places them within the generalized humanistic framework that Steichen first developed in *The Family of Man*, locating her subjects within the concept of "family" as a human universal. However, although her intention is to present public and positive images of lesbian mothers, Cade does not suppress bodily experiences of discomfort and emotional factors of anxiety. Both are made visually evident in her images. Cade's emphasis on the articulation of the individual, embodied female subject allows her to represent the social reality of lesbian motherhood with delicacy and power.

In the 1990s, photographers such as Jan Ballard began to integrate portraits of lesbian parents with their other work. In addition, several books of photographs of gay and lesbian families such as Barbara Seyda and Diane Herrera's *Women in Love: Portraits of Lesbian Mothers and Their Families* (1998), and Gigi Kaeser and Peggy Gillespie's *Love Makes a Family: Portraits of Lesbian, Gay, Bisexual and Transgender Parents and Their Families* (1999) have made their appearance.[18] Such books, which are in general bookstores as well as more specialized gay and lesbian venues, reach a wider audience than ever before.

Jan Ballard, "Partner,"
1991

Teen Pregnancy

Teenage mothers offer another source of serious challenge to traditional images of the ideal family. They have also served as a point of convergence for conflict over the distribution of social goods and services. Here again, the phenomenon is far from new. But photographic projects that seek to represent it are becoming increasingly important in establishing conditions for the dialectic of "positive" and "negative" imagery about teen mothers and the classed, raced and gendered discourse that goes with it.

Polly Brown has succeeded memorably in rendering the individual and social dimensions of pregnancy for three teenagers of diverse racial, ethnic, and class backgrounds. Formerly a teen mother herself, Brown became a trusted participant-observer who was granted comparatively open access to the daily lives of her subjects. Her 1982 photographic study owes much to the modernist documentary photo-essay tradition originating in the 1930s. Her photographs focus on the teenage mothers' experiences of pregnancy without ever isolating these young women from the other circumstances of their lives. Brown pictures the pregnant young women as supported by and embedded in a web of relationships with family and friends, at home, and in school. Her photographs portray the myriad ways, both gratifying and embarrassing, that a pregnant teenager becomes the focus of familial and institutional attention. Presented as lively individuals, the young mothers in these pictures counteract popular stereotypes of pregnant teens merely as social problems, while not disregarding the often difficult realities of their lives.

Polly Brown, "Tina and Her Mother," c.1982

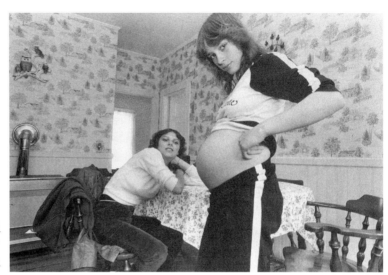

Polly Brown, "Rose and
Her Sister Debbie,"
c.1982

Several other photographers have also produced series of dignified portraits of pregnant teenagers that cross the domains of art and social advocacy. Notably, during the 1980s Nancy Stuart and Sandy Hale worked to provide an antidote to the widespread negative stereotypes broadcast about teenage mothers during struggles over welfare reform, while still attempting to portray their multiple needs. They picture them with kinship and community ties intact. Sandy Hale followed her subjects for over four years, from pregnancy through the first years of motherhood. Each time she photographed them, Hale asked her subjects to contribute a brief written statement about how they felt about their lives at that

Nancy M. Stuart, "Lela
and Wade, Aug. 6, 1987"

When I was younger I depende
on my mother.
my mother had to Look after me.
know I feel thats the way my
doughter feels.
I have to Look asther her
I don't have any body to Look
asther me..

Xiomara

Sandy Hale,
"Xiomara," n.d.

Kierra Walton, "Little
Sister Rubbing My
Belly," 1995

moment. These statements, published alongside the images in the subjects' own
handwriting, are often quite poignant. Four years after the birth of the babies,
very few fathers are still around. What she wanted to get across, Hale said, is that
"it's a difficult road."[19]

Teenage mothers themselves have also made images of their lives and spoken out on their own behalf. In a book that she made about her family in a workshop run by photographer Janice Rogovin, Kierra Walton included a pregnant self-portrait, accompanied by the optimistic words, "Well now that you've seen my generation another generation will appear because I'm about ready to deliver a baby girl. I, like my mother, am having her at a young age, sixteen, and I know it will be hard but with the support and help of my family I think I'll make it."[20] But despite its eloquence and political importance, this work has not been widely exhibited or distributed.

REPRESENTING REPRODUCTIVE POLITICS

During the 1980s, controversial technological interventions in the reproductive process achieved a dramatic public presence. Though advanced assisted reproductive technologies have been used only by a narrow sector of the population so far, they have already had a profound impact on how pregnancy is being reconceptualized. The traditional concept of pregnancy as a natural, and private, sequence of events that occurs within the confines of a woman's body had to expand to include a variety of possible interventions or intrusions.

Art photography has responded to this provocation. When viewed as single images, without accompanying text, scopic photographs do not expose their political stance. But in the period of exacerbated strife over the issue of public funding for abortion during the 1990s, works combining images and text emerged to address women's relationship to reproduction in an overtly political way. These photographs assumed the public nature of pregnancy, grounding it in social and political realities.

Some such efforts had been made before. W. Eugene Smith's photo-essay on midwives, published in *Life* magazine in 1959, is an early example of such an effort to portray reproductive practices in a social context. Eugene Richards' and Dorothea Lynch's pioneering collaborative book, *50 Hours* (1983), another example, politicized childbirth by placing it within the larger social context of an anti-nuclear demonstration, alternating images of emergent new life with images of protest against environmental degradation.[21] Early works like these clarified the public, collective, responsibility for the conditions in which women undertook pregnancy. But they were episodic and individualistic efforts.

In the 1990s, collaborative efforts aimed at politicizing our notions of pregnancy began to gather a certain amount of force. Kira Corser's two book projects, *The Struggle to be Borne* (1988) and *When the Bough Breaks: Pregnancy and the Legacy of Addiction* (1993), were extensive works of advocacy that addressed the social construction of pregnancy under the most difficult circumstances of poverty.[22] Combining her photographs with poetic text by Frances Payne Adler,

Corser sought in both book and exhibition form to find, educate and activate a community of viewers to take collective responsibility for such conditions of pregnancy. Her exhibitions were shown in the California State Capitol, where they influenced legislators to support prenatal care for women to whom it was otherwise unavailable.

Kira Carillo Corser, from *The Struggle to Be Borne*, 1988

Kira Carillo Corser, from *When the Bough Breaks:Pregnancy and the Legacy of Addiction*, New Sage Press, 1993

THE BELLY PROJECT

The Belly Project (1993), represents another kind collaboration that seeks to represent women's concerns as group concerns. A collection of images initiated by Lisa Kushner and photographed by Peggy McKenna, *The Belly Project* was a well-publicized and well-reviewed exhibition with an accompanying poster. Nan Goldin's 1980 photograph entitled "Ectopic Pregnancy Scar" is a precursor to this project because it addresses the physical aftereffects of reproduction on women's bodies. But whereas Goldin photographed a single woman, Kushner and McKenna photographed twenty women's bellies. Many of them exhibit graphically the wear and tear of their reproductive and medical histories as well as the passage of time. These frontal abdominal "mug shots," arranged in a grid, draw upon the vocabulary of informative but depersonalized medical imaging. The pictures include neither faces, which would have personalized the figures, nor breasts, which would have feminized them. Instead, the isolated bellies stand in for individual women, and for the experience of maternity in general.

The Belly Project draws attention to the bodily differences that result from, rather than cause, social experience. Whereas the full-term pregnant belly in its taut, expanded form has been theorized as phallic, the flaccid postpartum belly, with a fleshly inscription that signifies suffering and endurance rather than agency or power, is newly presented here to the public eye. The repetitive iconography of the project overall suggests the format of a police archive, yet the subject being thus classified is the maternal body, which is not generally thought of in criminal terms. Whereas the police archives of the nineteenth century attempted to identify physical types associated with certain individuals' behaviors or identities, *The Belly Project* draws attention to shared social experience. Captions that include first name, age, and a brief reproductive history encapsulated in list form (pregnancies, miscarriages, vaginal births, C-sections, abor-

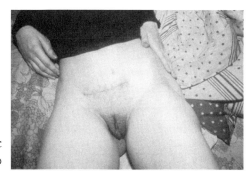

Nan Goldin, "Ectopic
Pregnancy Scar," 1980

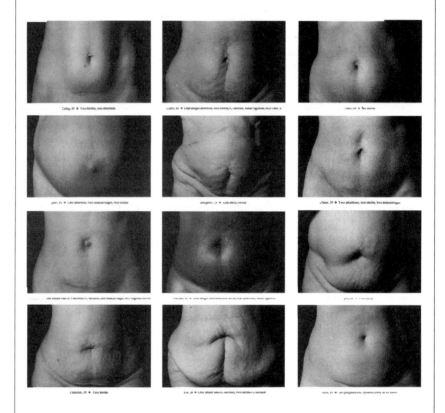

THE BELLY PROJECT

A Celebration of Women, Motherhood & Reproductive Choice

THE BELLY PROJECT
RR 1 BOX 2273, MORRILL, MAINE 04952

A PORTION OF PROCEEDS WILL BENEFIT REPRODUCTIVE RIGHTS ORGANIZATIONS

Peggy McKenna and Lisa Kushner, "The Belly Project," 1993

tions) accompany each image. Though the captions beneath the pictures seem to reveal information usually considered private, like a medical record, in reality they barely hint at the women's individual stories. The effect is of a generalized female subjectivity, conveyed through the cumulative effects of pregnancy upon many individual bodies.

TECHNOLOGY AND THE POSTMODERN SOCIAL SUBJECT

Evolving relations between pregnancy and medical technology largely determine both the individual experience and the social construction of childbearing. Artists have increasingly recognized a subject in this conjuncture.

Elaine O'Neil's tense and confrontational "Stess Test" (1992), for instance, pictures a woman dealing with the physical indignity of technical procedures for the sake of the assistance they may provide in case of medical difficulty. Meridel Rubinstein's "Fetal Monitor" (1982) uses the printout from a fetal monitor as one element of a visual meditation upon the close proximity of birth and death. Rubinstein portrays the fetal monitor's graphic markings as the drawing of a desert landscape, representing technology as a nonalienating basis for creative connection. Joanne Leonard's collage also appropriates the medical image, but in a somewhat different spirit. Leonard playfully positions a classic photograph from an obstetrical textbook as an element of collage within a drawing of a pear, subsuming the structures of medical intervention within a larger notion of fruitfulness. O'Neil's, Rubinstein's and Leonard's images levelly confront and accept technological innovations as an acceptable dimension of contemporary pregnancy and childbirth practices.

Robin Lasser's pregnant self-portrait, "Choice," and Mary Frey's "Body/Parts" are more ambivalent and ironic in their references to technology. Lasser uses graphic markings to inscribe a chart of chromosomes directly onto her own

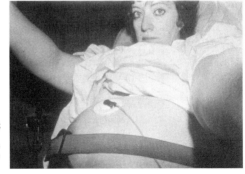

Elaine O'Neil, "Stress
Test, Cambridge, MA,
September 7, 1992"

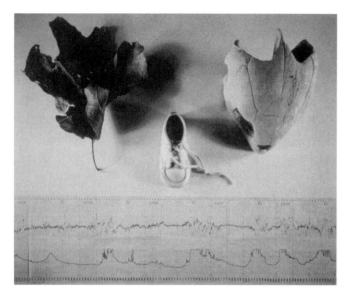

Meridel Rubenstein,
"Fetal Monitor," 1982

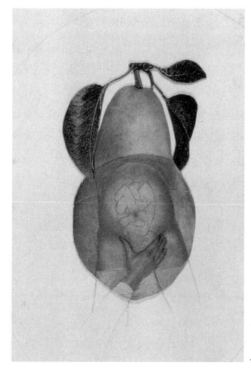

Joanne Leonard,
"Untitled," 1973 (from
Journal, 1973)

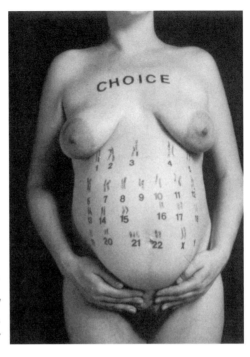

Robin Lasser, "Choice,"
from the *How's My
Mothering?* series,
1995–97

pregnant belly. The word "choice" bears an ambiguous inflection, referring not only to the decision of whether or not to have an abortion, but also to the custom options now potentially available for "designing" a child. The chromosome drawings function like labels on a package, establishing the pregnant woman as product too, rather than producer.

Mary Frey's profile of a pregnant torso, like Joanne Leonard's collage, resignifies the clinical gaze as uncanny. Her photograph associates the pregnant woman's medicalized appearance with several other historically unmoored visual references: Rafael's painting of the Three Graces holding apples, an anatomical drawing of the inside of the human head, and a formal portrait photograph of twin babies. These images, only loosely interconnected conceptually, are also kept visually separate. The intrigue and awkwardness of their association expresses unease.

CONCLUSION

As it moves through and beyond modernism, art photography offers an increasingly diverse array of photographs of pregnancy. They register a major cultural shift, from initial suppression of images and constraint of the gaze, to the emer-

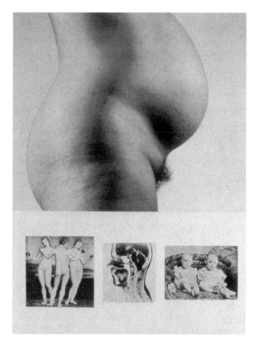

Mary E. Frey, "Number 21," from *Body/Parts*, 1989–91

gence of visual strategies that no longer depend solely upon the scopic distance. These construct a sense of pregnancy as both a socially malleable event and a liminal stage in an individual's private life. As the labors of art photography continue, their trajectory bears graphic witness to the tensions that have surrounded, and continue to surround, the identity, sexuality and social substance of the pregnant woman.

3) FAMILY PHOTOGRAPHS
AND THE PREGNANT POSE

> Photographic practice only exists and subsists for most of the
> time by virtue of its *family function* or rather by the function
> conferred upon it by the family group, namely that of
> solemnizing and immortalizing the high points of family life.
>
> —Pierre Bourdieu

Family photographs traditionally represent individuals who share ties of kinship
or household. They are made as records to be viewed by those who are in the picture, by their relatives, friends and acquaintances and by the generations to follow. The circle of viewers for a family photograph can narrow or widen significantly over time, depending upon whether the photograph is tucked away in an
album, drawer or attic, or finds its way into a public archive or exhibition space.
Each family photograph specifies a densely coded point in the flow of time.
Taken together and viewed with hindsight, family photographs tell stories of
growth, diminution and change in the family configuration.

Family photographs can be formal or informal, made by professionals or inti-
mates, and taken in a studio, at home or in another location. Pregnant women
have been photographed in all these ways. Whether formal or informal, however, taken by professionals or by other family members, family photographs are
ritually made and ritually viewed. They are among the most fetishistic of photographs, often carried on one's person in a wallet, where they function as sur-
rogates for the individual pictured. They can be viewed privately as personal
reminders, or they can be shared with friends and even strangers when one is
away from home. They mark uncanny presence and profound absence at the
same time.

The idea that family photographs are vehicles of pure, unmediated truth—
that they hold clues to the essence of individual identity and the character of formative relationships—is both powerful and widely held. Simon Watney writes of
insights he gained from viewing childhood family photographs:

I have always believed that I was a grotesquely fat and unattractive child, but the little boy who stares back rather cautiously from under his sun hat is neither of these things. I thought I was fat and ugly because I thought I was bad.[1]

Despite Watney's sophisticated critical approach to representation, the photograph here still serves as a truthful record to be compared with the distortions of memory.

Yet family photographs are also socially constructed artifacts. They operate at the juncture of private life and public mythology, naturalizing both. As Julia Hirsch explains, "Family photography is not only an accessory to our deepest longings and regrets; it is also a set of visual rules that shape our experience and memory."[2] These visual rules are grounded in class- and culture-based ideals of what a family should look like. Family photographs have always idealized the family according to the current norms. The more obviously studied formal photographs may be easier to see as constructs than snapshots are; however, candid snapshots made by participants in the scene have their scripts as well.

Within the last twenty years artists and critics have intensified their critique of photographs of the white middle class, pointing out that the "Kodak family" has been normalized to a degree that went far beyond its actuality in the culture. The gap between this wholesome image, still lingering, and social experience becomes all the more apparent as issues such as divorce, dysfunction and domestic violence make inroads into public consciousness. One wonders about the cultural work that family photographs perform. As Patricia Holland asks,

[F]or whom is this image so carefully, so spontaneously manufactured? Family photography is not expected to be appreciated by outsiders, yet there is a need to produce the correct pictures, as if the audience were the public at large. Is each individual looking for their own ideal image? Are members of the group presenting themselves for each other, or for unknown "others," for future generations? Is this a joint self-celebration, or is it a presentation of the imagined family group for the critical scrutiny of outsiders—even if those outsiders are never expected to see it?[3]

But clearly, family photographs are images made in commemoration of the presumably identifiable goodness of family life, and their subject matter is extremely selective; undesirable images of the family or any of its members are usually edited out of the album. The sick, the renegade, the moment of discord or strain—even the countless in-between moments of general confusion or disarray in family life—do not often figure in the family's visual archive.

THE FAMILY ALBUM

As ritual objects, family photographs are not only made according to specific conventions but are also viewed in culturally prescribed ways. More than the wallet (a traveling small-scale version of the album), it is the family album, even the guise of an unorganized box or pile of pictures, that comprises the central "text" of the family's ongoing narrative. People sometimes claim that if their house were burning, the possession most important to rescue would be the family album. In this way the album itself is a kind of fetish as well, a protection against the loss of one's extended identity.

For the family member, the album allows the construction of a kind of familial connective tissue that is richly layered and versatile. This process includes both making and viewing the family album. Making the album involves the deliberate arrangement of image and text in relation to one another, a kind of identifying ("marking") and placing of individual pictures. Assembling and captioning the pictures to create a coherent and personalized archive is kinship work often carried out by women. Family albums are then viewed instrumentally in ways that go beyond the scopic model of looking as knowledge. In them, visual and tactile experiences are combined with storytelling, as the pages are turned and their content enables the sharing and reconstruction of the past.

The family history that is constructed and transmitted in such a way has its own peculiar sense of chronology. Julia Hirsch describes the unusual sense of time in family albums by emphasizing its jumble of parallel but unequal moments:

> The living and the dead congregate; parents appear younger than their children; and all these faces in the midst of their respective lives are innocent of the destinies which will link them one to the other.[4]

The pictures of pregnancy that have recently entered the family album have extended the album's reach. Pregnant family photographs generally signify a particularly hopeful and forward-looking moment in family life, making them vulnerable to painful shifts in meaning if those hopes later go awry. But even more uncanny are ultrasound portraits of the fetus as an actor in the family which form a part of the album even before birth.

OUR FAMILY PHOTOGRAPH COLLECTION

We collected the family photographs of pregnancy that appear in this chapter in three principal ways: through personal networks of family, friends and colleagues, through audience donations after our public lectures on the *Pregnant*

Pictures project, and in response to queries we placed in *Mothering* magazine. Volunteering their personal photographs for an unknown project of a public nature, many of the women who answered our ads expressed the sentiment that such pictures needed to be seen. They sent their pictures in a collaborative spirit, with a wish to share. These women were predominantly but not exclusively white and came from rural and urban communities throughout the United States.

Like family photographs in general, the pictures of pregnancy in our collection in some ways evince a narrow range of recurring visual elements. In other ways, however, they show startling inversions and unexpected combinations of conventional family iconography. Our sample suggests that family photographs of pregnant women both conform to and depart from the customs governing the family album.

These pregnant family photographs function traditionally insofar as they are ritually made portraits, taken most often in domestic situations, and intended for viewing within a circle of family and friends. Yet it is clear that even in the relatively sheltered context of family photography, the pregnant body is neither an easy nor a comfortable subject for representation. Unlike other family photographs, which on some level function to signify the family as a stable social body, family photographs of pregnancy are about the body of the pregnant woman as a disruption within the family, where it signifies ongoing and impending change.

The twentieth-century photographs in our collection feature pregnancy as the primary and outstanding reason for the picture and insist on the visual distinctiveness, and often the separateness, of the pregnant woman in relation to the rest of family life. However, earlier photographs of pregnant women often did not make an issue of pregnancy one way or another. A mid-nineteenth century daguerreotype from the Burns Collection picturing a couple in a studio follows the conventions of formal portraiture without drawing attention to the woman's pregnancy. In a photograph from roughly the same period, four women and two horses stand in front of a sod house in Nebraska, and the pregnancy of one of the women also seems incidental to the picture. Another nineteenth-century photograph made in Oregon seems more about the formation of a large extended family grouping than about the obvious pregnancy of one of the women. These family photographs are formally posed, made in the studio or by itinerant photographers. Many more group portraits such as these must exist, in which at least one member of the group is pregnant, whether or not the pregnancy is visually evident. In their nonchalance about picturing the pregnant body as part of a larger scene, these photographs are extraordinary to the contemporary eye.

Untitled, n.d., Stanley
B. Burns, M.D., and
The Burns Archive

Nebraska State Historical
Society, Solomon D. Butcher
Collection, "Chrisman
Sisters," n.d.

Although informal amateur family photographs were also made in the nineteenth and early twentieth centuries, the amateur form known as the "snapshot" came into popular use in the United States only in the 1940s, encouraged by the marketing of lightweight, affordable cameras. The postwar period saw a great expansion of photography within the family. This is when the form of pregnant family photographs began to change, with particular attention being paid to the pregnant woman. The privacy and relative ease of having photographs made at home allowed intimacy that was accompanied, ironically, by the segregation of the pregnant woman.

Southern Oregon Historical Society, untitled, n.d.

POSING PREGNANT

Pregnancy is an experience of identity in transformation that proceeds on its own course within the woman's body, but not under the woman's direction. The pregnant woman is notably unable to claim a singular, cohesive being. Philosopher Iris Young suggests that the pregnant woman challenges the notion of a singular body, potentially offering new philosophical models of the self. To Young, pregnant subjectivity "entails the most extreme suspension of the bodily distinction between inner and outer."[5]

It is striking, therefore, that snapshots of pregnancy are often images of bodily self-delight and playfulness. If a pregnant woman chooses to have pictures made, it is usually because she is pleased to be pregnant. Pregnant snapshots often seem celebratory, at times even carnivalesque. Sensuality and humor, rarely found to the same degree in nonfamilial photographs of pregnant women, suffuse many pregnant snapshots.

The family snapshot apparently offers a special opportunity for the pregnant woman to think about what her pregnancy means to her, and these subjective meanings are expressed chiefly through the self-conscious use of posing. Family photographs of pregnant women are, overwhelmingly, carefully posed rather than candid. Snapshots of pregnant women are taken by family members or friends or, less frequently, by the woman herself. Yet it is the woman's pose, rather than the sensibility of the photographer-author, that dominates the picture. Although the pose is often a collaboration based on trust between photographer and subject, the photographer usually remains anonymous. This differentiates family snapshots from art photographs, in which one is quite aware of the constructive role played by the photographer, and only learns the name of the subject if he or she is famous. In family snapshots of pregnancy, it is the identity of the pregnant subject that matters.

In a landmark essay "Posing," Craig Owens notes the "fundamental duplicity of every pose," the bipartition which the subject undergoes when it assumes an image.[6] While posing, the subject is both performer and character, simultaneously assuming a role and monitoring it. The subject enacts a concept of herself and surveys herself in the process. In the case of family photographs, she is the primary viewer of the image as well, taking the opportunity to regard an external representation of herself beyond the self-survey found within the pose.

While women are hardly strangers to posing, posing pregnant is a special case. The pregnant body is already internally double or multiple; two or more bodies in one. When the pregnant woman poses, she can and often does use the elements of the pose to represent externally her double state, finding a visual echo of her shape in the world. In this way the doubling inherent in posing allows her to articulate her own multiplied being. The pregnant woman who exaggerates her rounded form in her pose is attempting to orchestrate her own spectacle, master the ambiguities in her pregnant identity, and declare herself an active subject. In a deliberate, signifying act she gives the shifting shape of her body momentary definition.

A playful pair of posed snapshots of pregnancy made in 1943, for instance, takes advantage of the sheltered confines of family photography to push the boundaries of picturing pregnancy beyond the expected portrait. In the first image, a pregnant woman appropriates a "movie star" pose. Her face and hair glamorously made up, she wears nothing but panties and pearls, and stands, spotlit, in an open and vulnerable position. This teasingly erotic image is paired with a laughing, unglamorous picture of the same subject, who stands, hands in pockets, dressed in plain maternity clothing, while flat lighting reveals a makeshift home studio. The transgressive expression of pregnant sexuality in the first picture is defused by the second, which seems to say, "Just kidding." Joan Riviere proposed in 1929 the idea that the sexualized stances associated with femininity serve the purpose of masking women's theft of male power, making

Anonymous, 1943

Anonymous, 1943

them appear less threatening and propitiating male anger.[7] When the woman is pregnant, however, it is her sexualized "feminine" stance that is threatening. In the case of these photographs, the potential threat posed by the first image is defused by the second, slightly embarrassed image.

These two photographs were, in fact, made by the pregnant woman's mother. In them, an imaginative, private collaboration between mother and daughter results in a union of the maternal image with cultural notions of glamour, nearly fifty years before Demi Moore's glamorous image was printed on the cover of *Vanity Fair*. Together, this remarkable pair of photographs conveys a sense of private pleasure in both women's experience of the pregnant body—the daughter's playful delight in being a "sight to behold," and the complicity of the mother with the daughter in sharing and rewriting maternity. They introduce important themes that recur in later snapshots: the theme of the pregnant woman deliberately playing, through self-caricature, with the idea of being a spectacle; the theme of pregnancy as sensual; and the theme of self-conscious posing.

Muriel Pader, photograph
by Morton Pader, 1945

Elsie Stewart

Sylvia and Vicci (Sylvia
pregnant with Gina),
photograph by
JackVeenstra, 1957

Muriel Pader's snapshot, taken two years later in 1945, is another instance of the new attention paid to the pregnant woman in family photography. It represents the pregnant woman as healthy and happy, standing outside her home in postwar Stuyvesant City. Here the emphasis is not so much on communicating the private bodily experience of pregnancy. Rather, the pregnant woman poses in a space that is simultaneously domestic and public, with an air of optimism.

The 1950s brought a more informal attention to the pregnant figure in family snapshots. Elsie Stewart is pictured pregnant in the mid-1950s, about to take a car ride, apparently amused by the idea of being photographed in her condition.

Melissa Christman

Julie Lynch

Vicci Veenstra's 1957 family portrait features herself and her pregnant mother posing comfortably in a chair. Unlike the nineteenth-century photographs of pregnant women that picture pregnancy incidentally, these home snapshots from the 1940s and 1950s begin to place the pregnant figure at center stage, both highlighting and isolating her.

CONTEMPORARY PREGNANT SNAPSHOTS

Family snapshots of pregnant women became much more common in the early 1970s, in conjunction with the women's movement. The new shots expanded on the iconography begun in the 1940s, extending the range and pleasures of playful self-presentation. Beginning in this period, family snapshots encouraged a humorous approach to pregnancy not seen in any other photographic domain.

The poses in these snapshots employ self-parody and physical clowning. In striking a humorous pose, the pregnant woman distances herself from her own body, then reclaims it as the creator-observer of her self-caricature.

In many humorous snapshots, the posing involves a kind of active doubling, even beyond the initial doubling implied by the posing pregnant body, which is achieved through exaggeration, repetition and active play around the pregnant form. For instance, some snapshots deliberately group other figures around the pregnant woman, enhancing the motif of multiplication. Melissa Christman's snapshot of herself posing belly to belly with another very pregnant woman and Julie Lynch's double portrait of herself with a pregnant friend at the ocean's edge are examples of a literal doubling that allows each woman to articulate both herself as a particular individual and the pregnant condition in general. Melonie Bennett's photograph extends the capacity to multiply across the gender gap to men by way of mimicry. Rhonda Wainshilbaum-Becker's snapshot of herself touching bellies with her young daughter, both of them nude, doubles the female belly across generations, the roundness of youth echoing the roundness of maturity. At the same time, their contact recalls their original umbilical connection. Karen Klugman dramatizes her pregnancy by appearing surrounded and happily overwhelmed by the children around her.

Sometimes objects or props are used as external representations of the woman's bodily state. For example, surrounding herself with large rubber balls, Wendy Cohan mirrors her own form. Her smile indicates her willing participation in the joke, which is both at her expense and for her pleasure. Ann Stinson,

Melonie Bennett, "Mary (Nine Months Pregnant)," 1995

Rhonda Wainshilbaum-
Becker, 1994

Karen Klugman

Wendy Cohan,
photographed by
David F. Cohan

Ann Stinson

Sabiyha Prince

M. L. Head

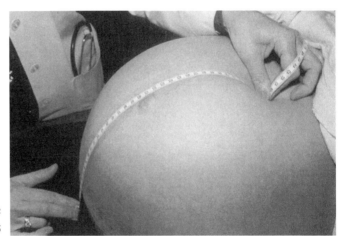

Dick Blau, "The Prize
Watermelon," 1995

seated nude under a spreading tree beside a stone Buddha, draws an exaggerated
(and cross-gender) parallel between her belly and his. For these women, objects
in the world become emblems of their own experience, and accessories to self-
expression.

But even without props, the pregnant woman can, and often does, deliberately point to her belly as the snapshot's central fact. Through this indexical
"pointing" to herself, she actively acknowledges her condition and can show it to
others. Sabiyha Prince's portrait of herself touching and displaying her belly is
both visual and tactile. M. L. Head articulates a more alienated sense of self in

taking the view of her own pregnant belly from below. In this image the belly becomes monstrous; she can barely peer over it to the other side. Few photographs other than snapshots take on the feelings of grotesqueness that can accompany pregnancy; in snapshots, expressing such feelings can be accomplished with a light touch. Dick Blau also points to the humor of the near-term pregnant belly, using clinical measurement as an ironic sign.

Strategic multiplication and indexical pointing within the pose nearly always result in caricatures of already exaggerated female bodies. The pregnant body is not represented in family photographs as too powerful, however. Humor mostly serves the function of enabling a subjective representation and, simultaneously, disarming it.

REPRESENTING THE EROTIC

Besides humor, family snapshots of pregnant women allow expressions of sensuality rarely found in other photographic contexts. In the domain of art photography, some aspect of the photograph generally mutes or counters an open representation of the pregnant woman's sensuality. But in family snapshots of

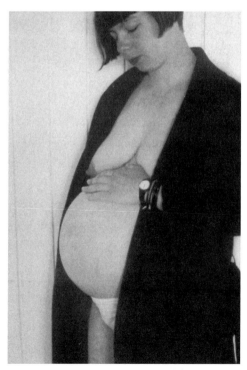

Ann Orsborn

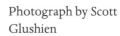

Photograph by Scott
Glushien

Trina Hikel

pregnancy sensuality abounds. Not only do pregnant women frequently pose
nude, but their poses often follow the cultural conventions of romantic or glamorous images of women. In snapshots, however, sensuality seems to function
primarily to represent the pregnant woman's relationship to her own body.
While her pose may be sexy, the sex she is referring to is not being invited; it has
already occurred and is being brought to fruition.

For example, in her snapshot of herself in the late stages of pregnancy, Ann
Orsborn strikes a sultry pose. She appears disengaged from her environment and
fully absorbed in observing her own body. More actively, even provocatively,
Trina Hikel displays her body in an image from an extended series of pregnant
self-portraits. She pictures herself nude, looking into a mirror with a camera in
one hand and the other hand on her hip. She is almost striking the pose of a
vamp, yet her saucy stance is for her own pleasure.

Erotically charged photographs of pregnant women can signify that pregnancy and childbirth are indeed sexual functions of women. In snapshots, sensuous poses allow the pregnant woman consciously to present herself to herself
as a sexualized subject, an attractive woman asserting the continuity of childbearing with other aspects of her sexuality.

Photograph by Peggy
Maisel

Photograph by Nancy
Floyd

Sabiyha Prince

"Deb, 4 Months after
Swallowing a
Watermelon Seed"

Sometimes family snapshots play with ideas about the connection between sex and reproduction. Scott Glushien's photograph of a pregnant woman holding an apple with a bite taken out of it refers to the biblical account of the loss of innocence and the acquisition of carnal knowledge, as well as punning on the idea of fruitfulness. Peggy Maisel's snapshot of a couple kissing awkwardly at an office party refers to the ongoing physical expression of affection during pregnancy, while Nancy Floyd's picture of a pregnant friend and her husband resting nude on their bed provides an unusual glimpse of marital intimacy during pregnancy. While portraits of expecting couples are relatively rare, Sabiyha Prince appears as a charming pregnant bride in a wedding snapshot. Deb Aldrich's snapshot, on the other hand, refers to an old joke about how babies are made with its title, "Deb, 4 months after swallowing a watermelon seed."

Catherine Nicol,
photograph by Alfred
Nicol

Elizabeth Butler

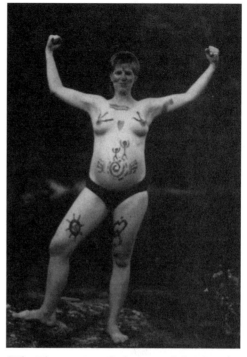

"The Blessing Way," photograph by s'myth

THE "NATURAL" PREGNANT BODY

Like art photographs, many snapshots place the pregnant figure in visual relation to aspects of the natural world, particularly bodies of water, domesticated animals and trees. In so doing, they comment on the natural power and mystery of pregnancy, choosing to de-emphasize historical or social dimensions of the experience. Catherine Nicol's photograph of herself with a flowering tree behind her makes a connection to the archetypal tree of life. Elizabeth Butler's image of herself practicing yoga at the edge of a lake expresses her sense of being a part of the larger natural world in more active terms.

Some snapshots also stretch the expected representation of pregnancy as part of nature by transgressively exploring the strength and agility of the pregnant body. These photographs playfully depict the kind of athleticism and physical ease found more typically in the representation of men or animals. Lorene Stanwick's "The Blessing Way," made by a photographer friend, is an image of herself standing, pregnant, on a rock flexing her biceps and wearing an expression of amusement. We associate Stanwick's pose with the conventional "muscleman" pose, which she mimics to signify power that is, in this instance, female. She wrote us that the photograph was made after completion of a pregnancy ritual designed by Stanwick and a group of women friends. The participants chose the symbols and painted them on her body in the hope of imparting strength and other needed qualities to Stanwick and her unborn child.

With so few images of pregnant female strength to draw on in contemporary Western societies, Stanwick and her friends pieced together a set of visual metaphors for the pregnant woman's relationships to nature and culture. The body paint and invented ritual were loosely appropriated from prehistoric and tribal images and contemporary performance art. Activating a kind of cultural fantasy, this photograph manages to construct an image of a strong and active pregnant woman.

Wendy Maude Buckmaster's exuberant snapshots of herself wearing nothing but high-top sneakers and clambering over what appears to be a ruined aqueduct on a mountaintop, challenge the passive, "expecting" image of the pregnant woman in a different way. She asserts here the wholeness of the pregnant body

Wendy Maude Buckmaster

that performs a difficult physical task with such agility. Her belly is not fetishized. A sense of danger accompanies her evident exhilaration as she perches high above the ground, abandoning the caution culturally mandated for pregnant women.

In these images, the pregnant woman is removed from the domestic scenarios of home and garden and pictured in a "wild" setting, evoking connections with the less benevolent aspects of nature. Unlike so many snapshots, Buckmaster's pictures do not portray a smiling figure who is mocking her own power.

IN AND OUT OF THE ALBUM

The 1980s saw the widespread use and rapid refinement of the sonogram as well as its institutionalization as a baby picture through the hospitals' custom of giving paper copies to the pregnant women. Sonograms have entered family albums in all social classes, functioning as a child's first portrait, implying special care and attention even before birth. The sonograms extend the range of the album to embrace the technologically enhanced exploration of the inner space of the pregnant woman.

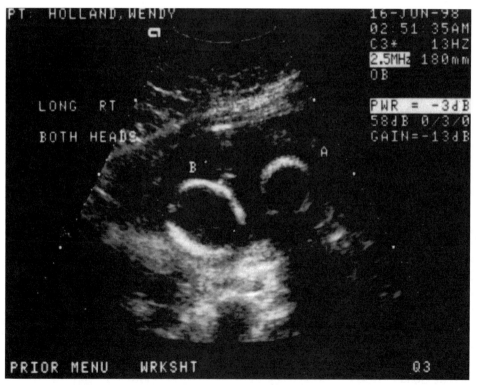

Wendy Holland, "Pictures of Emily and Lauren—Ultrasounds"

From *With Child*, photograph by Maggie Hopp, c.1992

During this same period, pregnant women extended their reach beyond the family album as well, going to professional photographers to have formal pregnant portraits made or even collaborating with artists to make images of their pregnancies that were more ambitious than home snapshots. Maggie Hopp and Paul B. Goode are among a small group of professional photographers who have photographed pregnant women in the studio and on location, pursuing extended artistic projects that also form part of the personal archive of their subjects. They picture individual pregnant women in sensuous and theatrical poses, drawing on a variety of cultural fantasies. Perhaps these photographs are framed on the wall, or kept aside for more private viewing. Hopp and Goode have each made efforts to publish their extensive work with pregnant subjects, but they report that, as of this writing, publishers have been squeamish about the subject. Mary Ann Halpin's book *Pregnant Goddesshood: A Celebration of Life* did get published in 1997, filled with portraits of fancifully costumed pregnant women, including "The Goddesses of St. Clair Avenue," in which pregnant women and

Paul B. Goode,
"Ramona and Ryan,"
n.d.

little girls dressed in harem costumes appear to be multiplying by spontaneous generation.

With the burgeoning of the Internet in the 1990s, personal Web pages have begun to beam photographs of pregnancies and births to far-flung family and friends electronically as well, once more shifting the public/private balance of family photographs. It is unclear what changes in family photographs will result from their wider and more rapid dissemination. Web sites displaying ultrasound fetal portraits, such as Richard and Wendy Holland's prebirth images of twin girls, combine a high-tech view into the womb with a public expression of excitement about an impending birth.

Mary Ann Halpin, "The Goddesses of St. Clair Avenue," from
Pregnant Goddesshood: A Celebration of Life, 1997

Family photographs do not fully participate in the scopic economy but are viewed instrumentally, usually within the confines of private life. Within this arena, it is clear that they can extend the representation of individual subjectivity. Yet they are also limited by their private context, remaining thematically close to a naturalized image of domestic life. While early family photographs did not dwell on pregnancy, family snapshots, particularly since the 1970s, foreground the pregnant woman as poser and performer. The humor and sensuality of pregnancy have been explored with more freedom in family snapshots than in most other forums. Interestingly, this shift coincided with the emergence of photographs of the fetus as a player on the public stage. Although family photographs of pregnancy may seem at first glance apolitical, their very existence is tied to changes in women's social options.

4) MEDICAL IMAGING, PREGNANCY AND THE SOCIAL BODY

> How long are we Americans to be so careful for the pedigree
> of our pigs and chickens and cattle—and then leave the
> *ancestry of our children* to chance or to "blind" sentiment?
>
> —American Eugenics Society, 1926

Obstetrical photographs, like all photographs, serve multiple purposes. In one sense they are comparatively specialized images. They come into existence as clinical case studies and therefore make their meaning within the scientific and humanitarian dimensions of medical discourse. They are sets of visual signs whose exhibition is largely confined to spectators within the medical field, a visual domain traditionally closed to noninitiates.

Yet obstetrical photographs also draw upon more general representational traditions. They employ symbolic vocabularies and transmit ideological messages that were originally formulated outside the clinical context. In fact, obstetrical photographs share many of the conventions for representing gender, race and class found in other kinds of photographs of women. In this respect, they are not just uniquely specialized images, but rich sources for examining cultural ideas about pregnant women's bodies both within and beyond medicine. As historian Sander L. Gilman points out in *Picturing Health and Illness: Image of Identity and Difference* (1995), even though "images, pictures, visual representations of all kinds have remained a stepchild in the writing of the history of medicine, the culture of medicine is as heavily involved with visual culture as any other aspect of modern cultural history."[1]

REPRESENTATIONAL LABOR

In this chapter we will inquire into the relationship between the representation of pregnant women in medical photographs over the past one hundred years and the shifting ideas of the eugenics movement in the United States. We will consider the photographs in each case as expressions of extant understandings of the meanings of pregnancy, and as productive sites where new meanings can arise.

The "eugenic idea," writes historian Daniel Kevles in *In the Name of Eugenics: Genetics and the Uses of Human Heredity* (1995), is that "physical, mental, and behavioral qualities of the human race could be improved by suitable management and manipulation of its hereditary essence."[2] The "obstetric idea," as stated by Dr. Herman Reinking in his presidential address to the State Medical Society of Wisconsin in 1899 when the specialty was just beginning to coalesce, is that "no one, except the educated physician, can ever give the parturient woman the aid, protection and amelioration of suffering to which she is entitled."[3] The eugenic idea has historically played an important, if not always overt, role in the social construction of the meaning of pregnancy. Eugenicists' claim to "suitable management" of the population resonates with obstetrical medicine's claim to superior "education." The voluminous production of medical textbook photographs of women with "normal" and "pathological" pregnancies often reflects eugenicist beliefs about the racial and class constitution of individual bodies.

Eugenic ideas are, of course, not the only themes played out in obstetrical photographs. They are, however, important enough scenarios in early obstetrical photographs to warrant particular attention, especially since permutations of the old themes have resurfaced in representations relating to reproductive technologies during recent years.

For our present purposes it will be useful to consider the changing appearance of obstetrical photographs of pregnant women over the last century in three phases. First, in the period from the turn of the century to the 1920s, the idea of differentiating between worthy and unworthy reproductive bodies first grew powerful and pervasive in Anglo-American thought. This period also coincides with the initial phase of the professionalization of American obstetrical medicine, during which medicalized childbirth gained dominance over the midwife's craft.

The second phase extends from the 1930s through the Great Depression, World War II, and well into the post–World War II era. During this period, childbearing moved into the hospital setting, and eugenic hopes, heavily discredited by Nazi endorsement and experimentation, were reconfigured as the promise of the scientific organization of health care to make progress for the population as a whole.

The third period comprises roughly the last quarter of the twentieth century, as genetics, combined with more and more potent assisted reproductive technologies, has positioned the unborn and the gene pool as eugenic targets for medical intervention and social control.

THE CLINICAL STANCE

The first appearance of photographs of pregnant women in medical textbooks toward the end of the nineteenth century coincides with the well-documented push to professionalize American medicine, at the expense of previous vernacular and/or female traditions of medical practice such as midwifery. Medical photographs of pregnant women were extensively used in this period in specialty textbooks such as Barton Cooke Hirst's 1898 *A Textbook of Obstetrics*.[4] They pictured both normal and abnormal conditions of pregnancy without the idealization or romanticization of pregnancy generally found in other venues.

The emphasis, however, was on abnormal situations that clearly called for "expert" consultation. Given their timing, and their uniquely unflinching representation of the sometimes horrific physical consequences of pregnancy, these images suggest not only the physical peril of pregnancy and childbirth at the turn of the century, but the benefits of placing pregnancy and childbirth under the care of physicians rather than allowing them to remain in the hands of midwives or general practitioners.

To the eyes of late-twentieth-century lay viewers, these early photographs may be quite disturbing, even shocking. They are not sentimental images, but they may nonetheless provoke deep empathy for the women who have found themselves in such distressing conditions. They powerfully portray the difficulties that individual pregnant women had to bear—and sometimes still must bear. Plates drawn from Barton Cooke Hirst's *A Textbook of Obstetrics* demonstrate the visceral power of these images. They constitute a theater of grotesque possibilities and ordinary disasters normally hidden from view.

A few turn-of-the-century images even were published as sets of stereoscopic views, a three-dimensional form of photography that reaches back into the nineteenth century and references voyeurism and spectacle as well as medical education. Other images were composed in artistic panels designed to look like Renaissance paintings, complete with skeletons as "memento mori." Apparently obstetricians were not opposed to being entertained as well as instructed by the evidence of their own success at meeting medical challenges. They even liked to re-encounter their "cases" as art.

Most such photographs, like those displayed by Hirst in one such "artistic" arrangement with captions that compare, for instance, "Spherical uterus of hydromania," "Fat, tympany, and anteversion," "Six months pregnant with a large, fibroid tumor. Seen in consultation with Dr. R. H. Handel," and "Breech presentation, at term," register the fact that clinical observation is a highly specialized activity. To the layperson, pregnant abdomens might look much alike, but physicians had to make more subtle distinctions. As Michel Foucault has argued, the clinical gaze lays claim to special power. It strives to be "a gaze that burns things to their furthest truth. The clinic no longer has simply to read the visible; it has to discover its secrets."[5] This looking beyond what is ordinarily visible required sophisticated training and advanced technology.

In the nineteenth century, photography was one such advanced technology. Images produced by mechanical reproduction were widely understood to be

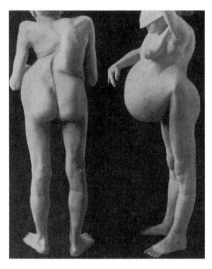

"Fig. 342. Kyphoscoliosus. Pelvis of rachitic type: C.V. 8.50 cm.(seen in consultation with D. Geo. I. McKelway)," Barton Cooke Hirst, *A Textbook of Obstetrics*, 1898.

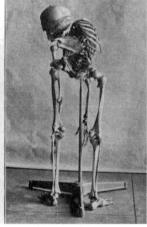

"Fig. 343. Skeleton of woman shown in Fig. 342, who died in consequence of labor," Hirst, 1898.

more "scientific" and "factual" than images produced in other ways. As David Green explains in "Views of Resemblance: Photography and Eugenics," the authority gained by photography "across a range of scientific, academic and technical disciplines" in the second half of the nineteenth century was due to "its apparent consistency with the empiricist assumptions and methodological procedures of naturalism."[6] Indeed, it was commonly thought that photographs did

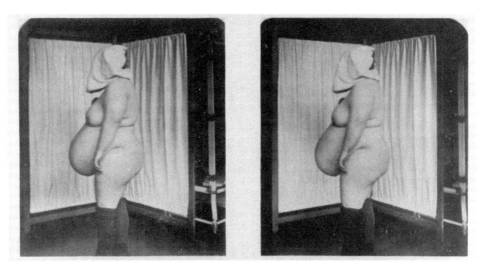

"Pendulous Belly," *The Edinburgh Stereoscopic Atlas of Obstetrics*, n.d.

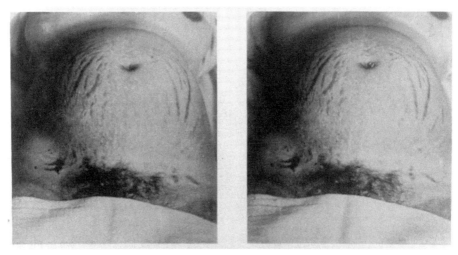

"Abdomen of Gravid Multipara," *The Edinburgh Stereoscopic Atlas of Obstetrics*, n.d.

not merely illustrate but actually increased the viewer's empirical perception by employing the penetrating lens of the camera to expose often subtle or hidden signs of difference and pathology.

These first attempts to integrate photographs of pregnant women into obstetrical textbooks supported the claim of special medical access to a gaze that saw through secrets in many other ways as well. For instance, before reliable pregnancy tests were developed, it was often difficult for physicians to differentiate a disease state from a pregnancy. Groupings of photographs helped physicians distinguish between abdominal conditions that were really due to pregnancy and those that mimicked pregnancy.[7] Conversely, the condition of

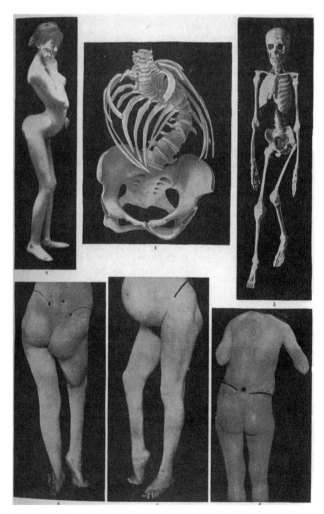

"Lumbodorsal Kyphoscoliosus (Schauta), and other conditions," Hirst, 1898

 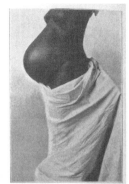

Fig. 132.—Spherical uterus of hydramnios.   Fig. 133.—Fat, tympany, and anteversion.

"Spherical uterus of
hydromania, and other
conditions," Hirst, 1898

pseudocyesis or "false pregnancy" was also pictured, as the "furthest truth" a physician might be called upon to pronounce in cases that involved paternity suits or special requests for lenient prison sentences made by female convicts who claimed that they were pregnant. It could be that a presumed pregnancy did not exist.

Obstetrical photographs, exposing both normal pregnancies and extreme abnormalities of pregnancy that are usually hidden—except from those who suffer them—simultaneously documented and increased the claims of obstetrical specialization. It was enough for the nineteenth-century physician to state that the subject was "a case of the author" for the photograph to seem appropriately scientific. Physicians-turned-photographers often cited their own consulting rooms or those of colleagues as the source of their photographic archives. By doing so they constituted themselves as a professional community whose specialized knowledge was both created and exchanged in part through photography.

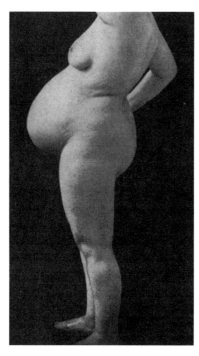

"Pseudocyesis: amenorrhea for 8 months, but vicarious menstruation from nose every month. The uterus is normal in size, position, moveability. The abdominal distention is due solely to tympanitis and fat," Hirst, 1898

Early medical images such as those in the Hirst textbook contain what is to our eyes now an oddly *ad hoc* arrangement of clothing and drapery, such as the socks and shoes left on some models' feet or the sheets wrapped clumsily around the legs of others. This apparent amateurism belies the sheer ambition for knowledge and power that was conveyed by these early images. In them one can see the use of clear visual conventions that allied the physician with other contemporary experts. In medicine the notion of the subject as "patient" easily blended in with the subject as "specimen," as "native," or as the "degenerate" of other discourses. For all, frontal, dorsal and lateral views delineated the subject of the photograph as an object of natural history, as in "Rachitic Dwarf." Nineteenth-century obstetrical specialists shared a visual vocabulary with anatomists, anthropologists and criminologists.

Categorization has always been one source of medicine's power, since it places the patient within the confines of an ordered system of knowledge. In the early medical photographs of pregnant women, this categorization often assumed the visual form of the grid. Clinical photographs such as "Mammary" from the second edition of Richard C. Norris' *The American Textbook of Obstetrics for Practitioners and Students* (1902) used grids to display body parts of many individuals so they could be compared and contrasted simultaneously.[8] These multi-

A   B

"Breech presentation,
head under ribs, and
other conditions,"
Hirst, 1898

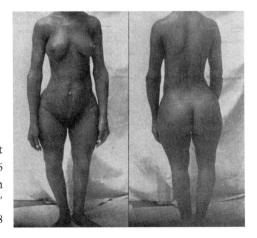

"Rachitic Dwarf: height
4 ft. 1 inch, conj. vera, 6
cm. Caesarian Section
(Howard Hospital),"
Hirst, 1898

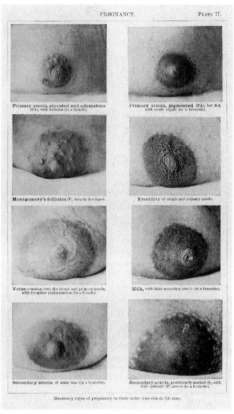

"Mammary," Norris, *The American
Textbook of Obstetrics for
Practitioners and Students*, 1902

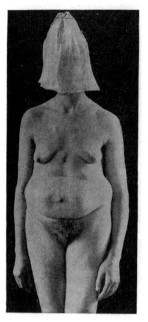

"Author's case of osteo-
malacia," Hirst, 1898

ple images simulated the quantitative advantage of the clinic, in which large
numbers of cases could be seen, implying encyclopedic knowledge. Like Galton's composite photographic images of racial "types" or Lombroso's photographic registers of criminal anatomies, the "Mammary" grid can be used to
identify the median and the mean, and to classify new examples.

The presentation of the patient's undressed body in so many of these photographic images was certainly very much at odds with normal life, both for the
patient and for the physician. Clearly, privacy was an issue. Often, as in "Author's
case of osteomalacia" by Barton Cooke Hirst, patients' faces were covered, lending the photographs an odd atmosphere of masquerade. But discomfort was not
the subject's burden alone. Restricted as late as the mid-nineteenth century from

looking directly at the genitals of his obstetrical patients, the trained physician by the end of the nineteenth century was supposed to have conquered false modesty.[9] In reality, however, he might still be struggling with what was and was not appropriate "exposure." One might conclude that one principal ideological function of early obstetrical photographs was to naturalize the masculine gaze at the female reproductive anatomy, and even at pregnant women's faces.

To publish photographic tableaux of physical abnormalities such as those available in Hirst's textbook was not the only strategy for naturalizing the medical gaze. Some turn-of-the-century obstetricians such as J. Clifton Edgar, in *The Practice of Obstetrics* (1904), and Richard C. Norris, in *The American Textbook of Obstetrics* (1904), chose another route. They published mostly pictures of healthy,

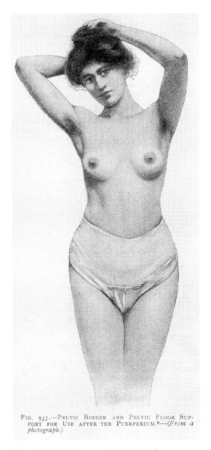

FIG. 937.—PELVIC BINDER AND PELVIC FLOOR SUP-
PORT FOR USE AFTER THE PUERPERIUM.*—(*From a photograph.*)

"Pelvic Binder and Pelvic Floor Support," J. Clifton Edgar, *The Practice of Obstetrics*, 1904

CONDUCT OF NORMAL LABOR.   PLATE 25.

Measuring the external conjugate: the black dots show the points from which the measurements are taken (from a photograph).

"Measuring the external conjugate diameter upon the living female (Dickinson)," Norris, 1904

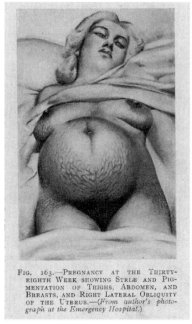

"Pregnancy at the thirty-
eighth week," Edgar, 1904

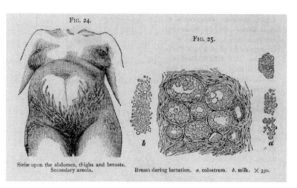

"Striae upon the abdomen thighs
and breasts," F. Winckel,
A Textbook of Obstetrics, 1890

well-cared-for, and sometimes even enticingly sexualized, pregnant women.[10] Norris' happy-looking young mother-to-be, for instance, presents her abdomen to the calipers with an introspective wistful gaze into the middle distance that propels her into the protected zone of white middle-class maternal fantasy. Her physical condition does not threaten to disrupt this fantasy. Edgar's model in "Pregnancy at the thirty-eighth week showing striae and pigmentation of thighs, abdomen, and breasts, and right lateral obliquity of the uterus" exhibits a passive, seductive pose that offers cosmetic feminine attractiveness to counter the gaze at the potentially alarming stretch marks that appear on the pregnant woman's body. In fact, Edgar was so eager to include this view of the striated abdomen that the image he labels his own—"from author's photograph at the Emergency Hospital"—is really a redrawing of a figure from his German colleague Dr. F. Winckel's 1890 *A Textbook of Obstetrics*, the translation of which Edgar himself supervised. But in Winckel, the woman has no head. Edgar added the sexualized woman's head himself.[11]

Such deliberately attractive images contrast dramatically with the graphic displays of bodily discomfort in Hirst. They seek to portray a doctor-patient rela-

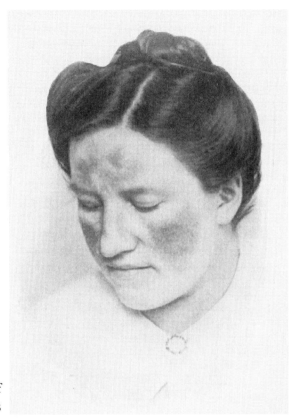

"The Mask of
Pregnancy," DeLee, 1913

tionship that is commensurate with the habitual social relations of everyday life. They emphasize the promise of the newly formed medical specialty of obstetrics, rather than dire warnings of what can happen if obstetrical care is not secured.

However, an illustration entitled "The Mask of Pregnancy" in *The Principles and Practice of Obstetrics* (1913) written by an important early-twentieth-century women's health advocate, Dr. Joseph B. DeLee, suggests certain difficulties that could arise with such positive visualizations.[12] The formal structure of this image conveys a classic "male gaze" at a pregnant woman, whose averted eyes and seemingly blushing, half-turned face represent a stereotypical femininity in repose. But upon closer inspection, the "blush" turns out to be a change in skin coloration called "the mask of pregnancy." The ambiguity on which the picture and the caption turn neatly expresses the conflict many obstetrical texts evince between portraying the pregnant woman as a feminized object of the male gaze, like any other woman, and portraying her as a clinical object whose sexuality must be hidden, or masked. Even in the domain of medicine, where hierarchical, empowered looking was the rule, the scopic gaze apparently ran into difficulty when it sought to incorporate sexuality along with the reproductive powers of a pregnant woman.

Nonetheless, the chief concern in late-nineteenth- and early-twentieth-century obstetrical writings is the most basic issue of survival. Because disease was rampant, maternal death was always possible. Though poor health reigned among the immigrant and working-class populations, it was in no way possible for obstetricians to guarantee maternal well-being for any woman at this stage, rich or poor, white or black, native born or immigrant. All were prey to a wide variety of life-altering physical dysfunctions associated with the physical stress of pregnancy and injuries of childbirth, not to mention the debilitating effects of chronic conditions such as tuberculosis, diphtheria, syphilis, and nervous disorders. It was obvious to many turn-of-the-century physicians that hospitals killed the poor, their main clients, through the unchecked transmission of deadly microbes. Yet the rich, confined in the comfort and supposed safety of home, died too, for reasons that were not well understood.

The 1910 Flexner Report to the Carnegie Foundation, which castigated the quality of medical education in the United States, singled out obstetrical training for special condemnation. It found that medical school lectures on obstetrics were "utterly worthless," practice with the mannequin was "of value only to a limited degree," "very little" hospital experience was provided for students, and out-patient work was "poorly supervised." Flexner believed that "principles, methods, technique, can be learned and skill acquired only in an adequately equipped maternity hospital."[13] The Flexner Report created a public uproar, led to new curricula and a tightening of standards for accreditation in the medical schools, and provided the rationale for the medicalization of birth and its shift from home to hospital in the ensuing decades. But pregnancy and birth become no safer for women.

Two years later Dr. J. Whitridge Williams published the results of his own survey on obstetrical teaching. Professor of obstetrics and gynecology at the Johns Hopkins Medical School and the author of the canonical textbook, *Obstetrics*, Williams was a towering figure in the late-nineteenth- and early-twentieth-century drive to provide healthier pregnancies and safer deliveries for pregnant women in the United States. His survey showed that the state of education in obstetrics in American medical schools was "deplorable."

Even students who graduated from his own university were "unfit on graduation to practice obstetrics in its broad sense, and scarcely prepared to handle normal cases." Williams concluded, "For many years I have regarded the general attitude toward obstetrical teaching as a very dark spot in our system of medical education, and the majority of the replies to my questionnaire indicate that my pessimism was more than justified."[14]

And in the introduction to his own textbook, *The Principles and Practice of Obstetrics*, Chicago physician Joseph B. DeLee asked in 1913, "Can a function so perilous, that in spite of the best care, it kills thousands of women every year, that leaves at least a quarter of the women more or less invalided, and a majority with permanent anatomic changes of structure, that is always attended by severe pain and tearing of tissues, and that kills 3 to 5 per cent, of children—can such a function be called normal?"[15] In 1920 DeLee proposed a policy of aggressive intervention with forceps, episiotomy, and the routine use of drugs such as scopolamine and ergot to standardize care, for he could not believe, he said, that "Nature deliberately intend[ed] women should be used up in the process of reproduction in a manner analogous to that of the salmon, which dies after spawning."[16]

Well into the twentieth century, this pessimism about the profession and anxiety about the most primal issues of safety in childbearing was evident in the textbooks. The frontispiece of J. Whitridge Williams' *Obstetrics*, which first appeared in 1903 and ran without a break in every edition until 1950, illustrates its focus on maternal survival under dire circumstances.[17] Drawn, apparently, after a photograph and entitled "Vertical Mesial Section Through Body of Woman Dying in Labour with Unruptured Membranes Protruding from Vulva," the frontispiece of his textbook shows a pregnant woman's torso sliced in half vertically by a saw. The fetus within her, trapped by "unbroken membranes," is itself sliced in two along the same vertical section line. That is, the fetus is treated in the same way as the mother; no physical distinction has been made between the two bodies.

The words of the caption, "Woman Dying in Labour," also subsume the fetus within the woman's story. If the woman is "dying," the fetus must be dying too, but no mention is made of that fact. Indeed, the sectioning of the fetus is superfluous if the point is to get information about *its* body, for a view of its own bones and internal organs can tell us nothing about the causes of its death. The section of the fetus simply mirrors the section of the mother, and has no existence separate from its mother, unlike contemporary fetal images.

What is most striking about this frontispiece may be that the woman's death is spoken of in the present tense. She is said to be "Dying in Labour" at the very moment that her body has been sawed in half. A highly improbable situation in reality, this violent conflation of birth and death and the confusion of times between the fatal outcome of the pregnancy and its depiction bespeak the peril that turn-of-the-century obstetrical medicine felt the birthing woman to be confronting.

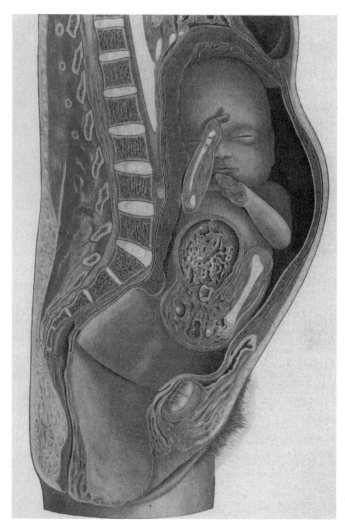

"Vertical Mesial Section
Through Body of
Woman Dying in
Labour with
Unruptured Membranes
Protruding from Vulva,"
J. Whitridge Williams,
Obstetrics, 1904

Significantly, although the woman has been cut in half, nothing visible within
her body gives a clue to the cause of her death. Would it have helped her had the
"unbroken membranes" been artificially ruptured? It is impossible to tell from
the image. Readers who for more than half a century opened copies of the many
editions of this canonical obstetrical textbook and studied its frontispiece sought
visible causes of tragedy that could only be discovered through the modes of
interpretation taught in obstetrical training. In effect, such a frontispiece is promotional material for medical education and intervention. It implies that if one

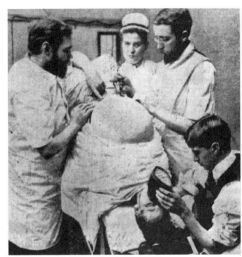

"Operation for Ovarian
Cyst," Harold Speert,
*Obstetrics and Gynecology
in America,* 1892

reads beyond the opening pages, one will gain the diagnostic insight necessary
both to interpret the visual image and to manage the peril it represents.

The woman's body was often portrayed in the early years of the twentieth
century as a natural obstacle for the fetus. Interest in visualizing the fetus growing within the mother was less an interest in the fetus per se, as it is today, than
in getting it out of the mother's body in any number of emergencies. The
nineteenth-century obstetrician was an "accoucher." That is, he saw his primary
job as ensuring that the mother got up again from the childbed; only secondarily
could he place a healthy infant in her arms. The womb was often reified as the
obstetrician's enemy in this process.

An 1892 photographic image of an "Operation for ovarian cyst," reproduced
by medical historian Harold Speert in *Obstetrics and Gynecology in America,*
broadly indicates the character and self-perception of an obstetrical surgical
team dealing with such a womb-obstacle.[18] In this case the swollen abdomen
only mimics pregnancy, a common look-alike against which many turn-of-
the-century pregnancy photographs attempted to establish a distinctive visual
typology. As Speert's caption notes, the photograph "demonstrates" a "new
gynecological operating table," and that "the surgeons' clothing [though not,
apparently, the nurse's] was protected by long rubber aprons."[19] The heroic conception of well-supplied medical gladiators refusing to be balked by an
intractable female organ conveys the idea that the distended womb presents a
formidable challenge for even a highly trained group of medical personnel to
surmount. The woman herself, although physically present in the image with

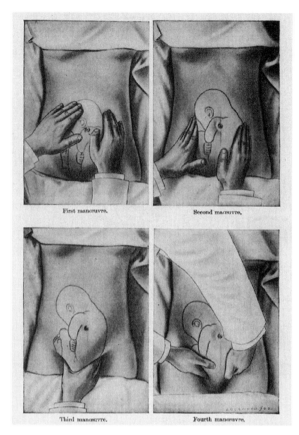

First manœuvre.   Second manœuvre.

Third manœuvre.   Fourth manœuvre.

"Palpation in Left Sacro—Anterior Presentation," Williams, 1912

her face even partially exposed, is virtually a lump of flesh. Anesthetized, she can give no entry for the viewer into her own suffering. The unseen womb within her body is the true protagonist here.

In another set of photographs—the 1912 illustration of "Palpation in Left Sacro-Anterior Presentation"—the contents of the womb are visualized in schematic drawings made directly on the woman's abdomen. In these pictures, the skill of the illustrator and the expertise of the attending physician are shown to be working actively together. This photograph conveys a graphic sense of the physicality needed for such maneuvers by rendering in dramatic perspective the hand's grasp of the fetal head through the skin and the arm movements of the physician in the fourth panel. Rather than serving to categorize, the four images in grid formation formulate a birth narrative, this time with the physician as protagonist.

Partly as a consequence of the underlying atmosphere of tension and antagonism, the boundary between photographs of the "normal" and the "abnormal" in early textbook illustrations seems unclear. Along with pictures of health and disease, images of medical "curiosities" are scattered about. Excerpts from so-called medical "museums" of "monsters," and examples of "anomalous and curious" cases from the historical past and from other cultures mingle with examples of the brand-new technological miracle of the X-ray image. Where and when the line between the ordinary and the extraordinary is being crossed is difficult to distinguish. And indeed, those in attendance probably felt that the one could easily become the other.

THE EUGENICS CONNECTION

Early obstetrical photographic grids and sequences that compared "normal" and "abnormal" pregnant women were not just striking arguments in support of obstetric education. They were also well suited to illustrate the conceptions of race, class and nation that circulated in late-nineteenth- and early-twentieth-century eugenics. Mainline eugenic thought in the United States took root at the same time as the earliest obstetrical photographs were published. It was divided into two strands: "positive eugenics," which emphasized, as Daniel Kevles puts it, "more prolific breeding among the socially meritorious"; and "negative eugenics," which "intended to encourage the socially disadvantaged to breed less—or, better yet, not at all."[20] But from either a prescriptive or a proscriptive orientation, it was the reproductive capacity of the female body— rather than, say, less fascinating environmental components of well being and public health such as clean air and adequate sewers—that was placed most directly under regulatory scrutiny.

Class prejudice was a constant of eugenic thought. However, in the United States, race was the more important category. The Anglo-Saxon was the ideal type implicit in almost all American eugenic rhetoric. But different races were thought to have different capacities for childbearing, and it was feared that Anglo-Saxons had become weak in that department. This meant that other races could soon outnumber Anglo-Saxons. Early eugenic thinkers in the United States had little difficulty, therefore, in advocating the exclusion of whole categories of people from full citizenship as supposed prophylaxis for the health and prosperity of the nation.

Clinical photography, like forensic photography and social documentary photography, helped to confirm such alleged relationships between reproduction, racial difference, and the social body. Even though medical images remained by and large a segregated set of images directed toward medical viewers, eugenically oriented physicians sought to educate the public about the importance of maternal health and the dangers of "degeneracy." It was "commonplace among eugenicists that men and women alike would be better equipped for race regeneration the more they knew about family and maternal health," writes Kevles. "Eugenics, concerned ipso facto with the health and quality of offspring, focused on issues that, by virtue of biology and prevailing middle-class standards, were naturally women's own."[21] Pregnancy has a unique capacity to signify biological "origins" both at the level of the individual and at the level of collective peoplehood. Early medical images of pregnant women easily functioned as screens for projected social narratives that related the quality and character of the population to maternal health or disease, wealth or poverty, to factors of whiteness or darkness and/or national origin.

Several important historical factors influenced the way the medical profession regarded the health of the pregnant woman during the original phase of the eugenics movement in the United States. At the turn of the century, rapid industrialization, urbanization and capitalization saw the continued impoverishment and disenfranchisement of rural blacks in the South. At the same time, large numbers of persons displaced from southern and eastern Europe by economic change and social revolution were immigrating to northern cities, the centers of obstetrical teaching and research, which subsequently witnessed a crisis in public health. The nation's imperial wars in the Caribbean and the Pacific brought contact with nonwhite, non-European peoples, some incorporated into the society against their will through territorial conquest. Many middle- and upper-class American whites became alarmed about the effect impoverished or "foreign" populations might have on the future of what they understood as Anglo-Saxon American institutions.

Such nativists became attracted at this time to positive eugenic ideas, such as notions of deliberate marriage for "race improvement." These ideas had first been called "eugenics" in Francis Galton's writings in 1883. Galton believed that eugenics principles "co-operate with the workings of nature by securing that humanity shall be represented by the fittest races. What nature does blindly, slowly, and ruthlessly, man may do providently, quickly and kindly."[22] Turn-of-the-century physicians, like settlement house workers and public health officials, urged greater attention to maternal health as one way of guaranteeing the vigor of "the race" as it rose to the challenges of contact and conquest. Eventually, this idea was expressed in the theory of selective breeding. "Improvement in social conditions will not compensate for a bad hereditary influence. . . . The only way to keep a nation strong mentally and physically is to see to it that each new generation is derived chiefly from the fitter members of the generation before."[23] Outspoken eugenicists such as President Theodore Roosevelt feared that a growing differential in reproduction between white and foreign or dark-skinned women would result in "race suicide" for American Anglo-Saxons. Roosevelt wanted all middle-class and upper-class white women to have a least four children for "someday we will realize that the prime duty, the inescapable duty, of the *good* citizen of the right type is to leave his or her blood behind him in the world," even though Roosevelt had lost his own first wife to complications of childbirth.[24]

Positive eugenics was dedicated to increasing the reproductive vigor of individual upper-middle-class white Anglo-Saxon women. Negative eugenics in this period also stressed maternal health. But rather than encouraging the Anglo-Saxon "fit" to have more children, it sought to suppress reproduction by those with deformations, diseases and depravities that would presumably "contaminate" the white American population. In 1891 statisticians discovered that criminality and mental deficiency were steadily increasing, and that immigrants were "breeding much more vigorously than native-born Americans."[25] There was great concern that left to themselves, the "defective classes"— that is, immigrants, poor people, people of color—who exhibited so many contagious diseases and social pathologies would soon be out-producing everyone else and populating the nation with "defectives."

Opinion was divided over the benefits to the nation and "the race" of offering medical care and social services to the poor. On the one hand, to do so would raise the general level of maternal and child health. On the other, as one social theorist reasoned, "advances in medical skills extended life 'for the members of weak and unsound stock' and—what was more significant—reduced their children's mortality rate.'"[26] Negative eugenics thus articulated an ambivalent stance toward scientific medical progress. In 1913 a contributor to the *Yale Review* warned that "defectives . . . 'breed back,' so to speak, to their degenerate ancestors, their very betterment but affording the opportunity for them to propagate their unfit kind."[27]

Medical participation in this branch of the eugenic campaign led to sterilization of alcoholics, drug addicts, epileptics, the mentally ill, criminals, poor people, and people who were "idiots," "morons" or "feebleminded." Scientists, government officials and American cultural institutions also were heavily invested. The Second International Congress of Eugenics took place at the American Museum of Natural History in 1921, and published its proceedings under the title "Eugenics in Family, Race, and State." By 1931, Donna Haraway writes, thirty state legislatures had passed eugenic sterilization laws.[28] "The logic of this selective thrust," write Carole H. Browner and Nancy Ann Press in "The Normalization of Prenatal Diagnostic Screening," was that "negative traits and behaviors were biologically transmitted from one generation to the next. Racism played no small part in these early eugenic efforts; non-whites constituted the overwhelming majority of those sterilized."[29]

"Specificity" was also an important concept in American medicine. The term meant the development of therapeutic regimes that took differences of age, gender, race, ethnicity, cultural and personal habits, climate, topography, and profession to be crucial factors in determining kinds and standards of care. According to medical historians Ronald L Numbers and John Harley Warner, adherents to American ideas of "specificity" had long proposed that "the therapeutic needs of the immigrant poor differed from those of native-born patients and, consequently, that information gained by observing pauperized Irish immigrants in a large urban hospital might be deceptive as a guide to treating middle-class private patients or even the hospitalized native-born."[30] In this milieu doctors expected obstetrical photographs to convey the patient's race and class.

For instance, several images in Hirst's *Obstetrics* joined previously pathologized figurations of "the African" to photographs of pregnant African-American women. A drawing made from a photograph captioned "Pendulous Abdomen in a Primapara with a Generally Contracted Rachitic Pelvis," printed in Hirst, offers much to think about along these lines. Even though its caption does not explicitly reference race, the image employs racial stereotypes in the way that it presents the pregnant figure. In fact, redrawing the image from a photograph even allows selective emphasis of particular features of these stereotypes, such as exaggerating the deformity of the lower legs. The image depicts a naked, dark-skinned, barefoot woman with her breasts as well as her belly fully exposed by her uplifted arm. Her face, though averted, is pictured as well. She is said to be suffering from a "pendulous abdomen" caused by a "rachitic pelvis," and her crooked legs and bent head makes it seem as if she does not stand completely upright as she walks.

But the problem presented here is not that of diagnosing her drooping abdomen or misshapen pelvis alone. It is also how to portray and understand the significance of these conditions in a "specific" subject. The black woman's nudity and her enigmatic facial expression are reminiscent of J. W. Zealy's daguerreotypes of South Carolina female slaves such as the portrait of "Delia" commissioned by Harvard Professor Louis Agassiz in 1850 to help him prove that Africans were a separate "creation" and did not derive "from a common center" with whites. Agassiz formally opposed slavery but, as Alan Trachtenberg remarks in *Reading American Photographs*, his belief in "polygeny," or separate creation, left him concerned to establish the specificity of presumed racial qualities and capabilities among Africans as well as those which differentiated them from whites.[31] Agassiz wanted the daguerreotypes to help "settle the relative rank among these races, the relative value of the characters peculiar to each, [and] to foster those dispositions that are eminently marked in them."[32]

The image presents a specifically African-American instance of "abnormal-ity," to which it applies typical conventions that marked the "primitive" body. The bare feet index "devolution," and imply that this barefoot patient might not require all the elaborate care of "civilization."

In the same textbook, a white woman with a rachitic pelvis is pictured differently. Even though the white woman's pregnancy is physically distressed in exactly the same way as that of the black woman, the photograph visually distinguishes her position as diseased subject from that of the black women along lines of class and race encoded in bodily signs. Here it is not "the slave" or the "primitive" that is the operative symbolic system, but Victorian pornography.

The pregnant nude white woman who stands with belly and breasts exposed clearly has followed orders to present herself in this manner. However, rather than being barefoot like the submissive black woman, she wears her shoes and her thick white stockings down around her ankles, as do female figures in numerous nineteenth-century bourgeois erotic scenarios. Even though she is not an "African," this woman submits to her photograph like a so-called white slave, or prostitute. In fact, the woman's coarse, heavy shoes give away her identity as

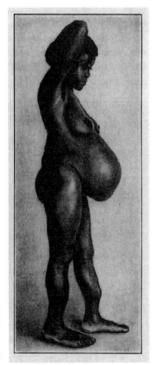

"Pendulous Abdomen in a Primapara with a generally contracted Rachitic Pelvis," Hirst, 1898

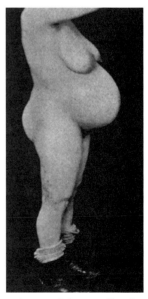

"The Pendulous Belly of Rachitis. Pregnant at term," Hirst, 1898

a member of the working class. Once again, the race and class "specificity" in the photographic image is meant to help determine how her physician will diagnose the "further truth" of her pregnancy, and what course of treatments he will recommend. Hers is an image of degraded whiteness, lacking even a head. The conventions of modesty and Victorian womanhood need not apply to her as she labors in a charity clinic or public hospital ward.

In another photographic grid taken from Gould and Pyle, *Anomalies and Curiosities of Medecine* (1898), black models are differentiated from whites by the addition of "African" cues, such as draping in sheets that resemble an idea of tribal dress. This draping is actually more modest than the fuller physical exposure of the bodies of the white models. However, in more than one image the drapery is also very oddly arranged around a chair, sticking far out behind the women in a bizarre echo of the "steatopygia" said at the time to be typical of black females and Italian prostitutes. To late nineteenth-century medical men, writes Sander Gilman, "the black female looks different. Her physiognomy, her skin color, the form of her genitalia mark her as inherently different. The nineteenth century perceived the black female as possessing not only a 'primitive' sexual appetite, but also the external signs of this temperament, 'primitive' genitalia and protruding buttocks."[33] A directed and constructed photographic image such as this has a clear reference point in drawings of Saartje Baartman, the "Hottentot Venus," who had been brought as a spectacle from South Africa in 1810 and was publicly exhibited in Europe until she died in 1815 at the age of twenty-five. Baartman's buttocks provoked fascination, and fantasies about her supposedly abnormal genitalia and sexual appetites proliferated, influencing even the form of this medical illustration almost a century later.

This particular grid in Gould and Pyle also presents the subject of race from another perspective. The most imperative distinction that is being made here is perhaps not the racial difference between black and white but the class difference implied between some women and others—that is, those who are immigrants, poor and working class, and those who are too wealthy, too protected to have their privacy violated by the publication of such photographs, even in the hope of obtaining help. Medical intervention into the lives of both white and nonwhite patients, *all* of whom are portrayed in this instance as pathological, is constructed as an intervention away from "depravity" on behalf of elite social progress.

Numerous photographs of this period also portray the increasing sense of social discipline that came with "positive eugenics." Military-style organization was an indirect but powerful theme. For example, J. Whitridge Williams' 1904 *Obstetrics* included an photograph entitled "Showing Relative Abdominal Enlargment at Third, Sixth, Ninth, and Tenth Month of Pregnancy."[34] In this photograph four images of a pregnant white woman with a handkerchief tied over her

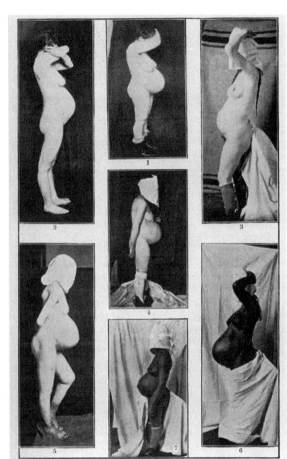

"Conditions simulating pregnancy," Gould and Pyle, *Anomalies and Curiosities of Medicine,* 1901

"Fat, tympany and anteversion," Hirst, 1898

face are lined up single file and naked, like new recruits at their army physical. The exactly repeated pose with the woman's hands each time clasped above her head echoes the repetitions of the modular form of the grid, allowing comparison of body parts. But it also homogenizes the pregnant body, unlike the images in the grids from the earlier period, which were often at great pains to illustrate aberrant occurrences within the pregnant woman's body and to show how distinct and "specific" each pregnant woman's body was.

In fact, the photographer has made virtually the same picture four times and combined all of them into a single image. The only thing that hints at something not standard in the image is the last recruit in line who is said to be in her *tenth* month. Among other things, the repetition of multiple healthy white bodies in the image suggests a camaraderie in pregnancy that is not similarly evoked by the isolation of the earlier representations of anomalous black and white women. One might even conclude from the image that a troop of confident, pregnant white women performs a eugenic "service" to the country.

The same edition of *Williams' Obstetrics* also ran an illustration of the "Same Full-Term I—Para in Vertical and Horizontal Position."[35] The image is designed to instruct the viewer about differences in how a normal pregnant abdomen looks when the pregnant woman is standing up and lying down. It is a lesson in the comparison of body parts, rather than the multiplication of bodies. But once again there is a soldierly cast to the photograph. The model's high socks look a

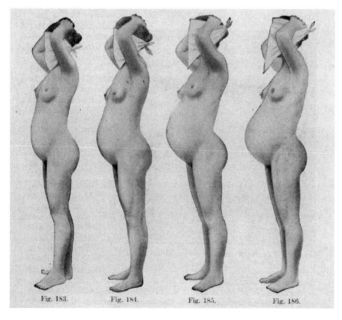

Fig. 183.   Fig. 184.   Fig. 185.   Fig. 186.

"Showing Relative Abdominal Enlargement at Third , Sixth, Ninth, and Tenth Month of Pregnancy," Williams, 1904

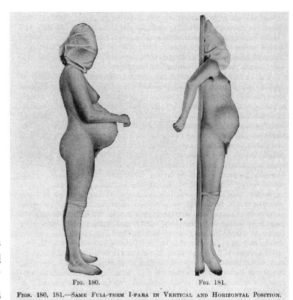

"Same Full-term I-para
in Vertical and
Horizontal Position,"
Williams, 1904

FIG. 180.   FIG. 181.

FIGS. 180, 181.—SAME FULL-TERM I-PARA IN VERTICAL AND HORIZONTAL POSITION.

good deal like boots or puttees, especially in comparison to the rumpled socks
swimming about the ankles of other models from the turn of the century. She is
militarized, rather than sexualized like her sisters. Her body in the "horizontal
position" looks very much like a casualty carried off the field of battle on a
stretcher.

PHASE TWO: REFORM

A second stage in American obstetrics textbook photography extends from the
Depression, through World War II, and well into the post–World War II period.
Advances in medicine were dramatic. In obstetrics specifically, the development
of penicillin and sulfa drugs during this period finally brought under control
infectious diseases like syphilis and tuberculosis, two of the most common complications of pregnancy. The interwar years saw the growth of modern hospitals
and maternity clinics patronized for the first time by middle-class—that is, pay-
ing—clients.

   In 1933 the United States created its first uniform procedures for reporting and
registering diseases, which in turn augmented the collection of public health statistical data. Such data stimulated practical alliances between government and
medicine, increased the local political power of physicians, and gave them a
greater say in national policy.

Dorothea Lange, "Calipatria (vicinity) Imperial Valley, CA, February 1939. In a grower's camp for migrant workers on the edge of the pea field. Public health nurse advises a prospective mother, aged 17, before the arrival of her first baby. The husband, age 23, is out picking: he made 73 cents this morning."

One result was that several plans to provide health care on a national, or mass, scale were developed and tested during this period. During the Depression, the New Deal created expanded models for the enterprise of public health that were funded, like the military, from national tax dollars, if never with the actual intention of nationalizing medicine. The Farm Security Administration, for instance, documented in several thousand photographs a federally administered direct relief program that brought medical care to no fewer than 120,000 families in more than one thousand counties throughout the United States.[36] Another model for national health care delivery was developed simultaneously by the Public Health Service, which also documented its activities extensively in photographs. The Farm Security Administration images compiled by John D. Stoekle and George Abbott White in *Plain Pictures of Plain Doctoring* show the delivery of medical services in the public sector during the 1930s and early '40s in terms of a vernacular ethos of primary care in a largely rural or small-town context. Dorothea Lange's FSA photograph of a pregnant woman living in a tent being visited by a health worker—one of the handful of FSA images to depict pregnancy—is consonant with this perspective. The Frontier Nursing Service launched a program that was similar in spirit to the FSA, as evidenced by Marvin Breckenridge's photograph entitled "Prenatal visit. Outside the cabin" which shows the rural, low-tech nature of the primary care the nurses delivered. But the Public Health Service collection, argues Sally Stein, "complicates" the picture Stoekle and White draw of 1930s medicine by offering another viewpoint. It

Marvin Breckenridge, "Prenatal Visit. Outside the Cabin," Frontier Nursing Service, Wendover, Kentucky, n.d.

"depicts a rapid changeover to an increasingly rationalized and centralized health system," which she asserts was "privileging research and development, capital intensive rather than labor intensive, with the lab assuming a central position in diagnosis, and popular media becoming a standard means of heightening public awareness of specific diseases and courses of prevention."[37] It is clear that the '30s and early '40s were a creative watershed for public sector health care. And all this does not even address, as Stein notes, the "private sector activities of the AMA (American Medical Association)," organizing in the interest of physicians.[38]

Militarization during World War II promoted an even higher level of health care organization within the armed services, and this translated into increased efficiency in civilian life and the widening perception that state "care" for industrial workers was in the national interest. Among the many changes World War II brought to American society was further participation of government in medical care, particularly through the funding of research by the National Institute of Health. "Preventive medicine had entered American culture with Flexner's medical reforms and at the insistence of Progressives in politics and society," observe John Stoeckle and George Abbott White. But "if the war demonstrated that women could do any task—even heavy, dangerous industrial work—it also demonstrated that the 'war effort' demanded a healthy population."[39] As one wartime poster read, "Your first line of defense is a healthy body."[40] Even though military medicine was not about the care of pregnant women directly, the increased attention and support of public health translated into better outcomes for the entire population. And infant mortality, "a symbolic indicator of national health standards," as Judith Waltzer Leavitt notes in *Sickness and Health in America* (1997), "during the first three decades of the 20th century decreased by more than 50 percent, and fell at an even greater rate during the next 20 years."[41]

Where the military goes, American industry follows closely behind. World War II and its aftermath were no exception to the pattern. Many technological innovations developed by the military, such as ultrasound, were adapted to peacetime medical uses. Such developments combined to bolster faith in the scientific-industrial model of the hospital, a health "factory" and research center now widely respected by doctors and middle-class patients alike as a safe and convenient institution. Even though the majority of births in the United States still took place at home until almost 1940, obstetrics was firmly established as a professional specialty and enjoyed the increased power and prestige of medicine generally.[42]

Significantly, the photographs published in obstetrical textbooks in this period were no longer made by the doctors themselves, working as amateur photographers in their own consulting rooms. Hospitals now had professional photographic staffs. The ad hoc arrangements of the earlier phase gave way to more standard formats in which both hospitals and patients followed definite protocols of modesty and display. The gain in uniformity makes these images more familiar to contemporary viewers; they are more like the kinds of instrumental images we have come to expect from scientific domains. Obstetrical textbooks no longer emphasized the heterogeneity of bodily states with which the physician would be confronted; instead they emphasized the wide array of standard expertise he could draw upon. If the physician was no longer the photographer, it was because as a specialist he had more pressing duties. On the one hand, since there were higher expectations than before that the result of pregnancy and labor would be a living baby and surviving mother, the neonate now came to occupy more of the obstetrician's field of vision. On the other hand, obstetrical practice divided more palpably into primary care and surgical branches, requiring increased specialization. The stereotype of the heroic gladiator continued, however, to advance obstetricians as humanitarian figures and to belie the fact that increasingly they worked in hospital settings within a bureaucratic hierarchy and strict division of labor.

In the textbooks of the late 1940s and early '50s, technological discoveries made by the military during the course of World War II began to appear in altered form. A prophetic image of a pregnant woman made in the early 1950s, and reproduced by Ann Oakley in *The Captured Womb* over a caption that reads: "recording of intrauterine pressure by transabdominal needle and seven channel external recording of uterine activity," illustrates the applied mechanical ingenuity that characterized the medical self-image in this era.[43] The unlikely looking contraption is a forerunner of ultrasound visualization, itself a World War II invention. Such technology augmented the ebullience of the postwar baby boom to reconstruct the pregnant woman's body as a national resource. Its reproductive power—regulated and domesticated—was no longer an obstacle but a secret weapon of American civilization.

The mid-twentieth-century obstetrician especially relied on an expanded range of visual technology. Obstetrical textbooks at mid-century increasingly featured images made by machines to be used as diagnostic tools for the supervision of pregnancy and labor. For example, by means of infrared photography the obstetrician was invited to visualize the veins under the skin of the living pregnant torso, as illustrated in an image from *Williams' Obstetrics* of 1950.[44] Making and reading X rays of the living fetus had long been part of his regular repertoire. The textbooks instructed physicians in X-ray pelviotomy, or measurement of the size of the pelvic outlet relative to the estimated size of the fetus, which previously had been done by palpation and guesswork. Early confirmation of pregnancy by X ray was common procedure until the rabbit test was developed in 1931, and even after, it was regularly used to check things like fetal size and to estimate due dates.

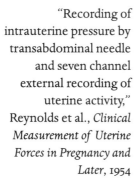
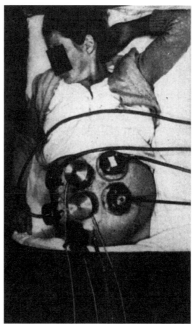

"Recording of intrauterine pressure by transabdominal needle and seven channel external recording of uterine activity," Reynolds et al., *Clinical Measurement of Uterine Forces in Pregnancy and Later,* 1954

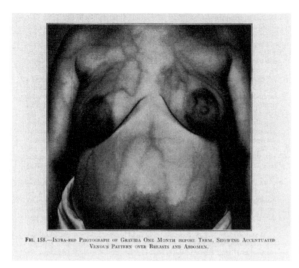

FIG. 158.—INFRA-RED PHOTOGRAPH OF GRAVIDA ONE MONTH BEFORE TERM, SHOWING ACCENTUATED VENOUS PATTERN OVER BREASTS AND ABDOMEN.

"Infra-red Photograph of Gravida One Month Before Term," Williams, 1950

The matter-of-factness with which the X-ray images appeared in obstetrical textbooks intimated that the procedure was standard practice. But as Bettyann Holtzmann Kevles writes in *Naked to the Bone*, "in 1926, an X-ray exam could take as long as an hour. There was so much tissue in the way, and the image before ten weeks gestation was so vague that this 'meant that the patient had to lie on her back with her pelvis elevated and with between 1.5 and 2 litres of carbonic gas injected into her peritoneal cavity.' This was no light matter, for 'occasionally it killed the fetus, and maternal death, even, has resulted from this procedure.'"[45] Yet the delicately beautiful illustration of an X ray of the fetus published in the 1913 edition of *The Principles and Practices of Obstetrics* by Joseph DeLee yields not the slightest suggestion of any such perils.[46] If one of the ways that photographs function as ideology is to disguise contradictions, then the mode in which X-ray technology was represented as safe in the obstetrical textbooks of this period was an ideological production of a very high order.[47]

The X-ray procedure eventually became less difficult for the mother and, Kevles notes, "by 1930 many obstetricians suggested routine prenatal pelvic X-ray examinations."[48] However, in 1956 a British epidemiologist named Alice Stewart demonstrated a correlation between deaths from childhood cancer and mothers who had been x-rayed while pregnant, and the regular use of X rays quickly ceased. But X rays were still used in uncommon cases. The 1950 Williams' *Obstetrics* includes X-ray images of multiple living fetuses, illustrating the presumption that it was acceptable to use radiation in anomalous situations.

Ultimately the most influential of the visualization technologies developed in

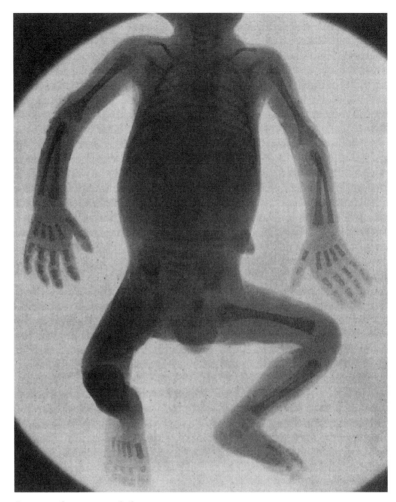

"X-ray of Fetus, Eighth
Month," DeLee, 1913

this era was ultrasound. Ultrasound investigation offered detailed information about the body's interior that clinicians had previously not been able to obtain. What is more, it translated the data from sound to image, and so delivered the information in visual form.

These new tools for managing pregnancy through visual surveillance meant that older, cruder, more massive kinds of physical intervention grew less and less

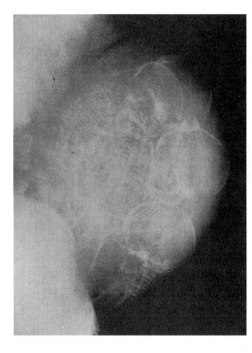

"Roentgenogram of
Quadruplets in Utero,"
Williams, 1950

prevalent. Textbook illustrations during this period evince a subtle change, with
fewer intimations of the "anomalies" that had been the rationale for the professionalization of obstetrics in the first period and more representations of the routine situations that called for the application of technology. Gone are the racially
inflected grids and the carefully composed comparisons that teach the viewer to
distinguish a "degenerate" body from a merely pregnant one.

In 1913, Joseph DeLee's advocacy of active intervention in almost all pregnancies attempted to bring discipline to the field by standardizing treatment. But in
1950 Nicholson J. Eastman, who became editor of *Obstetrics* after Williams died,
declared that "today's obstetrics is quite different from that of 20 years ago."
Eastman believed that "otherwise we should not have witnessed such a decline
in maternal deaths."[49] The difference Eastman noted was the now controlled
reaction of a more scientific obstetrics in the face of medical challenges that no
longer seemed so diverse and overwhelming. "It stresses conservatism in obstetric surgery and, above all, the avoidance of trauma," he observed of the field.
"Accordingly, the attendant who operates unnecessarily (and, by the same token,
often traumatically) practices the obstetrics of a quarter of a century ago and
will meet a corresponding mortality."[50]

Thus, in the postwar decades, as instanced in "Palpation in Left Sacro-Anterior Position" from the 1950 *Obstetrics*, the obstetrician is still pictured as laying hands upon the patient.[51] But the obstetrician's hand in midcentury textbooks is a vestige of what it once had been. These hands no longer imply that social barriers against violence must be broken to save the mother's life. Instead, they intimate that human reproduction has been brought under rational management. The pregnant body is now partly public and largely predictable; modern technology is the obstetrician's and the pregnant woman's best friend; surgery, when called for, is safe, clean and competent; the pregnant woman can yield without fear to the system. The presence of the obstetrician's hand is reassuring because the machine has supplanted its most aggressive penetrating functions.

But the mid-twentieth-century prototype of the bland and competent medical technocrat obscures, with a deceitful glamour, both the memory of the dire combat between man and the maternal body-as-obstacle that typified images from

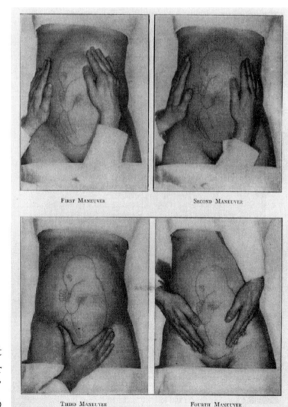

"Palpation in Left
Sacro—Anterior
Position,"
Williams, 1950

the recent obstetrical past, and consciousness of the anaesthetized sensibility of the present. The continuing social traumas of poverty and racism responsible for the assemblies of "abnormal" pregnant bodies that populate the earlier phase of obstetrical textbooks are not represented. At this stage, the class and race differences that matter are no longer conceptualized in terms of biological "specificity," but show up in the form of unequal access to medical attention. The photographic models in these new textbooks, healthier, wealthier and whiter than in the past, served as a kind of screen that rendered more opaque the depth of the social challenges that the earlier photographs had at least tried to depict.

The key to Eastman's assessment of the state of the profession is the motto: "above all, the avoidance of trauma." At midcentury, the obstetrician no longer starkly confronted the possibility of anatomical antagonism at every turn—not because difficult cases did not present themselves but because his technological tools made him feel more in control. He is trained to administer the same calm, sane logic of science for all female bodies.

New Eugenic Targets

Mainline eugenic thought subtly changed its target in the interwar period. Crude, full-fledged hysteria over the "devolution" of segments of the American population slowly lost the public ear. Obsession over the general standard of health of the entire body politic took its place. In part this shift honors the work of progressive reformers who fought hard on many fronts to improve social conditions and restrain the exploitation of the poor. In part it marks a change in perception consequent to more sophisticated research in genetics, to increased understanding in the relatively new social sciences of anthropology, sociology and psychology, and to better statistical methods that debunked earlier claims about the degradation of the health, intelligence and moral character of the immigrants. The impressive differential in the birthrate of "Anglo-Saxons" and other "races," for instance, turned out to be a fluke rather than a steady pattern. Racialized formulae for the meaning of social difference, which a decade before might have seemed unexceptional, now seemed more troubling and less clear.[52]

But in part this shift was also a result of the practical success of negative eugenic campaigns in United States. The fiercely restrictive Immigration Act of 1924 reduced the number of immigrants crowding into the cities from Eastern Europe to an inconsequential trickle. During the 1920s and early '30s, many state governments enacted compulsory sterilization laws for habitual criminals and mental "defectives," a policy with which 63 percent of Americans agreed, according to a *Fortune* magazine poll of 1937.[53] Looking for eugenic themes in photographs in obstetrics textbooks from this period, therefore, one wants to keep in mind how the object of professional concern has changed from the fearful degeneration spread by particular kinds of bodies to the health of the entire population. In an era that was discovering the power of statistics, racial and class codes that rationalized exclusion became less physically explicit and more quantitative.

Nicholson J. Eastman, who was J. Whitridge Williams' successor at the Johns Hopkins Hospital and the new editor of *Obstetrics*, observed in 1950 that the new standards of prenatal care, which ought theoretically to have been "equal" across the color line, were in fact no such thing. In an illustration that appeared in "Maternal Mortality"—a graph, not a photograph of a person—Eastman depicted his concern for the progress of obstetrical practice. This representation of the "percentage of Nonwhite Live Births with No Medical Attendant in 1946" sought to turn the old notion of medical "specificity"—that the rural, black population was not as healthy as the white urban part of the nation—into a new point about modern standards of care. It was time for the medical gaze to address inequality not by dwelling upon what made the races biologically "different," but by making treatment the same.

In the graph, Eastman correlates "nonwhite mothers," with "no medical attendant," and shows that they both are factors that result in "high maternal mortality." However, he does so without any mention of racism as a causative

"Percentage of Non-white Live Births with No Medical Attendant in 1946," from *Federal Security Agency U.S. Children's Bureau*. Based on data from The National Office of Vital Statistics, Williams, 1950

factor that underlies the inequities in medical care. The text underneath the graph informs the reader that "the phrase 'birth with no medical attendant' must be construed with its full implications." By this, Eastman means the

> dire poverty, faulty health education, poor hygiene, dietary deficiencies, no prenatal care, and delivery in a shack with no provisions for emergencies and in the hands of an inferior attendant—either the next-door neighbor, or an untrained midwife.

He continues,

> The high maternal mortality rates . . . for southern states become understandable in view of the large population of nonwhites in those areas coupled with the unfavorable environmental conditions and lack of medical attention which they experience. A vigorous attack on this problem is being made by various agencies.[54]

Eastman is clearly very aware of the social context in which pregnancy and childbirth were lived in southern states. He stresses lack of training rather than race as the problem. However, this formulation of the causes of maternal mortality may also subtly denigrate the African-American neighbor and the African-American midwife. On the one hand they are credited with providing outstanding service despite such "unfavorable environmental conditions"; on the other hand, their lack of training *is* one of those "unfavorable conditions." It is hard for anyone to win in such a situation. Eastman's assertion that "a vigorous attack" by various social "agencies" is making successful inroads against this medical problem is a powerful liberal evocation of the institutions of science, dedicated to a new era of equality through environmental reform. But millions of mothers and children who did not receive the benefit of new medical treatments would continue to suffer from the radical deformations of a racist society.

PHASE THREE: THE NEW GENETICS AND THE NEW EUGENICS

The mid-1960s added a new chapter to the eugenic narrative: the story of the fetus. Not the mother nor even the neonate but that which is *prior* to the neonate now came under scrutiny. The image of the fetus ignited intense political as well as medical debate.

Visualization of the living fetus did not, of course, begin in the 1960s. It started in the 1890s, with the invention of X rays, and was refined in the 1940s and '50s, by the introduction of sonograms. What distinguishes this third period of obstetrical illustration from the previous ones is thus not the existence of a technology of visualization per se, but new constructions of the *meaning* of these pictures. Whereas previously, as we have seen, the fetus was viewed as essentially a part of, or a mirror within, the maternal body, it now begins to figure as an individual in itself. The "unborn" become future citizens who would eventually gather a collection of "fetal rights."

Prior to this period, fetal visualization had been used primarily as a means to judge the physical needs of the mother and child as a unit during both pregnancy and labor. Was there a severe disproportion between the pelvic outlet and the size of the fetus? What position had the fetus taken at the outset of labor, and could it be altered by manual manipulation? Were there abnormalities in fetal development that predicted an emergency at birth? These were the kinds of questions that preoccupied physicians looking at such visualizations.

This single-minded emphasis on delivery is clear in the many editions of *Williams' Obstetrics* textbooks from the 1890s; they contain photographs of pregnant women's bellies on which outlines of full-term fetuses have been drawn in ink, together with spatial landmarks locating the position of the fetus in the womb. Such images are still primarily tactile guides. The obstetrician's hands touch the hidden shapes through the woman's skin, as in the 1950 illustration of the classic set of palpations.

In the mid-1960s, however, as the fetal image went public through the popularization of ultrasound, the touch itself gave way to vision as the obstetrician's premier diagnostic tool. Old- fashioned photographs of ink drawings on pregnant abdomens were now joined by new photographs of other kinds of ink drawings on pregnant bellies—literal targets, that locate the places where "receptors" should be placed so that the size and position of the fetus may be apprehended through visual technology.

These new images no longer celebrate touch. For example, "The nine areas used to identify the location of receptors in tokodynamometer determinations" reproduced by Anne Oakley in *The Captured Womb*, does not imply that hands will be placed on the woman's belly. Unlike previous guides to palpation, such as the quadrants drawn on the belly in the 1913 edition of DeLee's textbook, *these* markings on the pregnant abdomen do not feature the process of getting the fetus out so much as the problem of getting *in* to see it.

Whereas individual doctors and hospitals experimented in the 1950s with ultrasound visualization of many different organs, it took some time for the technique to become popular. Ultrasound competed at first with CT scans and MR images, and manufacturers apparently feared that the technology might soon grow obsolete. Even though ultrasound machines and images are comparatively inexpensive, multiple inventors in the early years made the commercial market seem tenuous to investors.

Indeed, ultrasound "might not have had a chance in the clinic were it not for two historical events," writes Kevles. The first was Stewart's 1956 study of the

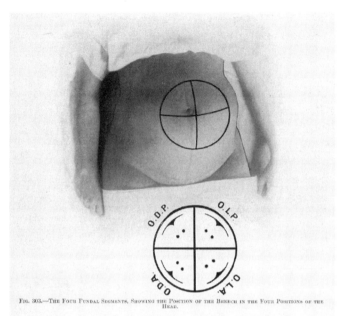

FIG. 303.—THE FOUR FUNDAL SEGMENTS, SHOWING THE POSITION OF THE BREECH IN THE FOUR POSITIONS OF THE HEAD.

"The four Fundal Segments," DeLee, 1913

effect of X-ray exposure on the fetus, because "when ultrasound appeared on the market in doctor-friendly form after 1970, obstetricians turned to it as a safe alternative technology." The second was "the new voice of women in the political arena who wanted to influence the practice of childbirth and abortion."[55]

In this period, women's health was highly politicized, and easy assumptions about how health professionals naturally work together in stable hierarchical teams could no longer be maintained. The politicization of abortion rights, especially after *Roe v. Wade* in 1973, provided more sites of contention. When a conflict between maternal and fetal health arose, the physician no longer had only medical and legal guidelines and his own ethical and religious beliefs to consult; now there were also politics to contend with. The feminist movement, the legal system, corporate interests and the religious right all contested the meaning of the fetal image. With the incidence of caesarian sections climbing and neonatal medicine growing more sophisticated, the obstetrician increasingly found himself, and now often herself, caught in the middle when political contention over how to treat the fetus erupted in the public sphere. The obstetrician's traditional understanding of the role of accoucheur now had to be balanced against new standards of care for the fetal "patient," whom visualization had made much more vivid.

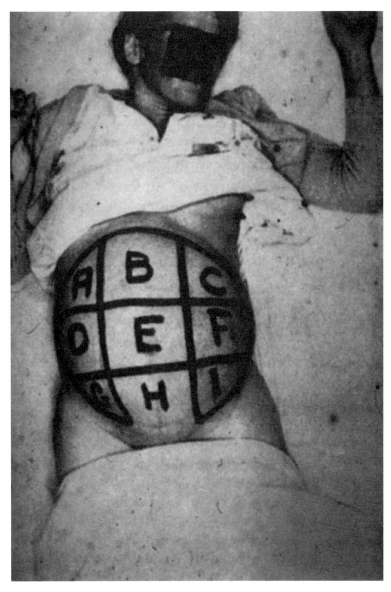

"The nine areas used to identify the location of receptors in tokodynamometer, from determinations," Reynolds et al., 1954

In this atmosphere, women who wanted more control over pregnancy provided the first mass market for ultrasound imaging. "Before ultrasound," Kevles explains, "there was no way to see eggs, a developing embryo, or a fetus at a early stage of development. Gynecologists and obstetricians were apt to regard the developing fetus as a kind of uterine tumor." But now, the image of the independent fetus as an unborn human with "rights that rivaled" the mother's altered this construction of the fetus in obstetrical practice forever.[56]

The fifteenth edition of *Williams' Obstetrics* in 1976 introduced "B-mode sonography" of the fetus, in which it took up to twenty minutes for the transducer to make a static image. Sonographic representations were at first fuzzy and difficult for non-experts, including most obstetricians, to interpret. But they soon began to conform to traditional ideas of what a fetus looks like. In the late 1970s, improvements cut the time to make the image to a tenth of a second, color greatly enhanced the appearance of the image, and computers could run these images together in "real time" simulation.

With a long discussion of the use of sonography for the diagnosis of pregnancy in the sixteenth edition of *Williams' Obstetrics*, the fetal patient in the obstetrical textbook came of age. Its visual hallmark is a medical illustration made neither by a doctor nor by a professional hospital staff photographer, as in previous periods, but by a machine. In the photograph of "fetal facial features at 20 weeks obtained by three-dimensional surface reconstruction" in *The Fetus as Patient*, edited by Asim Kurjak and Frank A. Chervenak (1994), it is evident how individual and expressive these machine-made images have become.[57] Pregnancy

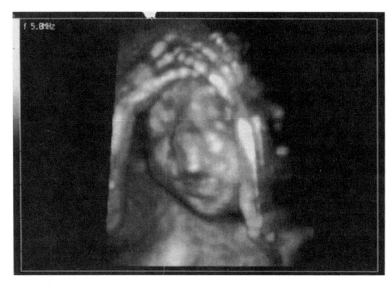

"Fetal facial features at 20 weeks obtained by three-dimensional surface reconstruction," from *The Fetus as Patient*, ed. by Asim Kurjak and Frank A. Chervenak, 1994

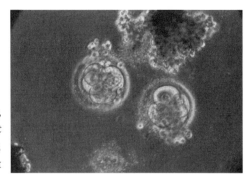

From Sherman J. Silber,
MD, *How to Get Pregnant
with the New Technology,*
1991

here takes on a new emphasis in reproductive medicine, one that concentrates on gestation as much as the older formulation thrust teleologically toward birth.

But fetal medicine also leads logically backwards, to the embryo and to genetics, with the result that clinical textbook images of pregnancy have once again undergone a dramatic shift in relation to eugenic symbolism. While certainly still devoted to maternal health, photographic illustration is comparatively more focused on fetal, and even embryological—read genetic—development than ever before. The fetus is now pictured not only as a patient for, but also a product of, medical science, as in Dr. Sherman Silber's photograph of a four-cell embryo.[58] The problem of freeing the fetus from its mother's body is simply one passage, not even necessarily the signal event, in its life course. After all, the embryo may have begun life in the first place with in-vitro fertilization outside its mother's, body, and the greatest drama of its birth might have to do with getting it *into* her rather than out again.

Conflict of interest between the maternal and the fetal patient can now be seen throughout the course of pregnancy, and not simply in the second stage of labor. This conflict largely replaces the earlier conflict between the manly force of the obstetrician and the female obstinance of the womb. The obstetrician, now an explorer in genetic space, is a principal player in the theater of "life" itself. Indeed, photographs have begun to demonstrate manipulation not only of the unseen but of the unseeable on a microscopic scale. These images document the power of assisted reproductive technologies that work not only in the intra-uterine but also in the intracellular space. There is no palpation in the petri dish.

Interestingly, power is now indicated by the delicacy of touch rather than the brute strength of heroic hands. The sophistication of fetal surgery or subtle and complex manipulations of single cells has all but obliterated public consciousness of the crude physicality of last century's violence, when "regular physicians bled, purged, and puked their patients."[59] The violence of contemporary representations arises rather in the flat, laconic manner in which they suggest that such interventions are always already technologically refined, medically desirable and uniformly beneficial from the often competing standpoints of society, the mother and the fetus-to-be conflict.

CONCLUSION

Race, class, and gender are configured differently in the current period than in the ones before. Whereas previously the particularities of the body were either exaggerated as at the turn of the century or deliberately ignored as at midcentury, they have now returned to view in the medical context, not as a matter of biology but as a result of culture and choice. The call for provision of safe, affordable and accessible elective abortions issued by mainstream white middle-class feminists has been joined by the demand for uniform access to health care and reform of sterilization abuse issued by working-class feminists and women of color. These demands, stemming from the increased political consciousness of the civil rights, antiwar and feminist movements, have deconstructed the supposed neutrality of midcentury color-blindness to insist once again on "specificity," now understood as accountability to local communities.

But there is an invisible dimension to this shift as well that interacts with the old eugenic concerns about "racial" or "national" supremacy. On the one hand, the possibility of sharing genetic material asexually across the class and color line proposes a new utopian model of miscegenation that biologically confounds the "ideal" of "pure whiteness," or "pure" anything else, for that matter. At the same time, however, the practice throughout the industry of explicit classification of egg and sperm donors not only by racial "types" but also by behavioral characteristics reinscribes the old racist and class-based "specificities." Also, because United States laws permit payment for egg donation unlike, for instance, Great Britain, it is unclear whether poor women or women of color within and beyond the borders of the United States may be increasingly identified as potential donors of genetic "material" for economically better-off middle-class consumers whose medicalized "infertility" can be "treated" with this material.

It is too early to determine whether genetic engineering and reproductive technologies will reinforce old specifications of race and class or make them less tenable. However, it is possible to speculate that so long as images of fetuses fail to expose the racial and class as well as the technological dimensions of these reproductive practices, the aspect of "new eugenics" will remain potent in ways that cannot be critiqued because they cannot be examined.

At stake in the social construction of reproductive technologies is not only which *women* or which newborn *babies* should or can be aided, but which *fetuses* can be created or altered, and how. Although the "dying woman" frontispiece disappeared in the 1950 edition of *Williams' Obstetrics*, the "endangered fetus" has largely taken her place as a cautionary figure, urging ever-greater scientific dedication and social control.

That is to say, the eugenic thread evident in images of pregnant women at least since the turn of the century has now wrapped itself around the image of the fetus as well. There is not a single, unchanging eugenic narrative. Late-nineteenth-century images that policed the boundaries between "normal" pregnancies and "abnormal" pregnancies were not the same as midcentury evocations of "good" and "bad" mothers, or late-twentieth-century evocations of "defective" and "effective" genes. But our study of images of pregnancy in medical textbooks leads us to conclude that the historical connection between eugenics and medical photographs of pregnancy persists.

5) PROMOTING PREGNANCY
Instruction, Advertising and Public Policy

> Photographs are no more, and no less, than fragments of
> ideology, activated by the mechanisms of fantasy and desire
> within a fragmentary history of images.
>
> —Simon Watney

In the early 1950s, three new groups of photographs of pregnancy came into
being to serve specific persuasive, instrumental agendas: instructional photographs for expectant parents, advertisements for maternity clothing and public policy photographs. All these photographs had roots in the social changes of
the 1930s and '40s. Instructional photographs were connected to interest in natural childbirth methods imported from Europe, advertisements to the nascent
maternity clothing industry, and public policy photographs to major social programs. These photographs of pregnancy specifically addressed female viewers
for the first time, bringing pregnant women into the public sphere as well as
identifying them as consumers.

VISUAL GUIDES TO PREGNANCY

Instructional photographs of pregnancy first appeared in the 1950s, published in
guidebooks for expectant mothers. This new domain for photographs of pregnancy coincided with the postwar baby boom in the United States and with a
growing interest in natural childbirth, as well as early genetic research. The photographs represented an unprecedented shift into the public sphere for images of
pregnant women. Not only did they target primarily a female viewer, they were
also on the shelves of bookstores and libraries for all to see.

The books in which they were published were often works of advocacy, first
for natural childbirth methods, then in the 1960s and '70s for the home birth

and midwifery movements, and for the women's health movement. The photographs were promotional, although they promoted practices and values rather than products. Later guidebooks, in the 1970s and '80s, became more specialized, addressing, for example, the concerns of physically disabled pregnant women, gay and lesbian parents, older first-time mothers, or infertile couples.

With the pregnant or soon-to-be-pregnant lay reader in mind, such instructional pictures showed aspects of childbearing that did not appear in other contexts. For example, photographs in guidebooks often featured pregnant women in social settings, placing them in relation to family, friends and health care professionals, rather than in the solitary poses so often found in art photographs. Yet while these photographs portrayed pregnant women in believable life contexts, the women were also consistently shown as sheltered from difficulty. The pictures generally provide a positive, encouraging view of pregnancy. Unlike medical photographs—another kind of specialized instrumental image—lay instructional photographs did not allow frightening aspects of pregnancy to enter the picture.

Yet these instructional photographs did cross other representational boundaries, sometimes in ways that shocked their viewers. For example, they provided the first explicit photographs of childbirth available to the lay viewer, who had to learn how to look at them. Marjorie Karmel, an early American proponent of the Lamaze method of psychoprophylactic childbirth, describes her first encounter with such images when she and her husband Alex took lessons from Madame Coehn in Paris during her first pregnancy. She writes that Madame Cohen:

> took a stack of photographs from the bookshelf and spread them out on the table. We had to stand up to look at them. At the first glance, my mouth dropped open and I nearly sat down again. She had set out in order a series of photos that showed minute by minute the emergence of the baby from its mother. The pictures were clearly of a real delivery; a real live woman giving birth to a real live baby. I had never even imagined what such a sight might look like, and I was so shocked and embarrassed that I could scarcely focus enough to see what she was pointing out to us. I glanced nervously at Alex to see what his reaction was. I could feel myself blushing. Strangely enough, Alex didn't appear to be the least bit disturbed by it. He gazed intently at the pictures, and seemed to be listening carefully to whatever Mme. Cohen was saying.[1]

Although this passage refers to explicit photographs of childbirth, which may be more startling than photographs of pregnancy, Karmel's reaction raises an important issue. Even as she recognizes that these are photographs of a "sight" or spectacle, she nevertheless experiences them viscerally in a way that renders them difficult to see (she could "scarcely focus"). Her physical response raises the possibility that instrumental photographs may be viewed quite differently from art photographs, that is, less in terms of scopic, distanced spectatorship and more in terms of bodily experience. Marjorie Karmel might feel embarrassed viewing photographs of childbirth, as she could have felt being observed herself, yet she could also actively incorporate the images and their meanings into her life.

Karmel's reactions suggest a model of viewing that does not depend on a purely visual epiphany or the exhilaration of identification across difference, and is not based on the emotional satisfactions of voyeurism or the formal control of visual tension within the frame. The viewer of instrumental images, seeking information relevant to her own experience, responds to the physical references in the pictures. The gaze, theorized as erotic in the scopic mode of viewing, is differently empowering in instrumental viewing. Rather than offering an abstract sense of visual mastery, these photographs provide information that speaks to the viewer's own questions and anxieties.[2]

One of the earliest sets of instrumental photographs was published in England by Grantly Dick-Read in the 1950 edition of his book *The Natural Childbirth Primer*.[3] Although this pioneering physician publicly championed a return to natural childbirth as early as 1930, his ideas did not begin to take hold in the United States until after World War II. In his campaign to popularize natural childbirth, he was one of the first to enlist photography as a visual aid.

Strikingly different from later instrumental images, the photographs in *The Natural Childbirth Primer* were made in a classroom where a group of pregnant women appear to be practicing special exercises in preparation for childbirth. The women, trim and well-groomed, wear identical white underwear; white masks cover their faces. They look rather like robots acting on the instructions of an invisible authority. Scientific legitimacy is implied by the anatomical diagrams that line the classroom walls. The room itself is an instructional space—neither home nor hospital—in which legitimacy can be lent to a new way of doing things. With their stiffness, their regimentation, and their strict attention to conventions of modesty, Dick-Read's photographs suggest, among other things, how difficult it was in 1950 to bring images of pregnancy into the public sphere.

These photographs also represent one of the first instances in which pregnant women were pictured in a group, rather than singly. Yet no interaction among the women is pictured; their movements are identical and parallel. Dick-Read's pictures take the suppressed sight of ungainly pregnant women in their underwear and present it directly and literally, with a decorum that makes it respectable. These pictures may strike the contemporary eye as surreal and unnatural. The instrumental photographs that followed later attempted, increasingly, to make the image of pregnancy more comfortable and familiar.

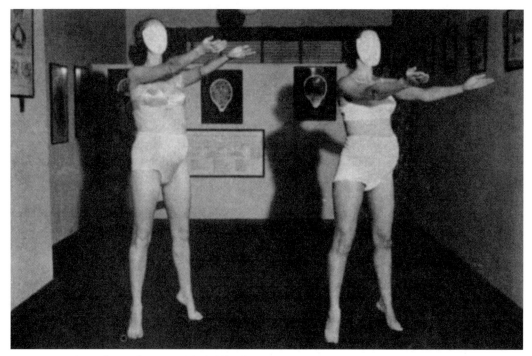

From Grantly Dick-Read, *A Natural Childbirth Primer*, 1955

From Grantly Dick-Read, *A Natural Childbirth Primer*, 1955

Timothy Maxwell, "Nel,
Lillian and Echo," 1981

Books like those by Dick-Read created an iconography of pregnancy that continued in the 1960s and beyond. It portrayed white, middle-class, usually stereotypically handsome couples in a classroom, home environment, or medical facility. In contrast to her solitude in art photographs, the pregnant woman in these books is often shown in relation to other people, all of whom appear to be providing support and nurture. Yet though she is the center of activity, she is a passive center, directed by medical personnel and her male partner. Particularly powerful are the occasional images of pregnant women together, such as Timothy Maxwell's photograph from the cover of the summer 1982 issue of *Mothering* magazine, for they depict pregnancy as an experience that can be deliberately shared among women. But such images continued to be comparatively scarce in the instructional context.

As in other image domains, in these promotional photographs pregnant women are almost never pictured working, beyond domestic or self-care tasks. A rare photograph of a pregnant woman at work was made by Mel Rosenthal in Managua, Nicaragua, and it was used on the cover of the 1984 book *Double Exposure: Women's Health Hazards on the Job and at Home*, an instructional book

Mel Rosenthal, "Textile
Factory, Nicaragua,"
n.d.

of a different sort.[4] The singularity of this picture is a reminder that cultural
influences from outside the United States have been crucial in expanding the
instrumental image base, and in introducing new approaches to thinking about
childbearing.

The Home Birth Image

During the 1970s, a movement to resituate birth out of the hospital, in the
home, and within the context of family—the home birth movement—gained
momentum. This movement, under the primary guidance of midwives rather
than obstetricians, generated a multitude of photographs that pictured pregnancy within a warm and loving community of family and friends, usually with
a traditional marriage at the core.

Ina May Gaskin's *Spiritual Midwifery* (1977) used photographs together with
drawings, diagrams, informational text and some seventy individuals' "amazing
birth tales" to communicate the holistic counter-cultural approach to childbearing that she developed on The Farm, an intentional community in rural Ten-
nessee. Perhaps because she positioned herself outside the cultural mainstream
to begin with, Gaskin was able, in text and photographs, to resexualize childbearing. She both described and visually represented how couples could use sexual intimacy to assist in the birthing process, and she wrote about the sexual
qualities of birth and nursing. For example, she quoted one of The Farm midwives as saying, "Over and over again, I've seen that the best way to get a baby

From Ina May Gaskin,
Spiritual Midwifery, 1977

From Ina May Gaskin,
Spiritual Midwifery, 1977

out is by cuddling and smooching with your husband. That loving, sexy vibe is what puts the baby in there, and it's what gets it out, too."[5]

At the same time, the photographs in her book are extremely modest. Although childbearing is seen as a sexual process, the pregnant woman is not sexualized; it is the sexuality of the *couple* that is pictured and discussed. Most of the photographs concentrate on the faces of individuals (including many pregnant women), small family groupings, and the interactions between pregnant women and midwives. Although the recognition and regulation of midwifery re-emerged as a charged political issue during the time this book appeared, neither its text nor its pictures were overtly political. *Spiritual Midwifery* celebrated the emotional processes that characterize childbirth in family-centered rather than specifically woman-centered images that are intense, positive and inclusive of community members.

The Women's Health Movement

In 1971, the Boston Women's Health Book Collective published the first edition of *Our Bodies, Ourselves.* The collective followed it with several updated ver-

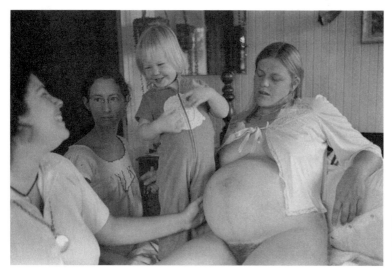

Suzanne Arms, from
*The New Our Bodies,
Ourselves*, 1992

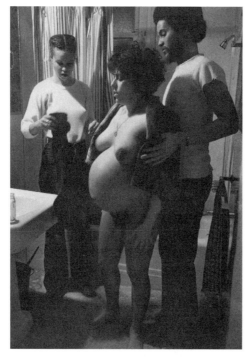

Suzanne Arms, from
*The New Our Bodies,
Ourselves*, 1984

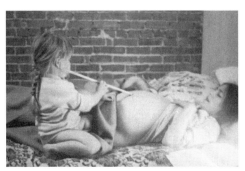

Ed Pincus, from *Our
Bodies, Ourselves*, 1971

David Alexander, from
*The New Our Bodies,
Ourselves*, 1984

sions including the 1984 *The New Our Bodies, Ourselves* and the 1998 edition, *Our
Bodies, Ourselves for the New Century*. The several editions of this book, which took
the subject of the female body as the basis for very broad discussion of women's
issues in a climate of support, became a handbook for several generations of
young women. It used photographs extensively and judiciously. For perhaps the
first time since *The Family of Man*, photographs appeared in print that represented pregnant women from a variety of cultural backgrounds and in a variety
of life situations. This representation of racial, economic and cultural diversity,

rare in previous childbearing guides, has made *Our Bodies, Ourselves* in all its editions a continuing resource for broadening thinking about the range of issues women face in the context of childbearing.

The photographs in *Our Bodies, Ourselves* are taken from several traditions usually associated with art photography: documentary work such as Suzanne Arms'; personal, home-based photographs such as Ed Pincus'; and studio photography such as David Alexander's. In this book they function instrumentally, providing a range of visual models for readers.

Frederick LeBoyer, from
Inner Beauty, Inner Light,
1978

Frederick LeBoyer, from
Inner Beauty, Inner Light,
1978

The Fit Pregnancy

Beginning in the 1970s, pregnant women were also pictured together in exercise manuals, the best known of which was *Jane Fonda's Workout Book for Pregnancy, Birth and Recovery*, first published in 1982.[6] Many of these books featured photographs of attractive groups of models in leotards shouldering the burden of bodily self-discipline already familiar to American women. In them, the pregnant woman assumes responsibility for maintaining her own attractiveness, while also being responsible for the health of the fetus.

There were, however, some interesting extensions of the idea of pregnant beauty. Frederick LeBoyer's 1978 book entitled *Inner Beauty, Inner Light* presented a remarkable series of photographs of a woman in her ninth month of pregnancy practicing yoga exercises in India.[7] Again, these photographs from outside the American cultural context provided a model of a pregnant woman who appeared much more active and energized than any in photographs from within the United States. LeBoyer writes that "pregnancy as well as delivery are far more than a mere matter of 'good health and fitness.' In simple words, it is all 'a spiritual experience' as one might call it. A matter of Life. And Death."[8] This extraordinary collection of photographs promoted an approach to the body and mind that went beyond customary Western ideas about body image. By the late 1980s, a variety of approaches to pregnant fitness could be seen, including less well known books such as Dr. Lynn Pirie's *Pregnancy and Sports Fitness*, which challenged and extended the visual iconography of American pregnancy by picturing a pregnant woman weight-lifting.[9]

A Child Is Born

While an instructional iconography was being developed for the pregnant woman in the contexts of home, gym and medical facilities, other instructional images of pregnancy—views of life within—were also generating a new iconography. In 1966, the first English-language edition of Lennart Nilsson's *A Child Is Born* was published.[10] Aimed at the same general readership as other instructional books, *A Child Is Born* combined two kinds of images: spectacular, technologically sophisticated photographs of conception and fetal development, and humanistic instructional photographs of white middle-class couples illustrating some of the physical and emotional stages of pregnancy and childbirth. The photographs of people serve as a backdrop for the epic biological drama. In this sense the photographer is omniscient: he sees and reconstructs a reproductive script in one set of images that is being blindly enacted by the adults in the other set of pictures.

If the protagonists are only dimly aware of the elaborate processes going on within them, the reader—who is likely to be pregnant herself—is privileged to see both levels of the drama, the human and the cellular. The power of natural processes and the technological mastery that makes possible their visualization are combined with the romantic story of a couple to elicit feelings of awe and wonder, and perhaps self-recognition in the viewer.

A Child Is Born is unusual in this integration of scientific and humanistic images of reproduction, and the viewing modes it invites are also dual. The scientific *in utero* photographs function as scopic images, made to be viewed voyeuristically, for a sense of penetration and mastery. The photographs of pregnant women at home and in medical environments function instrumentally, as sources of reassuring information. Taken together, the pictures in *A Child Is Born* place childbirth firmly within the medical context and under the management of professionals. The most powerful person in these images is not the pregnant woman but the photographer, a magician who unites with the touch of a finger the invisible forces of creation and the mundane events of daily life.

It is instructive to examine how the iconography of the humanistic images in particular shifts from one edition of this book to the next. There have been three English editions of *A Child Is Born*—1966, 1977 and 1990. Although the scientific photographs have become more vividly colored and detailed with each edition, their iconography has not changed substantively since 1966. The biggest change appears in the photographs of couples that are interwoven with the intrauterine images.

The 1966 edition follows one young, white middle-class couple through her pregnancy. It centers on several visits to a male doctor, and includes only three very circumspect images of the actual birth, with the husband present. Although the text mentions that the pregnant woman is employed, none of the photographs shows her at work. Rather, the couple is pictured in outdoor recreational settings like the zoo, the beach or the park—that is, when they are not at home or at the doctor's office.

The 1977 edition provides a wider range of social contexts for women than did the previous one. We find here a number of different women, all young and white, as well as doctors, nurses and midwives, nearly all of them female. The pregnant woman is also shown as less dependent on the doctor's information, as when, for instance, she administers her own pregnancy test.

Photographs in the 1990 edition follow the physical relationship of a glamorous couple, juxtaposed with other photographs showing elaborate medical instruments in relation to pregnant bodies, as well as images referring to environmental hazards. The pregnant woman here is pictured as having more choices as well as more to worry about.

The cover pictures of the three editions also track a shifting relationship between the fetus and the pregnant woman. On the cover of the 1966 edition, the fetus is pictured as a space traveler floating in a disembodied amniotic sac, with a fuel supply attached in the form of a placenta. The 1977 cover features a close-up of the face of a fetus sucking its thumb. The representation of face and hand, tropes of individuality, invokes its "personhood." In the 1990 edition, this same fetus-as-person has been reinserted via photo-collage into an image of a pregnant torso, but disproportionately enlarged so that the face and hand entirely fill the silhouette of the woman's belly. In other words, these covers describe a sequence that first separates the fetus from the pregnant woman, then establishes it as an independent individual, and finally reconstructs an image of pregnancy, via technical means, in which the emphasis has been placed on a fetus which no longer fits in the woman's body.

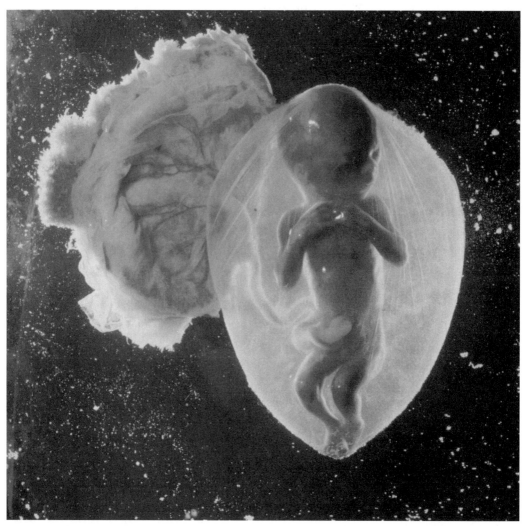

Lennart Nilsson, cover image,
A Child Is Born, 1966

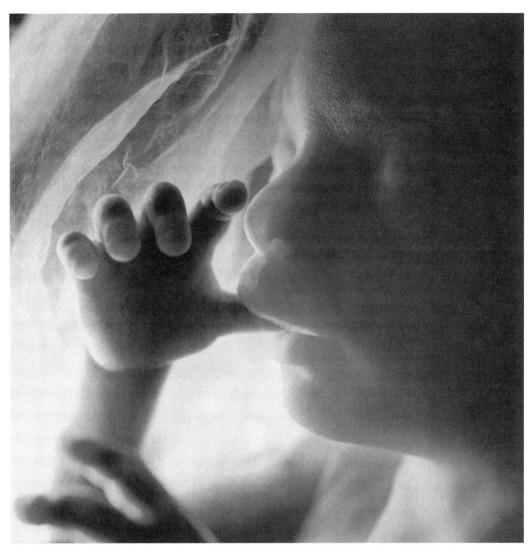

Lennart Nilsson, cover image,
A Child Is Born, 1977

Lennart Nilsson, cover image, *A Child Is Born*, 1990

Photographs in the three editions of *A Child Is Born* of the pregnant woman's first physical exam also illustrate changing attitudes toward both representation and maternal health care. In the 1966 edition, the photograph of the exam shows a conversation between an anxious young woman and a male doctor across a desk, taken from the point of view of an observer standing behind the doctor. A life-size plaster model of a full-term baby in a uterus is facing the doctor, not the woman, who must rely on the doctor to translate the inner workings of her body for her. In the 1977 edition, the exam is pictured from the patient's viewpoint as direct physical handling by a caring female doctor or nurse. In the 1990 edition, only the legs of the pregnant woman are visible, seen in stirrups from below, while the hands of a female doctor and attendant perform tests. The pregnant woman's body has become the visual background for technical procedures.

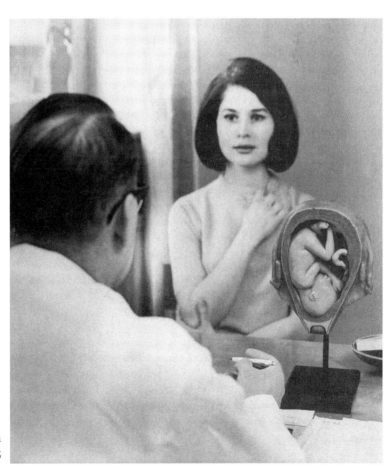

Lennart Nilsson, from
A Child Is Born, 1966

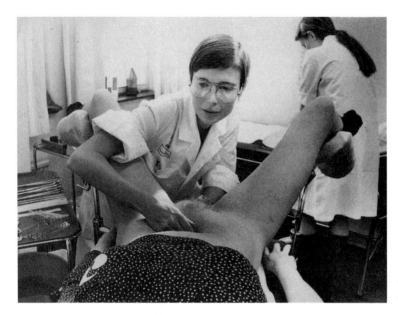

Lennart Nilsson, from
A Child Is Born, 1977

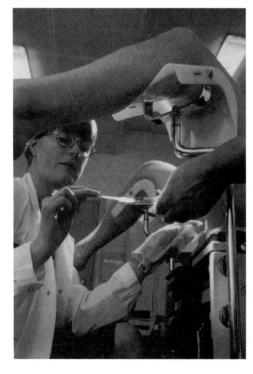

Lennart Nilsson, from
A Child Is Born, 1990

The 1990 edition introduced discussion of new reproductive technologies. These technologies increasingly make both male and female bodies potentially dispensable. Interestingly, in 1990 the visual affirmation of heterosexual romance and physical attraction is escalated, as if in response to this threat. Its numerous photographs of couples, printed for the first time in sensuous color, are more explicit in their sexual intimacy than photographs in previous editions. Although in 1990 fewer images of doctors or other health workers appear, the text still makes it clear that professional medical care and technology provide the appropriate framework for reproduction.

The Working Pregnant Woman

Images of pregnant women working outside the home are extremely hard to find in any photographic domain. The 1977 edition of *A Child Is Born* contains a rare cluster of such pictures. Although they do not call attention to themselves, five photographs of pregnant women in the workplace appear in the book, three of which are reproduced here. Small, seemingly casually selected, these images are unusual in the iconography of pregnancy because they bring the pregnant woman into the public sphere. They are also among the few photographs anywhere that indicate some of the physical awkwardness and discomfort of pregnancy, as, for example, in a photograph of a teacher bending to look over a student's paper while pressing her lower back with her hand.

These five photographs of working pregnant women were not present in the 1966 edition. By the 1990 edition, they had disappeared. Instead, two small photographs still showed pregnant women in work environments, but neither

Lennart Nilsson, from
A Child Is Born, 1977

Lennart Nilsson, from
A Child Is Born, 1977

Lennart Nilsson, from
A Child Is Born, 1977

showed the woman actively engaged in work-related activity. She appeared, rather, to be a visitor in both pictures. The emphasis in the text is on health hazards in the workplace, which the pregnant woman, presumably, has therefore left.

Photography and Social Change

Shifting iconography within the humanistic images in *A Child Is Born* demonstrates that as social practices surrounding reproduction change, visual representations also change. However, the relationships between changing images and changing practices are not transparent. Under some circumstances photographs illustrate the change itself, as did the five photographs of pregnant women in the workplace. When these images did not reappear in the 1990 edition, their absence may have signified that the figure of the pregnant woman at work had not yet found a comfortable place.

Another set of photographs in *A Child Is Born* can be read as providing a counterpoint to the changing social landscape. Photographs such as the romantic, sexualized images of couples appearing in the 1990 edition do not picture or illustrate changing practices, but offer reassuring counter-narratives. Coinciding with a discussion of new reproductive technologies that challenged traditional notions of sex in reproduction, these photographs responded to social anxiety by taking a conservative stance. A third possibility is that photographs themselves can produce change, as did the fetal images in *A Child Is Born*, which became intrinsic to changing cultural perceptions of the origins of human life.

The photographs in *A Child Is Born* attempt to present "universal" inner workings of pregnancy, unveiling the hidden processes of women's bodies while at the same time upholding conventional ideas of the middle-class family. The too-neat, overly literal fit between the scientific photographs and the humanistic ones glosses over a number of assumptions: that fetal photographs are the result of simple observation rather than active probing that might easily raise ethical issues; that childbearing belongs in the medical context; that the white middle-class family is natural and universal; and that the fetus has an identity independent of its mother.

Instrumental photographs in pregnancy guidebooks deliberately address a viewer who is intimately connected to the subject through her need to learn about matters directly affecting her own life. The emphasis on the experience of the mother that characterizes these photographs should be seen in light of simultaneous developments in reproductive technology and imaging that foreground the production and engineering of a fetus who is increasingly given priority as an individual over the mother. The isolation of most instrumental images in guidebooks for expectant parents permits, in some respects, a fuller representation of women's experience of pregnancy than can be found in other forums, but it also serves to keep these images marginal to debates over the control of reproduction.

ADVERTISING PREGNANCY

Another category of photograph that specifically addressed the pregnant viewer—advertisements for maternity clothing—also emerged in the 1950s. Though fewer in number than instructional photographs, advertising pictures introduced a number of compelling images of pregnancy into the marketplace.

The maternity clothing industry, with its roots in the 1940s, occupies a specialized, small-scale niche in the fashion market, and photographic ads for maternity clothing follow many of the conventions of fashion photography. They function both as scopic images—playing on voyeuristic fantasy—and as instrumental photographs, providing information that aims to turn the consumer of images into a consumer of products. Given that fashion photographs work explicitly with notions of attractiveness and desire, the very existence of advertising photographs that feature pregnant women might seem unlikely. Yet such photographs, in recent years, have broken new ground in the public representation of pregnancy.

At the same time, these photographs have had a history of being discreetly positioned. Advertisements featuring pregnant women have been carefully placed to maximize the probability that only "appropriate" viewers—pregnant or soon-to-be pregnant women, and people in the maternity clothing business—will see them. Photographs advertising maternity clothing are most often found in special brochures or catalogues that are distributed directly to interested individuals and groups, often modestly mailed in plain brown wrappers. They also appear in specialized women's magazines.

A small number of publications devoted to photographs of maternity clothing have had brief publication runs. For example, from 1987 to 1990 *Maternity Matters*, a lively trade magazine, circulated among maternity clothing retail dealers; still not fully out in public. In 1992 *Maternity Fashion and Beauty*, a magazine published, interestingly, by Larry Flynt Publications and devoted specifically to the pregnant body and its accoutrements, broke through to the public sphere. It was filled with images of glamorous and fun-loving pregnant women. *Maternity Fashion and Beauty* was on newsstands for just over a year before it went out of business. However, the historical trajectory of advertising photographs of pregnancy is to push the pregnant woman, as an attractive figure, out further into the public arena.

EXECUTIVE MATERNITY
FASHIONS

Mothers Work, c.1985

Mother's Place, 1987

Madison Avenue Pregnant

Although advertising for maternity clothing presents a range of products, from reasonably priced everyday apparel to expensive evening wear, and from comfortable work clothing to executive suits, the idea of luxury consumption is a constant theme in the photographs. These pictures represent pregnancy as a special time for women to take pleasure in their bodies, pamper themselves, and purchase garments and other items specific to the enjoyment of pregnancy.

Like other fashion photographs, advertisements for maternity clothing encourage viewers to construct a body image associated with desirability, and to view themselves as if their bodies were there primarily for display. They share with other forms of advertising the appealing motif of leisure, to the extent that even advertisements for maternity work clothing virtually never depict the model working. For example, a 1980s advertisement for Mothers Work pictures a smiling woman who poses playfully above the title "Executive Maternity Fashions." The pregnant woman, even when a professional, is most readily represented in a leisure-oriented setting. Since the 1970s, pregnant women have also often been pictured exercising in specially purchased maternity exercise clothing, in line with the goal of shaping a body image, as in the Mother's Place photograph above.

Early Motifs

In 1950s advertising photographs, models posed in maternity clothing in a variety of locations connoting leisure, as well as in the studio. The models appear to be quite slender, even by nonpregnant standards, apparently simulating a stylishly thin "pregnant" body and reflecting the medical advice of the time. They were usually shown alone or with one other person—a husband, another child who is most often a daughter, or a nonpregnant woman friend. When picturing a pregnant woman with a friend, '50s advertisements often showed the women enjoying each other's company apart from men or daily duties. This visual theme, recurring in later advertising as well, develops the idea of a "women's world."

Early photographs advertising maternity clothing already draw on codes of glamour, but are restrained in their use of sensuality, emphasizing instead dignity and poise. A photograph from the archive of the Chas. L. Lewis company pictures a woman standing in front of a decorative hearth poised with bag and gloves. She is at home but on her way out, dressed for the public sphere but not

Courtesy of Chas. L. Lewis, n.d.

Courtesy of Chas. L. Lewis, n.d.

Courtesy of Chas. L. Lewis, n.d.

quite there yet. In another early Chas. L. Lewis picture, an attractive "pregnant" model walks in high-heeled shoes down the street with an admiring and protective man, presumably her husband. This is one of the relatively few advertising photographs in which a man is pictured. The pregnant woman *is* out in public, not in a sheltered "women's world," but she is shielded by the presence of the man. The picture is structured so that the woman is looking toward the viewer, although her attractiveness is contained within the confines of marriage and family. The heroic angle here valorizes the couple, striding into the future, their teamwork forming an important building block of society.

The Pregnant Woman as Child

Early advertising photographs for maternity clothing often portray the pregnant woman as childlike, as do many other fashion photographs. In his 1976 book *Gender Advertisements*, Erving Goffman identified some of the visual elements used in advertising to present the middle-class woman as childlike.[11] Goffman

Courtesy of Chas. L. Lewis, n.d.

described a particular recurrent bending and lowering of the head, knee, or whole body which he calls a "cant," and which places the woman in a subordinate, childlike position. The pregnant woman is also often pictured in advertising with a head bend or knee cant, as can be seen repeatedly in the grid of 1950s photographs. She also often wears maternity clothing that is patently childlike, or exhibits little-girl facial expressions that are dreamy, coy or "cute." One photograph from the 1950s depicts a woman sitting demurely on the floor surrounded by maternity clothing; she is perhaps the recipient of gifts at a shower, or perhaps an overwhelmed shopper. She appears childlike and vulnerable as she contemplates a toy stork, protected by the circle of consumer goods around her.

Two more 1950s photographs from the Chas. L. Lewis company offer additional scenarios for blurring the boundaries between pregnant woman and child. In a postcard-style advertisement, a floppy pieced-together doll is dressed in maternity clothing and pictured carrying a basket of groceries and a young child. The pregnant woman is playfully constructed as both caretaker and lovable toy.

Another variant of "girlishness" appears in a photograph in which a pregnant mother and her preschool daughter appear together in matching maternity/play wear. The mother wears a little girl's bow in her hair, while the little girl is dressed

Courtesy of Chas. L. Lewis, n.d.

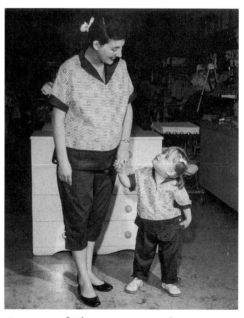

Courtesy of Chas. L. Lewis, n.d.

Mother's Place, 1987

as a mother-to-be. There is a kind of mutual mirroring around the theme of appearance and dressing up: the mother is transmitting important messages about self-presentation, and at the same time she is seeing herself mirrored in her daughter. This confusion of boundaries is represented as mutually pleasurable.

In later advertisements, the motif of pregnant woman as childlike is continued and in some ways expanded. The models are now visually identified with the activities of children, for example, holding teddy bears or playing children's games, as in the 1980s photograph from Mother's Place. Beyond simply representing the woman herself as a child, these pictures seem, however awkwardly and sentimentally, to be attempting to communicate something of the woman's relationship to the child growing within her. Motifs of the childlikeness of the pregnant woman continue to appear in maternity clothing advertisements through the 1990s.

Sensuous and Pregnant

In the 1980s, advertising photographs extended earlier representations of the self-centered pregnant woman, pictured outside of the family, in a world made up of and for pregnant women. The bodies of the models in these pictures began

Maternity Fashion and Beauty, 1993

Fifth Avenue Maternity, 1988

Fifth Avenue Maternity,
1988

to look more convincingly like those of actual late-stage pregnant women, and the images also began to focus increasingly on the pleasure the pregnant woman could take in her own body. In this way, advertising photographs of pregnant women began to stretch the narrow limits placed on the representation of pregnant sexuality in other domains.

Since the 1950s, many advertising images have featured two or more pregnant women together; in the 1980s these pictures became curiously powerful and sensuous images. While the pairs of women pictured in 1950s advertisements typically included one pregnant and one nonpregnant figure, the pregnant bodies were multiplied in 1980s advertising photographs, such as the group image from *Maternity Fashion and Beauty*. Given the redoubled emphasis here on heterosexual reproductivity, the advertiser enjoys a surprising freedom not only to represent pregnant women as sexualized, but also to represent eroticism among and between the women. When the women are pictured in pairs, for example, often

Maternity Fashion and
Beauty, n.d.

Japanese Weekend, n.d.

one will be in more masculine attire than the other, and they will appear to be a couple. The photographs from Fifth Avenue Maternity are particularly sultry and seductive.

In these images, the idea of a protected sphere for pregnant women, a "women's world" in which sexuality is sage, is continued and expanded. These images invite fantasies of carefree female companionship and camaraderie. The women pictured in such utopias appear to share the experience of pregnancy

Japanese Weekend, n.d.

Japanese Weekend, n.d.

with close friends, and to live in women's time and women's space, at leisure. These group photographs create an image that can appeal to women's fantasies of female power—the Muses, the Sirens, the Furies, the Amazons—without offending the possible male viewer, who can fantasize owning it all, a stable of handsome breeding women, a harem.

The sensual component of advertising photographs has been made still more overt in the 1990s. It even includes some gender play, as in the photograph from *Maternity Fashion and Beauty,* which depicts a model holding a very phallic water gun. Erotic references, so strictly prohibited in most other representations of pregnant women, seem to appear with relative ease in 1990s advertising photographs for maternity clothing, propelled at least in part by the economics of a competitive and volatile market.[12]

In the late 1980s, designers also began to align their maternity products more closely with avant-garde fashions. The San Francisco-based Japanese Weekend company, for instance, produced artistically designed ads featuring models in comfortable clothing, who posed in the studio or in urban locations. Yet although these pictures portray the pregnant woman as sophisticated, motifs of girlishness remain a subtext. In two pictures from Japanese Weekend, the models stand with a head or knee "cant," while a third young woman touches hand to chest in a tentative self-referential gesture. The figures combine the alleged self-confidence of the "contemporary woman" with isolation and vulnerability.

Lady Madonna, 1989

Crossing Racial Barriers

In addition to representing eroticism, 1980s and '90s advertising photographs also depict a racial mixture among pregnant women that is not found to the same extent elsewhere. In these photographs, beautiful women of many colors enjoy their leisure together, as in the Lady Madonna advertisements, although nonwhite women still generally constitute a minority in these group pictures.

While Annie Leibovitz's photograph of pregnant actress Demi Moore, published on the cover of *Vanity Fair* in August 1991, broke cultural barriers in showcasing the pregnant woman as glamorous and sexualized, African-American women have also had a very significant presence on these representational front lines. Going beyond posing for advertisements for maternity clothing, professional model Beverly Peele was featured pregnant in a major fashion spread in the November 1993 issue of the international haute couture magazine *Elle. Elle* published eight dramatic photographs of her, both nude and clothed, accompanied by a text that essentialized the sexiness and chic of pregnancy. Although her alluring poses were, for the most part, in keeping with the conventions of fashion photography, the title image of the spread, in which Peel poses nude, bears a very disconcerting resemblance to nineteenth-century photographs of African

Lady Madonna, 1989

Beverly Peele,
photographed by Gilles
Bensimon, *Elle*,
November 1993

Left: Silk
lamé T-shirt, lamé
scarf; Zoran.
Minimal makeup
and Max
Factor Interna-
tional's Moisture
Rich Lipstick
in Sheer Gold play
up Peele's
natural glow.
Makeup, Vincent
Longo for
Pierre Michel.
Right: Long
white cotton shirt,
Azzedine Alaia.
Makeup, Fran
Cooper for
the Stephen Knoll
Salon. For
details, see
Shopping Guide.

"I think I look the way every man wants a woman to look"

Beverly Peele, photographed by
Gilles Bensimon, *Elle,* November
1993

Beverly Peele, photographed by
Gilles Bensimon, *Elle*, November
1993

"racial types." Like some early medical photographs of pregnancy, this profile view emphasizes the African-American womans buttocks, referencing specifically the treatment of Saartje Baartman, the "Hottentot Venus." The design of the page draws further attention to Peele's anatomy by the placement of the letter "H" over her buttocks in a way that appears to measure and mark their dimensions. Thus the sexual attractiveness of the pregnant woman is associated with European racist fantasies about the hyper-sexuality of the African woman.

Since Peele was pictured pregnant in *Elle*, however, the image of pregnancy has been increasingly normalized in the public sphere. Other fashion models, actresses, socialites and celebrities have had their pregnant pictures published. There has been some fanfare but fewer shock waves than past experience would have led one to expect. With advertising photographs playing a key role, the image of the glamorous pregnant woman did emerge in the 1990s, achieving public visibility and growing public acceptance.

Public Policy and Persuasion

While the images of pregnancy made available in instructional and advertising contexts dramatically increased the public profile of pregnancy, political questions of reproductive control remain largely invisible in them. More overtly political is the openly ideological use of photographs of pregnancy, in the form of fetal images, by antiabortion activists. Photographs of fetuses are intended, in this context, to promote pregnancy per se, regardless of the circumstances. Antiabortion activists distribute an array of images on fliers and posters, or carry them on placards while protesting outside of women's health clinics that provide abortion services. These images range from pictures that look like sentimental baby photographs such as images of a fetus sucking its thumb, to horrific photographs of violated, dismembered fetuses. Certain prolife organizations also picture pregnant women in their promotional material, as decision-makers who have the power to choose to have their babies.

Like instructional and advertising photographs, these images invite instrumental viewing. They address the pregnant viewer dually, attempting to persuade her both by encouragement and threat to maintain her pregnancy. But unlike instructional and advertising photographs, these images also address the general public and government policy makers, exhibiting the same combination of encouragement and threat. Taking aim at the privacy doctrine that legally underpins the right to abortion, antiabortion activists have used images to deprivatize the issue and bring the inside of a pregnant woman's body into visibility as the center of bitter political debate in the public sphere.

This politicization of the pregnant woman's body through the use of images for advocacy in a public health arena, while dramatic, did not begin during the

Jack Delano, "Woodville, GA, June 1941.
At a cooperative prenatal clinic."

abortion wars of the 1970s, '80s and '90s. Rather, photographs of pregnant women were used in the public sphere as propaganda as early as the '40s, when FSA photographers such as Jack Delano and Marion Post Wolcott made images of public maternity clinics to illustrate the government's provision of prenatal care. After the New Deal, government programs as well as private family planning clinics continued to address the pregnant woman as viewer, employing encouraging images of healthy mothers who could expect healthy babies.

Such images stressed the positive aspects of both government-sponsored and private maternal and infant health care. There was, however, a negative history behind them as well. At the turn of the century, eugenicists became interested in portraying pregnancy as both an obligation and a threat to the nation, depending upon whose pregnancy it was. That is, enthusiastic reproduction was a social duty of the "superior" races and classes and a social danger when practiced by the poor. They evoked phantasmatic images of "inappropriate" or "socially unhealthy" families on posters displayed at exhibits at state fairs, conferences and

Marion Post Wolcott, "Schriever, LA, June 1940, Terrebonne, A Farm Security Administration project. A project nurse giving instructions and demonstrations during a meeting of the prenatal clinic."

other such public events, as elements of their campaign to limit reproduction by "defectives" —that is, the mentally retarded, the criminal, the insane, the indigent, the "colored races." Although one does not find this visual propaganda openly referenced now in public venues (discounting, perhaps, hate sites on the Internet), the eugenicist nightmare of socially undesirable pregnancy still has a tenacious afterlife in the form of historical associations even with visual images that have no deliberate connection to such ideas.

For example, in the image-savvy 1980s and early 1990s, certain nongovernmental social service organizations such as Planned Parenthood and the American Lung Association combined the kind of sophisticated graphic design used in mainstream advertising with public health instruction to create didactic and often humorously staged pictures aimed to dissuade teenagers from getting pregnant, to promote prenatal care or to discourage pregnant women from smoking and substance abuse. The March of Dimes also addressed smokers and drug users in their "Mommy . . . Don't" series, while Planned Parenthood sought the attention of young men in their "boyfriend" series, as in "If your girlfriend

American Lung
Association, n.d.

March of Dimes, n.d.

March of Dimes, n.d.

Planned Parenthood, n.d.

U.S. Department of Health and
Human Services, n.d.

gets pregnant, so do you." Some government public health brochures were published with Spanish-language captions, as in our example from the Department of Health and Human Services, making it clear that the intended recipients of particular family planning messages were Latina women.

The duality of persuasion and threat employed by these campaigns is a familiar mechanism. The meaning of the images, however, depends upon the political consciousness of their viewer. For some, the message can seem to be merely what it says. But for others, the fact that more than two thousand persons a year were involuntarily sterilized in the United States during the height of the eugenics movement between 1929 and 1941, and the history of racist and homophobic motivations for promoting fertility control among the poor and socially marginal populations give rise to a different perception of family planning and health services advice. An image that may have been intended to have an innocent appeal can from this perspective carry stereotyped and even genocidal overtones. Indeed, eugenic aims have so frequently been associated outright with, or not repudiated by, mainstream campaigns for women's reproductive freedom in the United States that these meanings are difficult for historically knowledgeable viewers to avoid.[13] Perhaps this is partly why Planned Parenthood has now ceased using images of pregnant women, at least for the time being, on its promotional material.

CONCLUSION

The images of pregnancy that have been made available in instructional, advertising and public policy domains constitute an archive of attempts to persuade viewers to take particular standpoints on the subject of pregnancy. Photographs found in childbirth manuals provide visual guidance and practical information for their viewers, inviting an instrumental mode of viewing that is keyed to viewers' particular needs. Advertising photographs for maternity clothing, on the other hand, represent pregnancy as an attractive state, moving the pregnant figure more fully into public visual space and setting it up for scopic viewing. Public policy pictures move pregnancy into the public arena in a different way, as images connected to active social advocacy and debate. All these photographs have been influential, opening up powerful ways of envisioning pregnant experience while also, at times, proscribing the behavior of pregnant women according to a variety of agendas.

Yet although the various agendas behind childbirth manuals and public policy images are far more important than the profit motive behind selling maternity clothing, it is advertising photographs which have expanded the visual vocabulary of pregnancy most significantly, through their appeal to fantasy. Although the social functions of these sets of promotional photographs are quite distinct, by the 1990s all can be seen as contributing to the construction of an image of the pregnant woman as an active consumer of products and options. The social costs and benefits of this model of pregnancy are still unfolding, and will be for a long time to come.

6) FROM FETAL ICON
TO PREGNANT ICON
Demi Moore and Clones

I'm a cloud, congealed around a central object, the shape of a
pear, which is hard and more real than I am and glows red
within its translucent wrapping. Inside it is a space, huge as
the sky at night and dark and curved like that, though black-
red rather than black. Pinpoints of light swell, sparkle, burst
and shrivel within it, countless as stars. Every month there is a
moon, gigantic, round, heavy, an omen.

—Margaret Atwood, *The Handmaid's Tale*

When *Life* magazine published Lennart Nilsson's photographs of living human
fetuses on April 30, 1965, as the first pictures of their kind, this was not strictly
true. In the first place, although the cover photograph seems to have been
appropriately labeled by *Life* as "the first portrait ever made of a living embryo
inside its mother's womb" because by "using a specially built super wide angle
lens and a tiny flash beam at the end of a surgical scope, Nilsson was able to
shoot this picture of a 15-week-old embryo," *all* the rest of the pictures were of
embryos that "had been surgically removed for a variety of reasons" from their
mothers' wombs. In other words, they were *dead* embryos.[1]

In the second place, obstetricians and embryologists had been using X-ray
visualizations of the living fetus inside its mother's womb for a hundred years
when the Nilsson images were published, and although such X rays had been discredited as unsafe for medical practice, they were by no means so crude or unin-
formative as "portraits" of the "the living embryo inside its mother's womb" as
the excited hyperbole for the new imaging technology would have us believe.
And, in the third place, in 1962 a similar, prior set of fetal photographs was compiled from medical archives by Geraldine Lux Flanagan, and published in a book
called *The First Nine Months of Life*.[2]

Yet it was Nilsson who won enormous attention on the day that *Life* published
his photographs. Nilsson's powerful configuration of the fetus as spaceman, floating in a starry sky, connected if at all to a mother only through an umbilical life-
support line, was, and remains, unforgettable. It rapidly became a cultural icon.

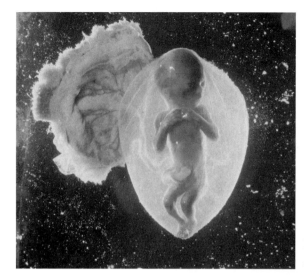

Lennart Nilsson, *Life*,
April 30, 1965

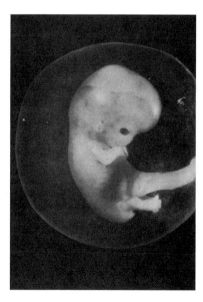

From Geraldine Lux
Flanagan, *The First Nine
Months of Life*, 1962

An icon is, in Vicki Goldberg's phrase, "a distilled and symbolic form" that expresses common and important themes in a culture.[3] At the same time it serves as a screen onto which individual viewers may project more personal meanings. In this way, the icon works to bring together the private and the collective. The specifically photographic icon is rooted in an historical moment, but it expresses concerns of that moment in ways that reach beyond its historical particularity.

At the time the Nilsson images were published, the race for outer space coincided with medical breakthroughs into the body's interior space, and particularly with intrusions into the inner space of the womb. As many have noted, Nilsson's image of the fetus as spaceman combines these two fields of exploration. Partly as a result, "planets, supernovas, and galaxies have been showing up alongside fetuses, embryos, and blastocysts during the past twenty-five years," notes philosopher Meredith Michaels.[4] At the same time, decolonization and civil rights movements extended personhood and expanded rights for new populations, genetic experimentation targeted the perfectibility of the human race, and the culture meditated upon the loss of innocence that accompanied such initiatives. The Nilsson image eventually acquired additional associations connected to these developments. It became a "patient," a person with "fetal rights," the ethical and religious figure called "the unborn," and even, as historian Barbara Duden has alleged, "Bambi," owing to what she calls Nilsson's "endearing concreteness" and his Disney-like skill in "eliciting epistemic sentimentality—a limitless concern for the most distant stranger."[5]

The Lux Flanagan images did not achieve the same iconic status. Coming as they did only slightly earlier in time, they too depict a fetal spaceman. He too floats in a capsule in the dark, primordial ether, but without the starry sky of space exploration behind. The Lux Flanagan fetus is also clearly a victim of medical aggression, trying in some images, with equivocal success, to escape from the sadistic prodding of a long, sharp needle, or folded into a coffinlike uterine box. Unlike the Nilsson spaceman, he is not a hero. The Nilsson fetus is much grander in conception. Nilsson inscribes him in a dramatic narrative of exploration and discovery and does not reveal that many of his photographs show dead fetuses. In addition, many of the images in Lux Flanagan's text are unattributed, whereas Nilsson appears in all his publications as author of his own images. The power to formulate the fetal icon became his.

As icons, Nilsson's pictures were often reproduced removed from their original context. They gave a common reference point or baseline for interpreting what was soon to be a spectacular growth in prenatal imagery. Even when the image was only a fuzzy blob on an ultrasound video monitor or a bloody pile of tissue on a cotton rag, the Nilsson fetus made it comprehensible. The pregnant woman herself, reading *Life* magazine or Nilsson's *A Child Is Born*, or any one of the many books that subsequently used Nilsson's illustrations, learned that she was carrying not the homunculus of earlier centuries or the Gerber baby of her fantasies, but the Nilsson icon. The physician learned that visualization of the fetus was not only increasingly possible, but that because it was now familiar, the

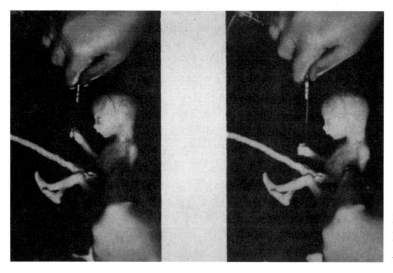

From Geraldine Lux
Flanagan, *The First Nine
Months of Life,* 1962

fetal image would increasingly support further intrusions upon the former secrecy of the womb. And statisticians, public health officials, and public policy makers discovered that once an image of the fetus was widely available, the fetus itself entered public life, along with imperatives for its physical protection, social enhancement, and civil rights that eventually rivaled the claims of its mother to those same social goods.

THE TRANSPARENCY OF THE MOTHER

Along with the currency of the fetus in the iconic form that it came to take through Nilsson's images came a corresponding change in the visibility of the mother. As we have shown, there already existed a long history of the suppression of the sight and the image of pregnant women. However, the focus on the inner contents of the womb at the expense of the womb's owner gave this taboo a new twist. It rendered her literally transparent. In the drive to visualize the fetus, it was the pregnant woman's role to dramatize how permeable a container her body could be. It is easy to mistake this development for an actual erasure of the mother. The mother is not absent in the fetal icon. Instead, like the seventeenth-century conception of God, she is nowhere and everywhere present at once. She is the enabling condition out of which "progress" comes, cooperating with and benefiting from the exploration of inner space. Actually erasing her would have produced a different set of less compliant archetypes.

This dynamic is easy to see in the earliest Nilsson or Lux Flanagan shots, which substitute a starry sky, or a completely blank surround, for the body of the

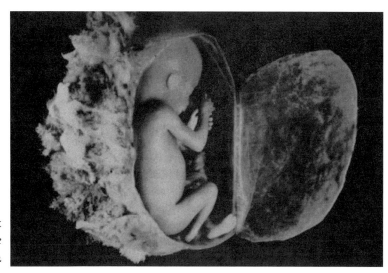

From Geraldine Lux
Flanagan, *The First Nine
Months of Life,* 1962

mother. In these images, the pregnant woman herself is of interest insofar as she
seems to have disappeared. This she gets better and better at doing as time goes
on. In the cover photograph of Nilsson's most recent edition of *A Child is Born*
(1990) (see Chapter 5), the pregnant woman has become even more vestigial and
insignificant. The physical presence of the fetus is enormous, while the pregnant
body, minus arms, legs and head, has inexplicably shrunk in comparative scale.

THE PREGNANT ICON

Against the general backdrop of the scarcity of photographs of pregnant women
in public places, and against the more recent and largely uncontested absorption
of the mother into the fetal icon, the August 1991 issue of *Vanity Fair* magazine
started a small revolution. Annie Leibovitz's cover photograph of actress Demi
Moore, pregnant and nude, was an instant scandal. It also opened the floodgates
to the public representation of pregnancy. Like Nilsson, Liebovitz crossed a
boundary at a ripe cultural moment, and with her image of the pregnant
woman, pregnant pictures crossed over into the public visual domain.

As with the Lux Flanagan precursors to the Nilsson images, a prior image of
a pregnant Demi Moore, also photographed by Annie Leibovitz and published in
the pages of *Vanity Fair* in May 1988, attracted no comparable attention. Like the
particular configuration of the Nilsson fetus as a spaceman, the particular form
of the 1991 image of a pregnant Demi Moore as "cover girl" was prescient. In the
earlier image, the pregnant Demi Moore and her then husband Bruce Willis
walk, embracing, on an empty beach. They could be castaways, or Adam and

Annie Leibovitz, *Vanity
Fair*, August 1991

Annie Leibovitz, *Vanity Fair*, May 1988

Eve, or any one of a number of other familiar pairings, but in any case the underlying fantasy is a tender and familial one. However, in August 1991, the pregnant icon, like the fetal one before her, escaped from such family ties.

Whereas the fetal icon was created by isolating the fetus and presenting it as an autonomous being, the image of a pregnant woman achieved iconic status by publicly appropriating the visual vocabulary of glamour. Leibovitz's photograph mixes the representation of female reproductive power, for so long de-eroticized and hidden, with the syntax of an image structured and positioned for voyeuristic, scopic viewing. After decades of closeting, the pregnant woman was being represented as most other women are in our culture: as an object of the gaze packaged to create and play on the desires of the viewer.

The *Vanity Fair* cover photograph raised an enormous hue and cry upon publication. The issue of the magazine was widely denounced as unfit for "family" reading. Several national chain stores refused to carry the magazine while the pregnant Demi Moore was on the cover. Obviously, the image was offensive to many viewers. However, it was neither its commodification of pregnancy nor the fact of commercial use of the image of a pregnant woman that was disturbing. Rather, it was the image of the pregnant body itself that registered as illicit. Newspaper reporters interviewed some newsstand customers who said that they saw nothing wrong with the image. "Giving birth," declared one man, "is a beautiful thing. There's nothing prettier than a pregnant woman."[6] But nevertheless, the August issue of *Vanity Fair* was sold all over the country except in New York City encased in a special plastic wrapper. This wrapper contained a plain white piece of paper that completely covered the image of Demi Moore from the neck down. In other words, rather than celebrate this image of pregnancy as a new visual empowerment for women, there was an attempt to censor it. This censorship authoritatively cemented the context of the image as pornographic. One letter to the editor read:

> Your August cover has provoked an intense response in our obstetrical-gynecological practice. To me, the photograph conveyed a sense of beauty and pride and I expected an overwhelmingly positive reaction from nurses and patients and their husbands. Unexpectedly, the opinions expressed were predominantly negative.
>
> Letter to the editor, *Vanity Fair*, 10/91

Another reader wrote:

> Pardon the thought of a dirty old lady—I'm seventy two—but after showing Demi Moore's huge belly, why not on your next cover have Bruce Willis with a huge erection? After all, he made the right connection.
>
> Letter to the editor, *Vanity Fair*, 10/91

In the controversy that followed, ninety-five television spots, sixty-four radio shows, fifteen hundred newspaper articles, and dozens of cartoons debated the merits of the cover. As Carol Stabile points out in her essay "Shooting the Mother: Fetal Photography and the Politics of Disappearance," the controversy over Leibovitz's image is evidence that,

> in a culture that places such a premium on thinness, the pregnant body is anathema. Not only is it perhaps the most visible and physical mark of sexual difference, it is also the sign for deeply embedded fears and anxieties about femininity and the female reproductive system. With the advent of visual technologies, the contents of the uterus have become demystified and entirely representable, but the pregnant body itself remains concealed.[7]

Cultural Contestation

Leibovitz's sexualizing of the figure of the pregnant woman occurred in the context of the ongoing development of reproductive technologies, which increasingly separate reproduction from human sexual acts. Thus in her photograph the pregnant woman is represented as a sexual being just at the moment in which in vitro fertilization has become a growing business, and there is public knowledge that embryos have become clonable, freezable, transportable. Just when heterosexual relations are no longer assumed to be a prerequisite for pregnancy, this photograph invites heterosexuality back into the picture. If the Nilsson icon celebrates male heroism, the Leibovitz icon is the apotheosis of female sexual valor on the eve of a new reproductive order.

In the photograph, Moore is entirely naked except for diamond earrings and a large tear-shaped diamond dinner ring that hangs below the knuckle of a well-manicured third finger. One of her arms cradles her bulging belly, the other encircles and protects her swollen breasts, delicately covering the nipples. The camera has been kind to Demi Moore's pregnant figure. Her thighs and rear are shaded out exactly where the flesh grows unfashionably wide and too softly dimpled; the torso in profile accentuates the lines rather than the heft of the pregnant belly. Demi Moore's three-quarter-frontal face looks up and away, ethereally disengaged from the weight of her body. Head and body are maximally displayed but treated separately, allowing later spoofs easily to substitute other heads atop her instantly recognizable figure. There is an ambiguity to both facial expression and bodily gesture: deliberate display works with an element of holding back in a power play that teases the viewer. Moore manages to combine direct eye contact with the classic feminine faraway gaze; she appears self-aware and self-protective, yet available to be viewed.

For the picture, Moore is scrupulously made up, moussed, and slightly greased so that she glows by reflected light. The overall effect is one of dramatic elegance and power—the kind of grooming and control over her own image that most third-trimester pregnant women probably feel is infinitely inaccessible to them. In this regard, the photograph is very much a woman's picture, playing to the female viewer's narcissism and masochism, as well as to the male gaze.

Like a row of shiny buttons down the front of a doll, the diamonds punctuate this message—that the woman can bear both the gaze and the child—written upon Moore's naked body. On each diamond there shines a spotlight that plays up the penumbra of a separate distinct region of that body. Reading downward, first the ear seizes the glitter, and then the breasts. But then there comes the belly. And this time the belly is alone in the spotlight; there is no signifying gem to show that the eye is resting upon what is precious. Instead, Moore holds to herself her vividly unadorned belly and breasts exactly as she might a bulging shopping bag from some boutique. The pregnant mother constructed by the era of reproductive technologies is a lady shopper, an enthusiastic consumer of reproductive "choices." The baby she "gets" is a perfectible product of a new genetic industry. It is the ultimate capitalist trophy.

In August 1992, exactly one year after her sensational cover photograph, Moore again appeared on the cover of *Vanity Fair*, once again photographed by Annie Leibovitz. This time she is dressed in what looks at first glance like a close-fitting man's suit. Upon examination, the suit is revealed to be expertly applied

Annie Leibovitz, *Vanity Fair*, August 1992

body paint. Moore's shapely, nonpregnant body is faintly visible under the illusion of men's clothing. Just as she had worn a pregnant belly a year before, seemingly an unmistakable marker of femininity, Moore now wears a masquerade of masculinity, demonstrating that all traces of the pregnancy have disappeared from her slim, fit body. The pregnant belly has here become a fashion accessory, to be donned for a certain time and then taken off. We have seen how the icon of the fetus was configured as independent of its mother; now we see an image of a pregnant woman whose pregnancy is a fleeting bodily performance, independent of its life-long repercussions. The image of the pregnant belly as a removable decorative appendage is a harbinger of technologically engineered pregnancies.

Replicating the Pregnant Icon

While some viewers had been scandalized by the appearance of a nude pregnant woman on a major magazine cover, others rushed to act on the new opportunity to picture pregnancy publicly. Leibovitz's photograph became a structure

Spy, September 1991

on which many agendas could be hung, a vehicle for making public statements. The pregnant icon unleashed a remarkable sequence of "clones"—public photographs that mimicked the form of Moore's pose while asserting their own political agendas. Leibovitz's photograph invited playful, transgressive responses. In the truly carnivalesque series of responses that followed suit, pregnancy was no longer a sequestered subject, but was available for public use.

Only a month after Leibovitz's photograph of Moore appeared on the cover of *Vanity Fair,* Moore's husband Bruce Willis, not to be outdone by his wife, appeared pregnant (in a computer-generated image) on the cover of *Spy* magazine. If the gendered boundaries of propriety were being crossed, why not go further? Advertisements for the film *Naked Gun 33 ⅓,* appearing on posters and in magazines, followed, with a photograph of the leading male actor's head over what appeared to be Demi Moore's body. The transgendered glamorous pregnant icon was being played as an outrageous eye-catcher. Several feature-length films on the theme of male pregnancy later followed suit.

The tabloids then took up the thread, with a cover image on the January 7, 1992, issue of the *National Enquirer* of a pregnant Ann Jillian captioned "My Pregnancy Secrets, She's Just 4 Weeks Away from Miracle Birth at the Age of 41." The cover on the July 7, 1992, issue of the *Weekly World News* featured the "First Photos Ever, Pregnant Man Gives Birth." The subjects being photographed in each of these pictures adopted Demi Moore's pose, hanging their own stories on its iconic form.

On August 1, 1992, exactly one year after the *Vanity Fair* cover, the lesbian feminist magazine *Metroline* published a Demi Moore "clone" on its cover with the caption, "Our Family Values: Creating Gay and Lesbian Families." In a grainy, harshly lit photograph reminiscent of a mug shot, a pregnant model in a bikini mimicked Demi Moore's pose. In this cover, the idea of pregnancy as glamorous was being spoofed, but the issue of its visibility, and the visibility of all kinds of pregnancies, was also being taken quite seriously. The new possibility of presenting a positive public image of pregnancy was seen as open to humorous interpretation, and at the same time enabling.

Metroline, August 1992

With African-American actress Whitney Houston's pregnant image appearing on the cover of *Ebony* in January 1993, the glamorous pregnant icon began to be accepted into the culture without irony. In striking contrast to the shock waves created by the Demi Moore cover, Whitney Houston's dignified image was received with great enthusiasm and pride by *Ebony* readers, who wrote in to the magazine to wish Houston well with her combination of career and motherhood.

While Houston's pose is related to the Moore photograph, Houston is not nude in the cover photo. She wears a black leotard and black veil-like skirt covering her belly. In an additional picture inside the magazine, she opens her skirt like a pair of wings, visually invoking African-American folk images of flying out of slavery. Pregnancy is thus made to speak of the hopes and ambitions of a people.

The August 1994 *McCall's* ran a wholesome cover photo of pregnant, and clothed, Genie Francis, leading lady of the soap opera *General Hospital*. Accompanied by the story of her own hard childhood, this smiling version of the icon celebrates pregnancy as part of the ideal of domestic happiness, '50s style.

Several months later, on October 24, 1994, *People* magazine ran a cover photograph of a young pregnant woman to accompany a feature article entitled "Babies Who Have Babies: A day in the life of teen pregnancy in America." A young white woman stood in a pose similar to Demi Moore's, but without

McCall's, August 1994

shielding her breasts. The sexualized pregnancy in this image is presented as dig-nified but not desirable.

Each of these pregnant cover girls, who appeared at regular intervals in the four years following the emergence of the Moore photograph, was used to artic-ulate a different social issue. From visibility for gay and lesbian families to pride in African-American culture, to celebration of traditional family values and the scapegoating of pregnant teenagers, the iconicity of Leibovitz's image meant it was translatable from the general to the specific and back again. It even entered the private sphere with snapshots such as Anne Stinson's parody.

In addition to these cover photographs, after the 1991 publication of the Demi Moore photograph, unprecedented images of glamorous pregnant women advertising fashionable clothing or appearing as pregnant celebrities were pub-lished within the pages of mainstream magazines. In 1998, the September issue of *Playboy* even featured a spread of nude photographs of a model in the early stages of pregnancy, although the opening photograph in the sequence shows her held firmly within her husband's encircling arms, her sexuality not fully avail-able as a spectacle. Leibovitz herself continued to push representational bound-aries, publishing her photographs of comedienne Roseanne Barr pregnant in

Mary Ellen Mark, *People*, October 1994

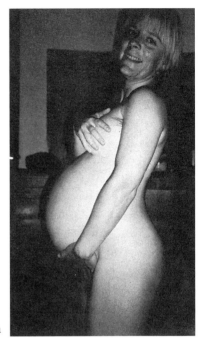

Ann Stinson

poses that simultaneously reified and undermined stereotypes of pregnancy. In Leibovitz's photograph published in July 1995 in the *New Yorker*, Barr poses at a desk, pregnant, slouched in a swivel chair in a messy room with crumbling walls, gazing into the distance, light falling across her body. Playing on the visual tropes usually associated with lyrical photographs of middle-class pregnant women, Leibovitz represents Barr as a solitary pensive figure at the office. However, Barr projects none of the expected transcendence of that tradition, but poses instead as a burdened and anxious working mother-to-be. A gifted comic famous for portraying an outspoken working-class woman, Barr here satirizes the glamour of the Demi Moore pose.

Leibovitz's "cavewoman" photograph, published in September 1995 in *Vanity Fair*, constructs a Neanderthal version of domestic happiness and traditional family values. The male figure, bearer of light, holds aloft a phallic torch. The female figure, Barr, stands close to the hearth, framed by the dark womblike entrance to the cave, striking a pose remarkably similar to Demi Moore's, her hands supporting and protecting her belly at bottom and top. Barr here appears to be a primal goddess of procreation, a statuesque earth mother, yet there is an element of irony to Leibovitz's placement of the cherished homemaker in a Stone Age setting.

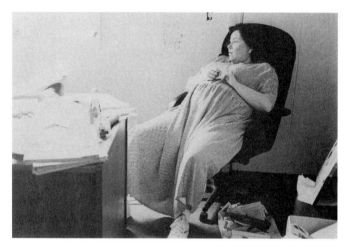

Annie Leibovitz, *The New Yorker*, July 1995

Annie Leibovitz, *Vanity Fair*, September 1995

The Pregnant Icon / Cultural Work

Why did photographs of pregnancy go public in the 1990s? Even though Leibovitz's image met considerable initial resistance, why was this picture successful in breaking the taboo against publicly picturing pregnancy where none had been successful before? Certainly its debut was facilitated by a cultural climate in which the connections among gender, sexuality, and reproduction had been loosened. And the public outpouring of response to the debut of the pregnant icon bespoke a pressing hunger felt by many to make pregnancy visible, despite the history of keeping its image under wraps and social construction under control.

It is the cultural work of an icon to administer visibility. An iconic image arises to give shape to a particular and pressing form of cultural experience, lending it a public presence and addressing the largest possible cross-section of viewers. At the same time, an icon also manages anxiety, keeping visible that which is merely disturbing and rendering inconsequential that which otherwise might overwhelm. In other words, the pregnant icon that emerged when Demi Moore's picture appeared on the cover of *Vanity Fair* in 1991 was a location of cultural triage, enabling and empowering the formation of certain meanings of pregnancy, and turning others aside. If we place a brief history of the previous quarter-of-a-century of pregnancy up against the run of Demi Moore clones, we can better understand both what the icon is imaging, and what it is deflecting.

Probably the most important cultural factor accompanying the emergence of the glamorous pregnant icon in the 1990s is the development and accessibility of new reproductive technologies. Let us recall, very briefly, how quickly these developments occurred and how swiftly they became common reproductive practices. Although the genetic research that enabled such procedures to succeed began in the immediate postwar era, the first child conceived by means of invitro fertilization and transferred into the mother's womb, was not born until 1978, in Manchester, England. Three years later, in 1981, a baby was similarly born in France. In 1984 the first frozen embryo was born in Melbourne, Australia. In 1986 twins were born from the simultaneous implantation of multiple embryos. Soon after, implanted quadruplets were born in Australia, then in Melbourne a pair of twins were born sixteen months apart. That is, the twins were fertilized on the same day, but the embryos were implanted at different times.

Such possibilities brought sensational and complicated surrogacy cases before the court. There was even a highly publicized instance in which a mother served as the surrogate for her adult daughter. By 1991, when the Demi Moore icon broke through, almost anything seemed possible, and marketable it should be added, by the brand new, highly profitable, international biotechnology industry.

Enter the glamorous, sexy, pregnant Demi Moore, whose desirous and desirable, consuming and consumable body is a broadly acceptable representation of reproductive "choice." The emergence of a pregnant icon into public consciousness gives the public a common image to relate to, as reproductive practice comes to resemble less and less the pictures in the mind. Like the fetal icon before it, the Demi Moore pregnant picture is a kind of fetish that (appears to) explain what we are seeing even when it is literally something else that is there.

Significantly, a kind of confusion in photographic representation occurred along with these changes in reproductive possibilities. Children produced in these new ways appear in the family photographs that festoon the offices of the doctors whom they have made famous: the gynecologist generally figures at the center of the picture, flanked by any number of mothers. The fathers usually remain off camera or on the periphery of this "family circle." Given the fact that only some fifteen percent of the couples who attempt in-vitro fertilization achieve success, the smiling solution in the doctor's office is somewhat deceptive.

Annie Leibovitz's cover photograph of Demi Moore did initiate a fuller representation of pregnancy in American popular culture. After the initial spate of copycat magazine covers, photographs of pregnancy began to appear, without fanfare, in many publications. The taboo against representing pregnancy in public has relaxed considerably since 1991, though by no means has it disappeared.

PREGNANT HYBRIDS

As public focus has shifted away from the role of the woman's body in reproduction, an ambiguous development from the standpoint of feminist theory, photography seems to have been freed to represent pregnant women in new ways. The most volatile reproductive issues as of this writing have to do with cloning—the prospect of reproducing humans from cells and DNA, bypassing both male and female bodies altogether. The pubic exploration of a new visual vocabulary for dealing with pregnancy, much of it drawing on earlier imagery, is taking place in the public domains of art photography, advertising and the popular press.

Several artists working in the 1990s have produced images that visually "hybridize" pregnant women with other creatures from the animal kingdom—domestic, wild and mythical. These works negotiate uncomfortable boundaries that under other circumstances would delineate the monstrous. Their sense of the relationship of pregnancy to nature goes beyond associating the pregnant woman with potted plants, kittens or even milk cows to suggest a direct reproductive link between animals and humans.

For instance, James Balog's disturbing photographs of a pregnant woman with a chimpanzee were made ostensibly to express the fantasy of greater harmony among life forms. Yet they raise questions about current reproductive

James Balog, "Pregnant with Chimp," 1993

Jill Gussow, from *The Other Side of Midnight/When the Animals Walk*, 1991

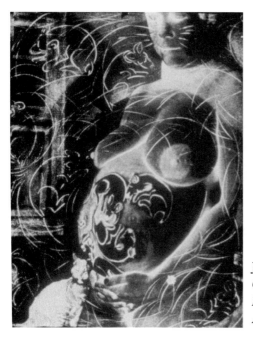

Jill Gussow, from *The Other Side of Midnight/When the Animals Walk*, 1991

technologies, many of which originate in animal science and utilize experimental cross-species "collaborations." One can read Balog's photographs as portraying a woman carrying a cross-species hybrid fetus.

Jill Gussow's work casts this idea in the more familiar terms of a pregnant woman's nightmare/fantasy of giving birth to lizards, turtles or mice. Referencing the drawings of fetuses on the pregnant belly that we have seen in some obstetrical photographs, her work also visualizes a new kind of creative power, located in the body of the pregnant woman. Aida Laelian's self-portrait as a pregnant creature already a cross between a woman and a zebra (what will the baby be?) is especially intriguing because she is pictured as a pregnant spectator, lifting up the focusing cloth of a large view camera on a tripod, about to be a voyeur onto some other scene. Michael Zide's photograph of his pregnant wife entitled "Jana and Ratleg, 1984" addresses the theme of human/animal hybridization with gentle humor.

Interestingly, we have not yet seen representations alluding to the placement of human embryos in animal wombs, a procedure that might imply an unacceptable sort of reproductive manipulation. In addition, while African-American women were among the first to be pictured as glamorous pregnant figures, exotically sexualized, we have not yet seen pictures of nonwhite women in a hybrid

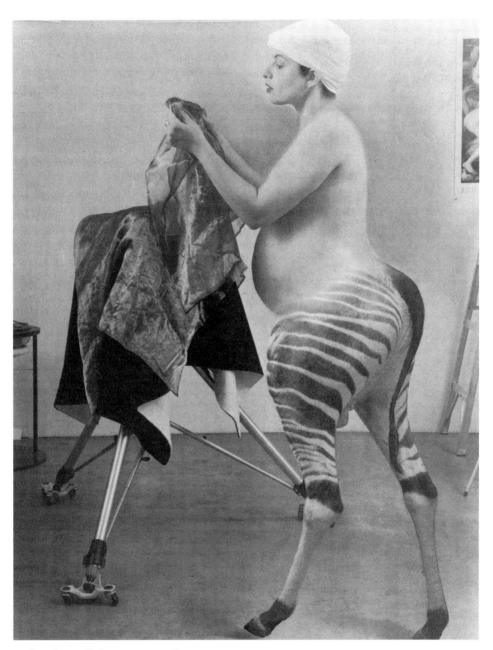

Aida Laleian, "The Memory of a
Vessel," 1992

relation to animals. This sort of picture might make historical associations with eugenics, breeding experimentation and human degradation too explicit.

However, the representation of the commingling of species was extended into a more public domain with the publication in November 1996, once again in *Life* magazine, of photographs of animal fetuses. Although none other than Lennart Nilsson had made these pictures over a period of years, their release in 1996 closely preceded epoch-making strides in cloning research. The photographs, soft, glowing and mysterious, are grouped to form a "multi-species family album," in which visual similarities between human fetuses and chicken, pig and various primate embryos are made graphically clear. *Life*'s recent interest in the use of such physiological parallels, visually represented, is akin to the use of physiognomy in the nineteenth century, although the images of easily interchangeable body formations invite the blurring rather than the codifying of boundaries. Once the site where fetal images first appeared to a large viewing public, *Life* continues to be the vehicle through which the public sees images that represent profound epistemological shifts in reproductive practice.

In September 1997 *Life* magazine also printed a photograph of a researcher in Japan (described as the "proud father"), in his lab with a plastic box serving the function of a uterus in which a goat is gestating. This picture vividly raised the possibility, for humans as well as goats, of going beyond disembodied conception to disembodied gestation and birth.

Adequate means do not yet exist for thinking through the implications of what these photographs allude to—the collaboration of humans, animals and machines in the creation and manipulation of new life. While the separation of sex and reproduction, the intermingling of species, and the appearance of new life out of something other than a womb or an egg appear in religious doctrine, folklore, mythology, and science fiction, we have not thought until recently of members of our own species being in control of these processes. The rationale for developing these gestational technologies is generally presented in terms of helping individual white middle-class couples with infertility problems, or of helping ailing individuals who need replacement organs or other body parts. But the stories of privilege and need frame the debate in terms of the individual, and obfuscate larger questions about the social control and ethical oversight of these practices.

ENVISIONING ISSUES

What role can photographs play in our evolving assessment of reproductive issues? Visual images in no way bear a simple relation to culture. Beginning with the observation that photographs of pregnancy were concealed from view, we have found that they also can be used to conceal underlying issues. We have seen

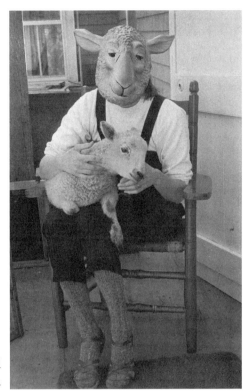

Michael Zide, "Jana and Ratleg," 1984

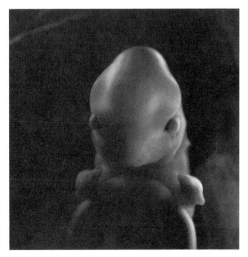

Lennart Nilsson, "Pig: 30 Days (Approximate Size: 7/8 Inch)," from *Life*, November, 1996

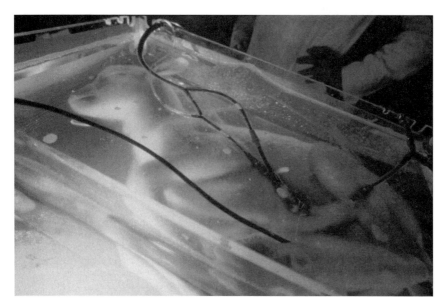

Tom Wagner, "Artificial Womb," from *Life,* 1997

that individual photographs—the Demi Moore icon, for example—may be read as a catalyst by some viewers, and as an offense by others. The repertoire of fetal icons has gone from Lennart Nilsson's visual removal of the fetus from its mother, to the actual removal of a gestating goat fetus to an artificial uterus, which is in turn represented in a published photograph which is likely to be prophetic. Similarly, we have moved from photographs of glamorous, sexualized, pregnant women directly to images of the reproductive linking of humans and animals. There are complicated relations between photographs and real-life events. Recent photographs that bring animals and machines into the human reproductive cycle may be preparing the viewer for boundary crossings ahead. They bear a relation to events that is different from other photographs of pregnancy we have studied—the idealized art photographs, the accessible, didactic images in childbirth manuals, the playful snapshots, sensuous ads and harsh medical photographs.

A plethora of contradictory ideas of pregnancy and reproduction currently coexist. The concept of reproductive choice has now been extended past the "shopping bag" model of a perfectible fetal product to the idea of a genetically engineered species. Images of pregnancy, once scarce, now proliferate as a powerful technological imperative drives the disembodiment of reproduction and secures its manipulation at the genetic level. The pregnant icon demands to be examined, for what it pictures and for what it leaves out.

EPILOGUE: PREGNANT PICTURES IN AN AGE OF MECHANICAL REPRODUCTION

> We must create new images that recontextualize the foetus:
> that place it back into the uterus, and the uterus back into the
> woman's body and her body back into its social space.
>
> —Rosalind Pollack Petchesky

THE REGENERATION OF GENERATION

At the turn of the twenty-first century the pregnant body has arrived at the possibility of a radically indeterminate status. Its gender, the time span of its potential fertility, even its transmission of genes to the fetus it carries are no longer biological givens. Once-visionary experimental technologies have reached a level of sophistication and practical application that challenges common definitions of human reproduction.

Many wonder how twenty-first century societies will define such reproductive possibilities, how variously each will grasp them, and how successfully individual women and men will be able to shape social resources to meet their own intimate needs. Technology, and the profit motive, are now firmly ensconced behind the wheel of human generation, where, to paraphrase the title of Walter Benjamin's famous essay on social effects of photography, their union has helped to drive pregnancy into a revolutionary new "age of mechanical reproduction."[1] But just as Benjamin warned that the mechanization of art could aid the spread of fascism, the power to re-create biological reproduction will be socially toxic if we do not find ways to direct it away from commerce, discrimination and exploitation.

Seeing/Looking

Many of the most recent advances in the biology of reproduction have been accompanied by significant visual representations. Some inhere in the procedures themselves, as in ultrasound visualization; some are artifacts of these procedures. But all these images are far more than transparent windows into the womb. They serve as guides to the further penetration, excavation, and transplantation of the bodily materials upon which assisted reproductive technology actively depends.

Yet, even while images have been helping to shape new technological possibilities, outside of medicine most photographs of pregnant women have hardly intimated the existence of these possibilities until very recently. Yet, for a long time, the "nature" of conception has not been as stable or as "natural" as is often presumed. Casual and formal surrogacy arrangements have always existed, as well as coercive and voluntary compliance. Records speak of alternative insemination at least since the late eighteenth century. But few images ever suggested that conception could be anything other than a purely "natural" procedure, if sometimes a violent one, until the late twentieth century. It follows that freer, richer expression of the changing social dimensions of pregnancy will not simply be a question of making freer, richer images. The framework itself must also be reconstructed, and the power to interpret is critical here.

Telling Tales

Such interpretation of images does not merely reveal; it generates connections—that is, stories. Careful articulation of images to the social contexts in which they are embedded is an active process of narration. Pregnant pictures function as representations of contemporary and historical conflicts over access to and control of reproductive resources. Determining the relation of images of pregnancy to social issues reveals the many political interests that the images can serve and the many ways that they can be made to serve them.

The stories we tell about pregnancy are the stage upon which meaning may be shared, but the meaning changes as the world around it turns. For instance, the old joke in which an unmarried woman claims to be "only a little bit pregnant" depicts a conservatively stabilized world of reproduction that has now lost its inevitability. The joke was funny because it expressed the hopeless attempt to defy necessity. It was a given that a woman's pregnancy already contained its big finale within its small beginnings, and from start to finish each step in the process of gestation implied the next. In the world of this joke, intervention is catastrophic for the fetus, not constitutive.

But with artificial insemination, embryo transfer and other highly technical interventions, it is no longer inevitable that a pregnancy carried to term must end up where it began. In fact, you need never to have been pregnant at all to be the genetic female parent of your infant. In other words, now you *can* be only a little bit pregnant and yet be the mother of a living child. The joke is resonant now for exactly the opposite reason: it registers liberation from the old constraints.

Similarly, old cultural restrictions upon definitions of masculinity and femininity no longer determine who is allowed to impregnate or to be impregnated. Lesbians and gay men who want to be mothers and fathers now commonly and openly create children through informal or even formal contractual relations that enable them to bypass heterosexual intercourse. The length of time that an embryo or fetus has to be contained within a growth environment that can only be supplied by a functional womb inside of a living woman has already been shortened by many weeks on either end of the ancient, nine-month gestational standard, and an artificial womb that may be used by men is certainly within the realm of possibility. One might say that the integrity of the old regime of sexual difference has now become obsolete, and with it even more of the original meaning of the old joke.

We would like to offer the term "optionally heterosexual reproductivity" as a transformation of Adrienne Rich's notion of "compulsory heterosexuality."[2] Rich's analysis of heterosexuality as both socially invented and socially enforced was so fundamental to feminist analysis in the mid-twentieth century that it is difficult to imagine what progress gender theory could have made without it. It made sense to separate sex from gender, as Rich did in the idea of the "homosocial continuum," greatly softening distinctions between women by downplaying sexual difference among them, when reproduction was thought to be tied necessarily to the habitation of a body that had a given biological function. Biology, presumably a given that could not be socially reconstructed, seemed less malleable than culture. It was not, therefore, to Rich, the important distinction.

However, now that component features of reproductive biology have yielded to technological intervention, the logical necessity for that binarism has also been undermined. With this release, as Shulamith Firestone predicted, comes a new mythos of pregnancy. Old longings, such as that expressed in George Platt Lynes' image of male gestation in "The Birth of Dionysis," or Harry Bowers' man-made fetal figure, are now newly prescient. For heterosexual couples, too, the relations of women and men in the sex/gender system have also been realigned. Suddenly there are increasingly heterodox reproductive positionings to inhabit, and increasingly unorthodox stories to tell. Pregnancy's new possibilities create an opportunity to think about restructuring social institutions that formerly were kept in line by the "realities" of gender. As Dion Farquhar observes in *The Other Machine: Discourse and Reproductive Technologies,* the belief that "women's bodies (indeed all bodies) are a natural given providing a constant and accessible source of uncontestable experience that is unmediated by and prior to discourse and interpretation" is no longer tenable.[3]

George Platt Lynes,
"The Birth of
Dionysus," n.d.

NEW IMAGES, OLD STORIES

If conventional appeals to the "universal experience" of pregnancy must now be
received with some skepticism, it does not mean that there will be no effort to
reconstruct a master narrative of reproduction. On the contrary, when "nature"
is now so obviously "culture" there may be new motivation to reassert the
inevitability of the social relations referenced in the old joke.

New images invite new stories. But they are not inevitable. Fetal images are a
case in point. Although ultrasound pictures are quite new, recycled notions of
motherhood have already been firmly overlaid upon them. These use the
increased visibility of the fetus to justify the old need to oversee the pregnant
body. For example, historian of science Barbara Duden reports that the guided
interpretation of ultrasound fetal images and their widespread circulation as
"baby photographs" has helped to shape a normative typology of maternal-fetal
"bonding" that publicly funded clinics may use to distinguish "good mothers"
from "bad."[4] Such designations can have significant consequences for the clinics'
pregnant clients if they are screened and streamed accordingly.

Duden finds that the most familiar archetype against which the fetus is con-

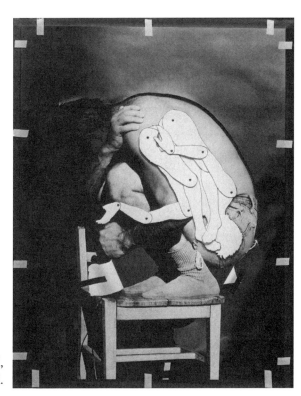

Harry Bowers, untitled,
n.d.

figured is that of an innocent creature of nature. This identification of the fetal image projects a notion of the fetus as an orphaned future citizen, and is construed as justification for the state to act preemptively to protect and acculturate it, *in loco parentis,* even when the fetus is still physically connected to its actual parent. On the other hand, the fetus as a "baby in a bottle," an image of monstrous birth that, according to Susan Squier, has also recurred "throughout the history of modern representations of reproduction," is a boundary-marking figure of a different kind, used to scare those who seek "unnatural" control over their own reproduction.[5] And lastly perhaps the commercial figure of the "Gerber Baby" best expresses the idea of the fetus as the perfect child delivered by genetic engineering to desperate and deserving white, heterosexual, married, middle-class couples who can afford to pay for a high-quality product.

What all these figurations of the fetus have in common is a tenuous relation to the scientific data conveyed by the image combined with a long and deep connection to societal myths. Using fetal images to produce dramas of the "bad" mother, or the "good" or "best" fetus, may not be the best way of understanding the biological, social or even spiritual relations of pregnancy, but they are both the most ancient dramas and the most ready to hand.

Out of Touch?

Precisely because it makes *visual* images, fetal imaging adds to what previously have been the crucial dimensions of knowledge about the fetus—touch and the personal testimony of the pregnant woman—the social relations of spectatorship. But again, the meaning of this shift to occularity is not predetermined. It depends upon the standpoint of the viewer at least as much as on the machine-made image. Photographers themselves have often tried to indicate their deep sense of the mutability of visual meaning. Joyce Tenneson's picture of a young woman who holds a frame over her nonpregnant-looking abdomen forcefully expresses the insight that meanings may be imposed and must be deliberately chosen. Ron Wohlauer's photograph of the image of a pregnant woman reflected in a framed mirror that sits on an easel in an artist's studio represents the layers of and mediation that determine interpretation.

And interpretation varies widely. Many feminists have argued, for instance, that sonograms "erase" the pregnant mother and create a dangerous, "unnatural" separation of the fetus from her body. Some have even expressed dismay over the alienation of what they believe to be a primal connection of the mother to the fetus. Others, however, have challenged this assumption of alienation, or a universal pregnant subjectivity. Kathleen Burdick points out that the "image of the fetus now serves as the cultural site where the unified maternal is restored. The fetus stands in, indeed, becomes, the lost image of the unified maternal, as it floats disembodied in its amnesiac ahistorical representational space."[6] Dion Farquhar also argues that "fetal imaging technologies achieve not only the usually reactionary social recognition of fetal personhood, but also the intensification of the pregnant woman-fetus relation."[7]

To see how individuals construe the effect of fetal visualization so differently is to discover the mistake of assuming too quickly the meaning of science's view of, or into, the pregnant body. As Rosalind Petchesky argued in "Foetal Images: The Power of Visual Culture in the Politics of Reproduction," the new visualization technologies, like all technologies, are inherently neither good nor bad, but depend on the context in which they are used.[8] Women are not simply victims of the new reproductive procedures, but individuals who are in some sense motivators and certainly consumers, who hold considerable power, and who often are helped by the images. Once again, it is the stories that matter.

In research conducted for her book *The Tentative Pregnancy*, Barbara Katz Rothman collected and examined these narratives. She compared interviews of

Joyce Tenneson,
untitled, n.d.

women who expected to undergo amniocentesis with women who didn't. Rothman found that those who did were far more "tentative" in their early bonding
with the fetus, while they waited the necessary weeks for test results that might
indicate serious problems and the possible question of abortion. Rothman concluded that

> a diagnostic technology that pronounces judgements halfway through the
> pregnancy makes extraordinary demands on women to separate them-
> selves from the foetus within. Rather than moving from complete attach-
> ment through the separation that only just begins at birth, this technology
> demands that we begin with separation and distancing. Only after an
> acceptable judgement has been declared, only after the foetus is deemed
> worthy of keeping, is attachment to begin.[9]

Rothman concluded that current bonding ideology is an artifact of male doctors'
visual literalism concerning pregnancy, since for men, she argues, emotional
attachment does follow upon a visual experience first. "The technology [of prenatal diagnosis] assumes," she wrote, "and thus demands of women, that our

Ron Wohlauer, "Pregnant
Nude," 1981

experiences parallel men's, that we too start from separation and come to intimacy—and only with caution."[10] But some women *may* in fact "come to intimacy" with their fetuses only tentatively and "with caution." And some men may be quite emotional about an "infant" who is far from visible. It is unclear why this kind of experience would necessarily "parallel men's."

Rothman's research suggests that maternal testimony about the emotional power of bonding with a fetal sonogram is also a far more complex story than can be taken at face value. For if a mother may bond only with an image of a fetus that she has already decided to keep, then it is not ultrasound images in themselves that inspire feelings of attachment, but the context in which they are received and interpreted.

But naivete about visualization is rampant. Bettyann Kevles notes that the "assumption that no woman could see a sonogram and go ahead with an abortion" has led "some [conservative] legal scholars [to suggest] that every abortion seeker see a sonogram of her fetus" as part of an effort to persuade her to change her mind. And she adds in a footnote what is even more egregious, that "this was the argument used against aborting the fetuses of the Muslim women raped in Bosnia, almost all of whom abandoned their babies upon delivery. The anticipated 'bonding' never happened, and the babies were warehoused, adopted if possible, or died from neglect."[11]

Fetus Unbound

Rarely do such stories break entirely free of past conventions. Clifford Grobstein, Professor Emeritus of Biological Science and Public Policy at the University of California, San Diego, is a case in point. In his thoughtful and provocative *Science and the Unborn: Choosing Human Futures* (1988), Grobstein tried to show, on the cover of his book, the new possibilities that are implied by reproductive research. The cover surrounds an image of the iconic Nilsson fetal spaceman with phrases appropriated from the pro-life vocabulary such as "the unborn" and "choosing human futures." But Grobstein used these conventional phrases to help explicate a highly unconventional argument about the importance of fetal personhood, not to conserve life as we know it on earth, but to invent life as it will be in outer space. He proposed that "the most precious cargo carried by a colonizing space ship will be its human genetic heritage—the product of millennia of interaction between life [sic] and Earth, now to be tested in unearthly environments." These "colonial jewels," Grobstein predicted, will consist of "carefully selected reproductive adults, frozen pre-embryos, or perhaps even 'spare parts,' lengths of DNA for later transfer of particularly important stored genes."[12]

Grobstein also proposed an elaborate vision of the uses of frozen sperm:

Space colonization may well have consequences for the status of the unborn, because of the logistics and economies of space travel and the biology of small founding populations. The first places a premium on small numbers of travelers and the second on wide genetic variation. A colony of travelers even on nearby Mars would be substantially isolated reproductively from the reproductive population on Earth.

Small sexually reproductive populations of any kind have greater difficulty maintaining themselves over generations than larger ones because inbreeding is likely to bring out unfavorable recessive characteristics. On Earth this is a recognized problem in the biology of small islands and of attempts to rescue endangered species such as the California condor. Human founder populations, whether on space arks or stable extraterrestrial sites, will have to carry more genetic variation than will be allowed by the logistics of transit of persons. Enter the unborn in the frozen state.[13]

Transport of frozen pre-embryos would minimize required space and resources and, if the pre-embryos were carefully selected from Earth's genetically diverse human population, could enlarge and diversify the gene pool of the new colony.

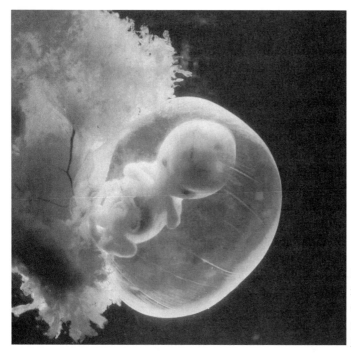

Lennart Nilsson, cover image for Clifford Grobstein's *Science and the Unborn: Choosing Human Futures,* 1988

Such a conception, in both senses of the word, is not without difficulties and complications. Among other things, it presumes that pre-embryos might be created to be transported and to be raised by foster parents in a distinctly strange land and with very little in the way of informed consent.

This certainly sounds at first like an original scenario, but in fact it generates highly conventional representations and erasures. What Grobstein cites as the "human genetic heritage" is not just the result, as he suggests, of some abstract and axiomatic "interaction between life and Earth," but of the strenuous reproductive labor performed by historically specific men and women during "millennia of interaction," which he ignores. Where Grobstein finds Earth's human population to be an "earthly stew" that is overflowing "its existing confines" and "showing signs of unhealthy fermentation and rising pressure [which] might be relieved, before it becomes explosive, by broadened perspectives that direct it outward into the openness of space," his sense of this new emergency is also the ancient claustrophobia of human "confinement" where the fetus may be subject to "unhealthy fermentation" and "rising pressure" within its mother's body.[14]

The idea of genetic "colonial jewels" also represents not a new fetal metaphor but the return of eugenics. Grobstein values diversity chiefly for its genetic contribution to the exploration of space, an old epic of conquest and control. It is a cellular characteristic, frozen and transported in "pre-embryos," disconnected from its meaning in lived lives.

The tale concludes by comparing all life that now exists on Earth to one giant, collective pregnancy, in which "humanity spreading from the earth is a new birth . . . [and] all we have so far been may be as if we are yet unborn." But not once in this account of the achievements of biotechnology does Grobstein mention the word "woman" or "man" or "black" or "white" or any other specific category of personhood.

This fantasy risks reinstating the old hierarchies of power simply by enfolding them as logical givens within an evolutionary framework that would change the terms of global "life," but never of particular lives.

Nilsson Revisited

Grobstein clearly draws upon Nilsson's fetal spaceman icon to embody his fantasy about fetuses in space. There exists, Grobstein asserts, a fundamental historical interrelation between "space technology" and "biotechnology."

It is not happenstance that space technology and biotechnology surged forward in the mid-twentieth century. The surge derives from the close and mutually supportive interaction that has evolved between advancing science and technology—especially manifested in the rich connections and crossfeeding among the diverse technologies derivative from science and now dominating our culture. The integrative nature of this technological web provides the link between the almost simultaneous, and seemingly fortuitous, burgeoning of otherwise largely unrelated space and biological science.[15]

Within this "web," the visual image has been firmly linked to pregnancy in ways that are as productive, and as irreversible, as they were unimaginable a generation ago. As Grobstein senses, fetal images are only "seemingly fortuitous." His tale of the extraction of resources from "inner space" to use in colonizing "outer space," expresses in condensed form many of the important connections that underlie the legibility of the fetal icon.

But the Nilsson fetus reproduced on the cover of Grobstein's book is not the strange new explorer who captured the world's imagination on the cover of *Life*. Instead, it is a much less familiar Nilsson image of the fetus as a technician busily repairing some mechanical malfunction. The "rich connections and crossfeeding among the diverse technologies derivative of science and now dominating our culture" that Grobstein discloses apparently evoked not the just the new archetype of the species but a figure who was more familiar. The way in which Grobstein altered the Nilsson icon reveals how much even the notion of the fetus as space explorer is historically and ideologically embedded.

NASA's Pregnant Picture

Certainly aspects of Grobstein's narrative are disturbing. But compared to NASA's discomfort with picturing human sexuality, Grobstein's fetal engineer seems progressive. In August and September 1977, two spacecraft called Voyager I and II were launched on a journey to continue past Jupiter and Uranus beyond the solar system of Earth. Attached to each was a record of almost "90 minutes of the world's greatest music; an evolutionary audio essay on The Sounds of Earth; and greetings in almost sixty human languages (and one whale language)." The spacecraft bore the following written message from President Jimmy Carter:

> This Voyager spacecraft was constructed by the United States of America. We are a community of 240 million human beings among the more than 4 billion who inhabit the planet Earth. We human beings are still divided into nation states, but these states are rapidly becoming a single global civilization. We cast this message into the cosmos. It is likely to survive a billion years into our future, when our civilization is profoundly altered and the surface of the Earth may be vastly changed. Of the 200 million stars in the Milky Way galaxy, some—perhaps many—may have inhabited planets

and spacefaring civilizations. If one such civilization intercepts Voyager and can understand these recorded contents, here is our message: This is a present from a small distant world, a token of our sounds, our science, our images, our music, our thoughts and our feelings. We are attempting to survive our time so we may live into yours. We hope someday, having solved the problems we face, to join a community of galactic civilizations. This record represents our hope and our determination, and our good will in a vast and awesome universe.[16]

The record also contained "118 photographs of our planet, ourselves and our civilization." The team that worked on selecting the pictures proposed the inclusion of a photograph of a young, white, handsome, nude couple holding hands, the woman visibly pregnant, in the Voyager capsule, "to show recipients how our bodies look."[17] NASA officials rejected the photograph and allowed a substitute: a silhouette of the two figures, with a schematic fetus drawn on the woman's belly.

While the discarded photograph specified particular kinds of bodies, the approved silhouette was more physically ambiguous. Concerned to protect the future of the human race as it projected it into the unknown, NASA apparently

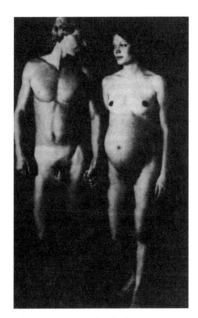

Photograph included in
Voyager proposal, n.d.

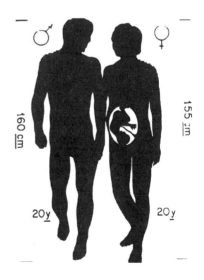

Jon Lomberg, "Silhouette of
Pregnant Couple," 1977

judged it better to schematize than to represent the new Adam and Eve as raced and sexed social beings. It is striking that NASA assumed nonhuman beings in space might be able to make head or tails of any photograph at all. It is even more striking that race and sex and pregnancy were harder realities to confront than space travel itself.

IMAGES AND ALCHEMY

For images to yield new meanings, rather than merely cement the old defeats, new stories must interrupt old discourses. But this is very difficult to do. Lawyer and social theorist Patricia Williams has given the matter of race more extensive thought. In *The Alchemy of Race and Rights* (1991), Williams too indulges in a utopian fantasy of "race-less" reproduction. After pondering the social implications of the new biotechnology, she writes:

> In a technological age, guerrilla warfare must be redefined. I dream of the New Age "manifesto": We must all unite, perhaps with the help of white male college graduates who are willing to smuggle small hermetically sealed vials of black sperm into the vaulted banks of unborn golden people; we must integrate this world from the inside out. We must smuggle not the biological code alone, but the cultural experience. We must shake up biological normativity; bring our cause down to particulars, to the real terms of what is at stake in the debate. We must be able to assert the battle from within, and in the most intimate terms conceivable.
>
> I suggest guerrilla insemination to challenge the notion of choice, to complicate it in other contexts: the likelihood that women would choose black characteristics if offered the supermarket array of options of blond hair, blue-green eyes, and narrow, upturned noses. What happens if it is no longer white male seed that has the prerogative of dropping noiselessly and invisibly into black wombs, swelling ranks and complexifying identity? Instead it will be disembodied black seed that will swell white bellies; the symbolically sacred vessel of the white womb will bring the complication home to the guarded intimacy of white families, and into the madonna worship of the larger culture.[18]

Like Grobstein, Williams dares to dream about a new humanity. But while neither Grobstein nor Williams shrink from embracing the possibilities of using reproductive technology to effect fundamental social change, the image of the fetus that is a sign of liberation to one, is a sign of cultural limitations to the other.

Williams' fantasy was provoked not by Nilsson or NASA but by reading a report in the *New York Times* of a lawsuit that was brought by a white woman who had deposited the sperm of her terminally ill husband in a sperm bank. When the wife returned after her husband's death to be artificially inseminated, she was apparently impregnated with the "wrong" (i.e., not her husband's) sperm, for she gave birth to a visibly black daughter. The mother sued the fertility clinic for financial damages on behalf of herself and her daughter because "her insemination became a tragedy and her life a nightmare" on account of the "racial taunting of her child."[19]

William's fantasy expands upon the Demi Moore pregnant icon of a glamorous white woman holding her blooming belly like a full shopping bag. Like Tanya Marcuse's trenchant visual elaboration of this idea in her image of a full-bodied pregnant torso made from a delicate and sensuous material, Williams at first accepts the promise of such enticing choice. Williams' narrative indulges for a moment in the liberatory implications of the idea of reproduction as consumption by imagining luxurious new possibilities of a genetic "supermarket."

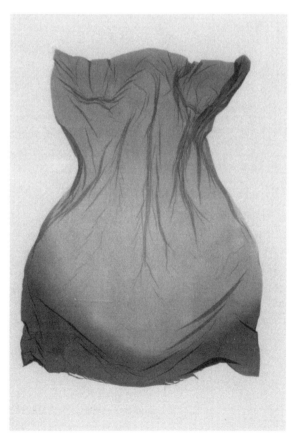

Tanya Marcuse, "Torso #XXII," Polaroid Emulsion Transfer on Mylar, 1996

But almost immediately Williams decides that something is wrong with the story. A dissatisfied customer, the white woman in Williams' story, wants her money back because the baby she took home from the fertility clinic turned out to be the wrong color. Better shoppers would presumably manage to secure "blond hair, blue-green eyes, and narrow, upturned noses." "Black characteristics" would remain on the shelves.

Guerrilla insemination, Williams finally concludes, "won't work." Racism still infuses the cultural matrix within which only the gender poles of reproduction have become unstuck. Such a strategy would end with "yet another generation of abandoned children, damaged in the manufacture, returned to the supplier, and sued for in the effort to undo their existence by translating the disaster of them into compensatory dollars and cents."[20] Ultimately, what Williams wants to challenge is the notion of choice embedded in the contemporary pregnant icon. All narratives of biological origins, even the most unlikely ones, are readings that have to be negotiated with the racial balance of power that already exists.

What Is Wrong with This Picture?

Criticism of the racialized subtext of the pregnant icon as shopping bag that is implicit in Williams' story of the supermarket is rendered much more explicit by another African-American woman law professor, Dorothy Roberts. In *Killing the Black Body: Race, Reproduction and the Meaning of Liberty*, Roberts rubs several contemporary photographic representations of the "new reproduction" against the grain to expose their racial bias:

A friend of mine recently questioned my interest in a custody battle covered on the evening news. A surrogate mother who had agreed to gestate a fetus for a fee decided that she wanted to keep the baby. "Why are you so always so fascinated by those stories?" he asked. "They have nothing to do with black people." By "these stories," he meant the growing number of controversies occupying the headlines that involve children created by new methods of reproduction. More and more Americans are using a variety of technologies to facilitate conception, ranging from simple artificial insemination to expensive, advanced procedures such as *in vitro* fertilization (IVF) and egg donation.

In one sense my friend is right: the images that mark these controversies appear to have little to do with Black people and issues of race. Think about the snapshots that promote the new reproduction. They always show white people. And the baby produced often has blond hair and blue eyes—as if to emphasize her racial purity. The infertile suburban house-wife's agonizing attempts to become pregnant via IVF; the rosy-cheeked baby held up to television cameras as the precious product of a surrogacy arrangement; the complaint that there are not enough babies for all the middle-class couples who desperately want to adopt; the fate of orphaned frozen embryos whose wealthy progenitors died in an airplane crash: all seem far removed from most Black people's lives. Yet it is precisely their racial subtext that gives these images their emotional appeal.[21]

Roberts argues that although some single women, and lesbians and gay men have been able to use them to circumvent barriers to reproduction, in general the ways our society explores the new technologies are "more conforming than liberating: they more often reinforce the status quo than challenge it." This conformity includes repetition of the eugenic pattern of encouraging and helping white people to transmit their genes while restricting Black access by means of economic barriers and racial steering. According to Roberts, "one of the most striking characteristics of the new reproduction is that it is used almost exclusively by white people."[22] Can one really imagine, she asks, "a multi-billion dollar industry designed to create Black children!"[23]

Roberts also points out that "media images of the new reproduction mirror this racial disparity." Whether they appear in news magazines "plastered with photos of the parties (all white) battling for custody of Melissa [Baby M]," or advertisements for eggs and sperm that emphasize the whiteness of the donor as a desirable feature, or as part of a four-part series in the *New York Times* on "The Fertility Market," that "displayed a photograph of the director of a fertility clinic surrounded by seven white children conceived there" and "a picture of a set of beaming IVF triplets, also white," these images assert the importance not simply of genetic ties, but of *white* genetic ties.[24]

Meanwhile, as Roberts also observes, when we do read news accounts involving Black children created by these technologies, they are usually sensational stories intended to evoke revulsion precisely because of the children's race:

In The Netherlands in 1995, a woman who gave birth to twin boys as a result of IVF realized when the babies were two months old that one was white and one was Black. The Dutch clinic mistakenly fertilized her eggs with sperm from both her husband and a Black man. A *Newsweek* article subtitled "A Fertility Clinic's Startling Error" reported that "while one boy was as blond as his parents, the other's skin was darkening and his brown hair was fuzzy." A large color photograph displayed the two infant twins, one white and one Black, sitting side by side—a racial intermingling that would not occur in nature. The images presented a new-age freak show created by modern technology gone berserk.[25]

Those who publish these images seem to assume that the viewer will use them to confirm a particular narrative.

> *Newsweek* ran a cover story entitled "The Biology of Beauty" reporting scientific confirmation of human beings' inherent obsession with beauty. The article featured a striking full-page color spread of a woman with blond hair and blue eyes. The caption asked rhetorically: "Reproductive fitness: Would you want your children to carry this person's genes?" The answer, presumably, was supposed to be a resounding, universal "Yes!"[26]

But Roberts, like Williams is looking to undercut the unthinking racism of this kind of representation by articulating a quite different response: "Not necessarily!"

EXPECTING SOMETHING?

Certain photographs by artists working in the 1990s address these public and private dimensions of contemporary reproductive imagery in ways that are particularly cogent. First, Robin Lasser's outrageously funny yet sobering image in which, via computer, she has placed photographs of four pregnant torsos on a billboard invokes prophetic scenarios imaginable within the framework of technologically assisted pregnancy. Against the backdrop of a pleasant-looking residential neighborhood, and with the words "Expecting Something?" as a sardonic and somewhat sinister text, the four panels on the billboard highlight different aspects of the changing social construction of pregnancy. Reading from left to right we see a man's body with a detachable, hairy pregnant belly; a woman's body sporting a pregnant body cast printed across the breasts with the words, "How's My Mothering? 1-800-510-SUCK"; a woman's pregnant torso inscribed with prohibitions that a pregnant woman must follow; and a large, pregnant torso painted in the coloration of a cow, with rubber nipples protruding from the actual nipples, a ring through one of them.

Underlying all four figures is a concept of the pregnant body as an intersection of public and private spheres. The pregnant body is something literally to be written on, in language that the public can read. Both torsos that have words on them refer to the public surveillance of maternity and to the self-surveillance that accompanies it. One refers to the "How's My Driving?" signs that are sometimes put on trucks, suggesting that the figure is subject to discipline as a member of the working class. The other refers to toxins embedded in contemporary culture and to luxury items ("no hot tubs, no sushi"), identifying the figure as a member of the middle class burdened with the self-discipline of fetal quality control. By its reference to cattle, the bovine figure alludes to the interspecies experiments currently going on in animal husbandry as well as to the treatment of women as breeders. The rubber nipples relate to the collaboration of human, animal and machine that is accelerating in genetic research and the biotechnology industries. But far from appearing monstrous, this figure is sassy and hip, her nipple ring sporting a child's sticker image of a cow just like her. And finally, the male figure relocates pregnancy outside the female body, this time bearing the burden. Lasser's image, a site for theatrical masquerade, both foregrounds and foreshadows ethical ambiguities in contemporary human reproduction: the

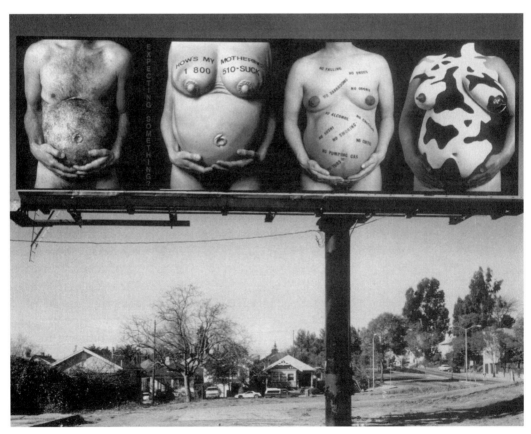

Robin Lasser, from the *How's My Mothering?* series,
1995–1997

crossing of gender and species boundaries, and the increased surveillance of women's bodies.

The "HIDE-ing project, image 4; a collaboration of Renee Cox, Maggie Hadleigh-West, Jenny Polak and Juana Valdes," on the other hand, also depicts a quartet of figures, equidistant from one another and in parallel formation. The project deals with issues of visibility and assimilation in multiethnic relationships. These four nude women, two white, two black, represent a small sample of female bodies, none of them conforming to the culture's ideal body image. Together they project a vision of female solidarity across difference and despite technology.

Significantly, their togetherness is pictured in an empty white studio, a space apart. The only object in the space in addition to the figures is the camera's cable release. It extends from the photographer's body to the lower edge of the frame, like an umbilical cord connecting the pregnant woman to the unpictured world outside the frame. Although all four women appear to be of reproductive age, only one, the photographer, looks pregnant. The other three may or may not be occupied with reproduction. This image foregrounds the women's bodies in a deliberately prosaic way. The women are shown in a group but not because they are sexually inviting or exotic, "natural" or "other." Pregnancy by whatever means is just one possibility among many.

Each woman gazes at the viewer with a somber look. The meanings of reproduction are shifting in the world outside the frame. Is there to be a world in which women's biology does not determine their destiny? Language for addressing the changes that are developing remains elusive, but the space of these women remains connected to the world outside by the cable of an image-making machine.

Lasser's photograph and the HIDE-ing Project put forward two views of the future of pregnancy. Lasser presents a vision of public control and manipulation in which women figure as body parts, elements of a larger picture, albeit elements with attitude. The HIDE-ing Project dramatizes a diverse community of women in which the pregnant woman is distinct but not separated, and has the power of the gaze.

Intervention in reproductive processes is not new. What is new is what Grobstein calls "the rising capability to intervene directly in the deep structure and developmental expression of life's hereditary core."[27] Which pictures, which stories of reproduction will prevail? Pregnant pictures both structure and constrain our understanding of these developments, and offer the opportunity to grapple with the choices we must make.

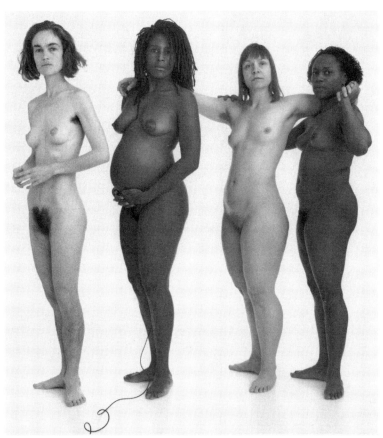

Renee Cox, Maggie
Hadleigh-West, Jenny
Polak and Juana Valdes,
HIDE-ing Project,
image 4, 1993

Notes

Chapter 1

Epigraph: Iris Marion Young, "Pregnant Embodiment: Subjectivity and Alienation," in *Throwing Like a Girl and Other Essays in Feminist Philosophy and Social Theory* (Bloomington: Indiana University Press, 1990), 160.

1   Sherry Ortner, "Is Female to Male as Nature Is to Culture?" in *Woman, Culture and Society*, ed., Michelle Zimbalist Rosaldo and Louise Lamphere (Stanford: Stanford University Press, 1974), 67–87.

2   See Rachel Roth, "At Women's Expense: The Costs of Fetal Rights," in *Women and Politics*, 13 (3–4, 1993), 117–135, and Cynthia Daniels, *At Women's Expense.*

3   Maria Mies, *Patriarchy and Accumulation on a World Scale: Women in the International Division of Labour* (London: Zed, 1986), 54.

4   Linda Gordon, *Woman's Body, Woman's Right: Birth Control in America* (Harmondsworth, England and New York: Penguin Books, 1986), 95.

5   Simone de Beauvoir, *The Second Sex*, trans. H. M. Parshley (New York: Vintage, 1974); originally published by Alfred A. Knopf, 1953, and in 1949 in France by Librairie Gallimard as *Le Deuxième Sexe: I. Les Faits et les Mythes. II. L'Experience Vécue*, 32–33.

6   Ibid. 33.

7   Ibid.

8   Shulamith Firestone, *The Dialectic of Sex: The Case for Feminist Revolution* (New York: William Morrow, 1970), 198, 206.

9   Ibid. 206.

10   Ibid. 226

11   Ibid. 11.

12   Julia Kristeva, "Motherhood According to Giovanni Bellini, "*Peinture* 10–11 (December 1975), reprinted in Julie Kristeva, *Desire in Language* (New York: Columbia University Press, 1982), 237.

13   Susan Stewart, *On Longing: Narratives of the Miniature, the Gigantic, the Souvenir, the Collection* (Baltimore: The John Hopkins University Press, 1984).

14   Adrienne Rich, *Of Woman Born: Motherhood as Experience and Institution* (New York: W. W. Norton, 1977), 48.

15   Ibid. 152–153.

16   Jacques Lacan, "The mirror stage as formative of the function of the I," in *Ecrits, A Selection*, trans., Alan Sheridan (New York and London: W. W. Norton, 1977), 1–7.

17   Adrienne Rich, *Of Woman Born*, 6.

18   Ibid. 156.

19   Ibid. xvii.

20   Ibid. 13.

21   Laura Mulvey, "Visual Pleasure and Narrative Cinema," in *Visual and Other Pleasures* (Bloomington: Indiana University Press, 1989).

22 J. C. Fletcher and M. I. Evans, "Maternal Bonding in Early Fetal Ultrasound Examinations," *New England Journal of Medicine* 308 (1983), pp. 282–293, cited in Petchesky, "Foetal Images: The Power of Visual Culture in the Politics of Reproduction," in *Reproductive Technologies: Gender, Motherhood, and Medicine*, Michelle Stanworth, ed. (Minneapolis: University of Minnesota Press, 1987), 59.

23 "Response to the Silent Scream," by Planned Parenthood of Seattle, King County.

24 Lynn M. Morgan and Meredith W. Michaels, *Fetal Subjects/Feminist Positions* (Philadelphia: University of Pennsylvania Press, 1999), 4.

25 Rosalind Pollack Petchesky, "Foetal Images: The Power of Visual Culture in the Politics of Reproduction," 62.

26 Ibid. 71.

27 Ibid. 72, 73, 74.

28 Luce Irigaray, *This Sex Which Is Not One*, trans. Catherine Porter with Carolyn Burke (Ithaca: Cornell University Press, 1985), 23–33.

29 Susie Bright, *Susie Bright's Sexual Reality: A Virtual Sex World Reader* (Pittsburgh: Cleis Press, 1992), 100, 101.

30 Ibid. 101.

31 Iris Marion Young, "Breasted Experience: The Look and the Feeling," in *Throwing Like a Girl and Other Essays in Feminist Philosophy and Social Theory* (Bloomington: Indiana University Press, 1990), 199.

32 Ibid.

33 Iris Marion Young, "Pregnant Embodiment," 46.

34 Donna Haraway, "A Cyborg Manifesto: Science, Technology, and Socialist-Feminism in the Late Twentieth Century," in *Simians, Cyborgs and Women: The Reinvention of Nature* (New York: Routledge, 1991), 149–182.

35 Judith Halberstam and Ira Livingston, eds. *Posthuman Bodies* (Bloomington: Indiana University Press, 1995), 2.

36 Petchesky, "Foetal Images," 78, 79.

Chapter 2

Epigraph: Susan Sontag, *On Photography* (New York: Farrar, Strauss and Giroux, 1977), 28, and Roi Partridge, quoted in Judith Fryer Davidov, *Women Camera Work Self/Body/Other in American Visual Culture* (Durham, NC: Duke University Press, 1998), 466 n 71.

 1 Susan Sontag, *On Photography* (New York: Farrar, Strauss and Giroux, 1977), 102.

 2 See Pierre Bourdieu, *Photography, A Middle-Brow Art* (Stanford: Stanford University Press, 1990), 73–98 and *Distinction: A Social Critique of the Judgment of Taste* (Cambridge: Harvard University Press, 1984) 35–40.

 3 Pierre Bourdieu, *Photography, A Middle-Brow Art*, 87, 88, 193 n 14.

 4 Susan Sontag, *On Photography*, 167.

 5 Laura Mulvey, "Visual Pleasure and Narrative Cinema," in *Visual and Other Pleasures* (Bloomington: Indiana University Press, 1989).

 6 Pamela Allara, "'Mater' of Fact: Alice Neel's Pregnant Nudes," in *American Art* (Spring 1994), 16.

7   Excerpt of a written statement accompanying Gerard Malanga's photograph, which was sent to us in response to a query we placed in *Afterimage.*

8   Russell Lee, quoted in James Guimond, *American Photography and the American Dream* (Chapel Hill: University of North Carolina Press, 1991), 120.

9   Edward Steichen, *The Family of Man* (New York: Museum of Modern Art, 1955).

10 Julia Scully, *The Family of Woman* (New York: Grosset and Dunlap, 1979).

11 Quoted in James Guimond, *American Photography and the American Dream* (Chapel Hill: University of North Carolina Press, 1991), 120.

12 Quoted from slide taken of original artwork. Courtesy of Kent Gallery, New York.

13 This information was sent to the authors in a personal communication from Joel-Peter Witkin, 1997.

14 Mary Russo, *The Female Grotesque: Risk, Excess and Modernity* (New York: Routledge, 1994), 8.

15 This image was one of the very few of pregnant subjects that appeared in a particularly important collection of women's photographic self-portraits, *In/sights: Self-portraits by Women,* ed. Joyce Tenneson Cohen (Boston: David R. Godine, 1978).

16 Cheryl Younger, quoted in Joyce Tenneson Cohen, *In/sights,* 134.

17 Iris Marion Young, "Breasted Experience: the Look and the Feeling," in *Throwing Like a Girl and Other Essays in Feminist Philosophy and Social Theory* (Bloomington: Indiana University Press, 1990), 198.

18 Barbara Seyda and Diana Herrera, *Women in Love: Portraits of Lesbian Mothers and Their Families* (New York: Little, Brown, and Co., 1998), and Gigi Kaeser and Peggy Gillespie, *Love Makes a Family: Portraits of Lesbian, Gay, Bisexual and Transgender Parents and Their Families* (Amherst: University of Massachusetts Press, 1999).

19 Personal communication with the authors, 1999. See Sandy Hale, *Child Mothers* (Hartford: Connecticut Association for Human Services, 1989).

20 Kierra Walton, *My Family* (Boston: self-published limited edition artist's book, 1995).

21 See William S. Johnson, ed., *W. Eugene Smith: Master of the Photographic Essay* (Millerton, NY: Aperture, 1981); *Life* (December 3, 1951), and Dorothea Lynch and Eugene Richards, *50 Hours* (Wollaston, MA: Many Voices Press, 1983).

22 Kira Corser and Frances Payne Adler, *The Struggle to Be Borne* (San Diego: San Diego State University Press, 1988), and Kira Corser and Frances Payne Adler, *When the Bough Breaks: Pregnancy and the Legacy of Addiction* (Portland, OR: New Sage Press, 1993).

Chapter 3

Epigraph: Pierre Bourdieu, *Photography: A Middle-Brow Art*, 19.

1   Simon Watney, "Ordinary Boys," in *Family Snaps: The Meanings of Domestic Photography,* ed. Jo Spence and Patricia Holland (London: Virago Press, 1991), 29

2   Julia Hirsch, *Family Photographs: Content, Meaning and Effect* (New York: Oxford University Press, 1981), 13.

3   Patricia Holland, Introduction to *Family Snaps: The Meanings of Domestic Photography,* 7.

4   Julia Hirsch, *Family Photographs,* 126.

5   Iris Marion Young "Pregnant Embodiments: Subjectivity and Alienation," *Throwing Like*

a Girl and Other Essays in Feminist Philosophy and Social Theory (Bloomington: Indiana University Press, 1990), 163.

6 Craig Owens, "Posing," in *Beyond Recognition: Representation, Power, and Culture* (Berkeley and Los Angeles: University of California Press, 1992), 212.

7 Joan Riviere, "Womanliness as a Masquerade," in *The Inner World and Joan Riviere: Collected Papers 1920–1958*, ed. Athol Hughes (London: Karnac Books, 1991), 90–101.

Chapter 4

Epigraph: From an exhibit placard at the American Eugenics Society display, Sesquicentennial Exhibition, Philadelphia, Pennsylvania, 1926. Quoted in Daniel Kevles, *In the Name of Eugenics: Genetics and the Uses of Human Heredity* (Cambridge: Harvard University Press, 1995) 62–63.

1 Sander L. Gilman, *Picturing Health and Illness: Images of Identity and Difference* (Baltimore: Johns Hopkins University Press, 1996), 10.

2 Daniel Kevles, *In the Name of Eugenics: Genetics and the Uses of Human Heredity*, ix.

3 Dr. Herman Reinking, as quoted in Charlotte G. Borst, *Catching Babies: The Professionalization of Childbirth, 1870–1920* (Cambridge, MA: Harvard University Press, 1995), 90.

4 Barton Cooke Hirst, *A Textbook of Obstetrics* (Philadelphia: W. B. Saunders, 1898). Unless otherwise noted, all illustrations from Hirst discussed in the text are drawn from this edition.

5 Michel Foucault, *The Birth of the Clinic: An Archeology of Medical Perception*, trans. A. M. Sheridan Smith (New York: Random House, first Vintage Books edition, 1975), 210.

6 David Green, "Veins of Resemblance: Photography and Eugenics" in Patricia Holland, Jo Spence, and Simon Watney, eds. *Photography/Politics: Two* (London: Comedia Publishing Group, 1986), 9.

7 See, for instance, Barton Cooke Hirst, *A Textbook of Obstetrics*, 5th ed. (Philadelphia and London: W. B. Saunders, 1907), 207–212, which tries to distinguish the visual appearance of pregnancy from obesity, hernia, sarcoma of the liver, ovarian cyst, uterine carcinoma, tuberculosis, fibroid tumor, and distended bladder.

8 Richard C. Norris, *The American Textbook of Obstetrics for Practitioners and Students* (Philadelphia and London: W. B. Saunders, 1902), 17.

9 See Harold Speert, *Obstetrics and Gynecology in America: A History* (Chicago: American College of Obstetricians and Gynecologists, 1980), 78–79. Speert notes that in 1848 Charles C. Meigs, professor of midwifery at the Jefferson Medical College in Philadelphia, wrote that he hoped "the day is far distant when the spectacle shall be seen in our hospitals, of troops of women, waiting in succession, for a public examination of their genitalia, in presence of large classes of medical practitioners and students of medicine." As late as 1850, an editorial in the *Buffalo Daily Courier* reminded readers that "in this branch of medicine the eye is to be blinded," and asked, "What possible good can come of such exposure?" 78–79.

10 Richard C. Norris, *The American Textbook of Obstetrics*, 409; and J. Clifton Edgar, *The Practice of Obstetrics: Designed for the Use of Students and Practitioners of Medicine*, 2nd ed. (Philadelphia: P. Blakiston's Son & Co., 1904), 121.

11 See F. Winckel, *A Textbook of Obstetrics including the Pathology and Therapeutics of the Puerperal* State *designed for Practitioners and Students of Medicine* (Philadelphia: P. Blakiston's Son & Co., 1890), 72.

12 Joseph DeLee, *The Principles and Practice of Obstetrics* (Philadelphia and London: W. B. Saunders, 1913), 110.

13 Abraham Flexner, *Medical Education in the United States and Canada*, report to the Carnegie Foundation for the Advancement of Teaching (Carnegie Foundation for the Advancement of Teaching, 1910; reprint, Washington, D.C.: Science and Health Publications, 1960), 117. Quoted in Borst, *Catching Babies*, 101.

14 J. Whitridge Williams, "Medical Education and the Midwife Problem in the United States," *Journal of the American Medical Association* 58 (1912), 1–7. Quoted in Borst, *Catching Babies*, 105–109. Ellipses deleted.

15 DeLee, xii–xiii.

16 Joseph B. DeLee, "The Prophylactic Forceps Operation," *American Journal of Obstetrics and Gynecology* 1 (Oct. 1920). Quoted in Judith Walzer Leavitt, *Brought to Bed: Childbearing in America 1750–1950* (New York and Oxford: Oxford University Press, 1986), 179.

17 J. Whitridge Williams, *Obstetrics: A Textbook for the Use of Students and Practitioners* (New York and London: D. Appleton, 1904) n.p. Unless otherwise noted, all illustrations discussed in the text are drawn from the 1904 edition of this work.

18 Speert, *Obstetrics and Gynecology in America*, 39.

19 Ibid.

20 Kevles, *In the Name of Eugenics*, 85.

21 Ibid. 64.

22 Francis Galton, "Eugenics: Its Definition, Scope and Aims," *Sociological Papers* 1 (1905), 50. Quoted in David Green, "Veins of Resemblance," 14.

23 Ethel M. Elderton, "The Relative Strength of Nurture and Nature" (Dulau, 1912), 33; quoted in Kevles, *In the Name of Eugenics*, 40.

24 Kevles, *In the Name of Eugenics*, 85.

25 Ibid. 72.

26 W. C. D. Wetham and D. D. Wetham, *The Family and the Nation: A Study in Natural Inheritance and Social Responsibility* (Longmans, Green, 1909), 87–88. Quoted in Kevles, *In the Name of Eugenics*, 74.

27 William Henry Carmalt, review of *Heredity in Relation to Eugenics* in the *Yale Review* 2 (July 1913), 797. Quoted in Kevles, *In the Name of Eugenics*, 72.

28 Donna Haraway, *Modest_Witness@Second_Millennium. FemaleMan_Meets_OncoMouse* (New York and London: Routledge, 1997), 224, 237.

29 Carole H. Browner and Nancy Ann Press, "The Normalization of Prenatal Diagnostic Screening," in *Conceiving the New World Order: The Global Politics of Reproduction*, eds. Faye D. Ginsburg and Rayna Rapp (Berkeley, Los Angeles, and London: University of California Press, 1995), 307.

30 Ronald Numbers and John Harley Warner, "The Maturation of American Medical Science," in *Sickness and Health in America: Readings in the History of Medicine and Public Health*, 3rd ed., eds. Judith Walzer Leavitt and Ronald L. Numbers (Madison and London: University of Wisconsin Press, 1997), 136.

31   Alan Trachtenberg, *Reading American Photographs: Images as History, Mathew Brady to Walker Evans* (New York: Hill and Wang, 1989), 52–60.

32   Louis Agassiz, quoted in Stephen Jay Gould, *The Mismeasure of Man* (New York and London: W. W. Norton, 1981), 78–79.

33   Sander L. Gilman, *Difference and Pathology: Stereotypes of Sexuality, Race and Madness* (Ithaca and London: Cornell University Press, 1985), 85. See also Sander L. Gilman, "Black Bodies, White Bodies: Toward an Iconography of Female Sexuality in Late-Nineteenth-Century Art, Medicine, and Literature," in *"Race," Writing and Difference,* ed. Henry Louis Gates, Jr. (Chicago and London: University of Chicago Press, 1986), 223–61.

34   Williams, *Obstetrics*, 161.

35   Ibid. 149.

36   John D. Stoekle and George Abbott White, *Plain Pictures of Plain Doctoring: Vernacular Expression in New Deal Medicine and Photography* (Cambridge and London: MIT Press, 1985), 80.

37   Sally Stein, "Seeking the Photographic Cure," *Exposure* 25:2 (summer 1987), 53, note 15.

38   Ibid.

39   Stoekle and White, *Plain Pictures of Plain Doctoring,* 184.

40   Ibid.

41   Judith Walzer Leavitt and Ronald Numbers, *Sickness and Health in America: Readings in the History of Medicine and Public Health* (Madison: University of Wisconsin Press, 1997), 4.

42   One historian reports, "By 1940, 55 percent of America's births took place within hospitals; by 1950, hospital births had increased to 88 percent of the total; and by 1969, outside of some rural areas, it was almost unheard of for American women to deliver their babies at home." Neal Devitt, "The Transition from Home to Hospital Birth in the United States, 1930–1960," *Birth and the Family Journal* 4 (1977), 47–58. Quoted in Leavitt, *Brought to Bed,* 171.

43   Oakley, *The Captured Womb,* 191.

44   Nicholson J. Eastman, *Williams' Obstetrics* (New York: Appleton-Century-Crofts, 1950), 211.

45   Bettyann Holtzman Kevles, *Naked to the Bone; Medical Imaging in the Twentieth Century* (Reading, MA: Addison-Wesley-Longman, 1997), 230.

46   DeLee, *Principles and Practices of Obstetrics,* 57.

47   See Simon Watney, Jo Spence and Patricia Holland, *Photography/Politics Two* (London: Comedia, 1986). See also Lisa Cartwright, *Screening the Body: Tracing Medicine's Visual Culture* (Minneapolis: University of Minnesota Press, 1985).

48   Bettyann Holtzman Kevles, *Naked to the Bone,* 230.

49   Nicholson J. Eastman, *Williams' Obstetrics* (New York: Appleton-Century-Crofts, 1950), 16.

50   Ibid.

51   Ibid.

52   See discussion in Kevles, *In the Name of Eugenics.*

53   Ibid, 114.

55 Nicholson J. Eastman, *Williams' Obstetrics*, 5.

55 Bettyann Holtzmann Kevles, *Naked to the Bone*, 245–246.

56 Ibid. 247.

57 Asim Kurjak and Frank A. Chervenak, *The Fetus as Patient: Advances in Diagnosis and Therapy* (New York and London: Parthenon, 1994).

58 Leavitt and Numbers, *Sickness and Health in America*, 5.

Chapter 5

Epigraph: Simon Watney, "On the Institutions of Photography," in *Photography / Politics Two* (London: Comedia, 1986), 196.

 1 Marjorie Karmel, *Thank you, Dr. Lamaze: A Mother's Experiences in Painless Childbirth* (Philadelphia: J. B. Lippincott, 1959).

 2 Our model of instrumental viewing derives from Jonathan Crary's discussion of an embodied mode of viewing, which, he writes, emerged in the 1820s and 1830s. We differ from Crary in thinking of instrumental viewing as a longstanding mode that operates concurrently with other possible viewing modalities. For Crary's discussion, see Jonathan Crary, "Modernizing Vision," *Vision and Visuality*, ed. Hal Foster, Dia Art Foundation Discussions in Contemporary Culture No. 2 (Seattle: Bay Press, 1988), and Jonathan Crary, *Techniques of the Observer: On Vision and Modernity in the Nineteenth Century*, 7th printing (Cambridge: MIT Press, 1996).

 3 Grantly Dick-Read, *The Natural Childbirth Primer* (London: William Heinemann, 1950).

 4 Wendy Chavkin, *Double Exposure: Women's Health Hazards on the Job and At Home* (New York: Monthly Review Press, 1984).

 5 Ina May Gaskin, *Spiritual Midwifery* (Summertown, TN: Book Publishing Company, 1990).

 6 Femmy DeLyser, *Jane Fonda's Workout Book for Pregnancy, Birth, and Recovery* (New York: Simon and Schuster, 1982).

 7 Frédérick LeBoyer, *Inner Beauty, Inner Light* (New York: Alfred A. Knopf, 1978).

 8 Text of a personal letter written to the authors by F. LeBoyer, August 1999.

 9 Lynne Pirie, *Pregnancy and Sports Fitness* (Tucson, AZ: Fisher Books, 1987).

 10 Lennart Nilsson, Claes Wirsen, and Axel Ingelman-Sundberg, *A Child Is Born: The Drama of Life before Birth* (New York: Dell, 1966).

 11 Erving Goffman, *Gender Advertisements* (New York: Harper and Row, 1976).

 12 Maternity clothing companies go rapidly in and out of business. Most of the advertising photographs printed in this chapter are from companies that are no longer in business.

 13 This history is documented by Linda Gordon in *Women's Body, Women's Right: A Social History of Birth Control in America* (New York: Penguin Books, 1977), and Dorothy Roberts in *Killing the Black Body: Race, Reproduction and the Meaning of Liberty* (New York: Vintage, 1999).

Chapter 6

Epigraph: Rosalind Pollack Petchesky, "Foetal Images: The Power of Visual Culture in the Politics of Reproduction," in *Reproductive Technologies: Gender, Motherhood and Medicine*, ed. Michelle Stanworth (Minneapolis: University of Minnesota Press, 1987), 78.

1   *Life* magazine, April 30, 1965.

2   Geraldine Lux Flanagan, *The First Nine Months of Life*, 2nd ed. (New York: Simon and Schuster, 1962).

3   Vicki Goldberg, *The Power of Photography: How Photographs Changed Our Lives* (New York: Abbeville, 1991), 135.

4   Meredith W. Michaels, "Fetal Galaxies: Some Questions about What We See," in *Fetal Subjects/Feminist Positions*, Lynn M. Morgan and Meredith W. Michaels (Philadelphia: University of Pennsylvania Press, 1991), 125.

5   Barbara Duden, *Disembodying Women: Perspectives on Pregnancy and the Unborn* (Cambridge, MA: Harvard University Press, 1991).

6   *New Haven Register*, Thursday, July 18, 1991, 6.

7   Carole A. Stabile, "Shooting the Mother: Fetal Photography and the Politics of Disappearance, *Camera Obscura: A Journal of Feminism and Film Theory* 28 (January 1992), 191–92.

Epilogue

Epigraph: Margaret Atwood, *The Handmaid's Tale* (New York: 1984), 73–74.

1   Walter Benjamin, "Art in an Age of Mechanical Reproduction," in *Illuminations*, ed. Hannah Arendt (New York: Schocken Books, 1969).

2   Adrienne Rich, "Compulsory Heterosexuality and Lesbian Existence," in Elizabeth and Emily Abel, *The Signs Reader: Women, Gender, and Scholarship* (Chicago: University of Chicago Press, 1983), 140.

3   Dion Farquhar, *The Other Machine: Discourse and Reproductive Technologies* (New York and London: Routledge, 1996), 19–20.

4   Barbara Duden, *Disembodying Women: Perspectives on Pregnancy and the Unborn* (Cambridge, MA: Harvard University Press, 1991), 25–29.

5   Susan Merrill Squier, *Babies in Bottles: Twentieth-Century Visions of Reproductive Technologies* (New Brunswick, NJ: Rutgers University Press, 1991), 10.

6   Kathleen Burdick, "Stranded Histories: Feminist Allegories of Artificial Life," in *Research in Philosophy and Technology: Technology and Feminism* 13 (1991), as quoted in Farquhar, *The Other Machine*, 172–73.

7   Dion Farquhar, *The Other Machine*, 173.

8   Rosalind Petchesky, "Foetal Images: The Power of Visual Culture in the Politics of Reproduction," in *Reproductive Technologies: Gender, Motherhood and Medicine*, ed. Michelle Stanworth (Minneapolis: University of Minnesota Press, 1987).

9   Barbara Katz Rothman, *The Tentative Pregnancy: Prenatal Diagnosis and the Future of Motherhood* (New York: Viking, 1986), 114.

10 Ibid. 115.

11 Bettyann Holtzman Kevles, *Naked to the Bone: Medical Imagining in the Twentieth Century* (New Brunswick, NJ: Rutgers University Press, 1997), 250, 339, n 34.

12 Clifford Grobstein, *Science and the Unborn: Choosing Human Futures* (New York: Basic Books, 1988), 162.

13 Ibid. 159.

14 Ibid. 162.

15 Ibid.

16 President Jimmy Carter, quoted in Carl Sagan et al., *Murmurs of the Earth: The Voyager Interstellar Record* (New York: Random House, 1978), 28.

17 Sagan et al., *Murmurs of the Earth*, 79.

18 Patricia Williams, The *Alchemy of Race and Rights* (Cambridge, MA: Harvard University Press, 1991), 188.

19 Ibid. 186.

20 Ibid. 188.

21 Dorothy Roberts, *Killing the Black Body: Race, Reproduction and the Meaning of Liberty* (New York: Vintage, 1999), 246.

22 Ibid., 25–51.

23 Ibid. 271.

24 Ibid. 251.

25 Ibid. 252.

26 Ibid. 251.

27 Clifford Grobstein, *From Chance to Purpose: An Appraisal of External Human Fertilization* (Reading, MA: Addison-Wesley, 1981), 10.

Permissions

Permissions are listed in the order that the art appears in the book. Every reasonable effort has been made to obtain permission for all art reproduced.

INTRODUCTION

Unable to locate copyright owner

CHAPTER TWO

Copyright Manuel Alvarez Bravo

Copyright Gerard Malanga

Modotti, Tina. *Mother and Child, Tehuantepec, Oaxaca, Mexico.* (c. 1929) Gelatin-silver print, 8 7/8 x 5 15/16" (22.6 x 15.2 cm). The Museum of Modern Art, New York. Given anonymously. Copy Print 1998 The Museum of Modern Art, New York.

Copyright The Dorothea Lange Collection, The Oakland Museum of California, City of Oakland. Gift of Paul S. Taylor.

Copyright Collection Center for Creative Photography, The University of Arizona.

Copyright Hideo Haga. Courtesy of Haga Library Inc., Tokyo, Japan.

Copyright Helen Levitt. Courtesy Laurence Miller Gallery, New York.

Copyright Helen Levitt. Courtesy Laurence Miller Gallery, New York.

Copyright Bob Saltzman

Copyright Tammy Cromer-Campbell

Copyright Shawn Walker, Photo-Arts Studio

Copyright Paul Himmel

Copyright Elliott Erwitt/Magnum Photos

Photograph by Imogen Cunningham. Copyright 1978 The Imogen Cunningham Trust.

Courtesy of the Library of Congress

Copyright Barbara Morgan, 1942, Pregnant.

Copyright 1999 Artists Rights Society (ARS), New York / VG Bild-Kunst, Bonn

Copyright Ruth Bernhard/All Rights Reserved

Copyright Jack Welpott

Copyright Bob Saltzman

Copyright Bruce Davidson/Magnum Photos

Copyright Marion Hoben Belanger

Copyright Jack Welpott

Copyright Joel-Peter Witkin, Courtesy Pace Wildenstein MacGill Gallery, New York City, and Fraenkel Gallery, San Francisco.

Copyright Joel-Peter Witkin, Courtesy Pace Wildenstein MacGill Gallery, New York.

Copyright Joanne Leonard

Copyright Sandy Hale

Photograph by Mable Walton, courtesy of Kierra Walton

Kira Carrillo Corser, from *The Struggle to Be Borne*, San Diego University Press, 1988

Kira Carrillo Corser, from *When the Bough Breaks: Pregnancy and the Legacy of Addiction,* New Sage Press, 1993

Copyright Nan Goldin, courtesy Matthew Marks Gallery, New York

Copyright Peggy McKenna

Copyright Elaine O'Neil, Cambridge, MA 1992

Copyright Meridel Rubenstein

Copyright Joanne Leonard

Copyright Robin Lasser

Copyright Mary E. Frey

CHAPTER THREE

Courtesy of Stanley B. Burns, M.D. and The Burns Archive

Courtesy of Solomon D. Butcher Collection, Nebraska State Historical Society, Lincoln.

Courtesy of Southern Oregon Historical Society, Photograph #877. Anonymous contribution from a private collection.

Courtesy of Ellen Pader

Courtesy of Vicci Veenstra

Courtesy of Kane Stewart

Courtesy of Melissa Christman

Unable to locate copyright owner

Copyright Melonie Bennett

Courtesy of Rhonda Wainshilbaum-Becker

Courtesy of Karen Klugman

Unable to locate copyright owner

Unable to locate copyright owner

Unable to locate copyright owner

Courtesy of M.L. Head

Copyright Dick Blau

Unable to locate copyright owner

Courtesy of Trina Hikel

Copyright Scott Glushien

Courtesy of Peggy Maisel

Copyright Nancy Floyd, courtesy of Beverly Naidus

Unable to locate copyright owner

Unable to locate copyright owner

Courtesy of Catherine Nicol

Unable to locate copyright owner

Copyright s'myth, courtesy of Lorene Stanwick

Unable to locate copyright owner

Courtesy of Richard Holland

Copyright 1998 Maggie Hopp
Copyright Paul B. Goode
Unable to locate copyright owner

CHAPTER FOUR

Public Domain
Public Domain
Public Domain
Public Domain
Public Domain
Public Domain
Public Domain
Public Domain
Public Domain
Public Domain
Public Domain
Public Domain
Public Domain
Public Domain
Public Domain
Public Domain
Public Domain
From *Obstetrics*, J. Whitridge Williams, MD, 1912 edition, copyright © 1912 The
    McGraw-Hill Companies, Inc., reproduced by permission of the McGraw-Hill
    Companies, Inc.
Public Domain
Public Domain
Public Domain
Public Domain
Public Domain
Public Domain
Public Domain
Courtesy of the Library of Congress
Copyright Marvin Breckenridge, Courtesy of the Frontier Nursing Service, Wendover,
    Kentucky
Courtesy of Charles C. Thomas, Publisher, Springfield, Illinois.
From *Williams' Obstetrics*, Nicholson J. Eastman, ed., 1950 edition, copyright © 1950 The
    McGraw-Hill Companies, Inc., reproduced by permission of the McGraw-Hill
    Companies, Inc.
Public Domain
From *Williams' Obstetrics*, Nicholson J. Eastman, ed., 1950 edition, copyright © 1950 The
    McGraw-Hill Companies, Inc., reproduced by permission of the McGraw-Hill
    Companies, Inc

From *Williams' Obstetrics*, Nicholson J. Eastman, ed., 1950 edition, copyright © 1950 The McGraw-Hill Companies, Inc., reproduced by permission of the McGraw-Hill Companies, Inc

From *Williams' Obstetrics*, Nicholson J. Eastman, ed., 1950 edition, copyright © 1950 The McGraw-Hill Companies, Inc., reproduced by permission of the McGraw-Hill Companies, Inc.

Public Domain.

Courtesy of Charles C. Thomas, Publisher, Springfield, Illinois.

From *The Fetus as a Patient*, by Asim Kurjak and Frank A. Chervenak, 1994. Courtesy Kretztechnik AG, Austria

Sherman J. Silber, MD, *How to Get Pregnant with the New Technology*, 1991 Warner Books, from St. Luke's Hospital, St. Louis, Missouri

CHAPTER FIVE

Estate of Grantly Dick-Read

Estate of Grantly Dick-Read

Copyright Tmax

Copyright Mel Rosenthal

Courtesy of Book Publishing Company, from *Spiritual Midwifery*, by Ina May Gaskin, copyright 1990.

Courtesy of Book Publishing Company, from *Spiritual Midwifery*, by Ina May Gaskin, copyright 1990.

Copyright Suzanne Arms

Copyright Suzanne Arms

Copyright Ed Pincus

Copyright David Alexander

Copyright Frédérick LeBoyer

Copyright Frédérick LeBoyer

Photo Lennart Nilsson / Albert Bonniers Publishing Company

Photo Lennart Nilsson / Albert Bonniers Publishing Company

Photo Lennart Nilsson / Albert Bonniers Publishing Company

Photo Lennart Nilsson / Albert Bonniers Publishing Company

Photo Lennart Nilsson / Albert Bonniers Publishing Company

Photo Lennart Nilsson / Albert Bonniers Publishing Company

Photo Lennart Nilsson / Albert Bonniers Publishing Company

Photo Lennart Nilsson / Albert Bonniers Publishing Company

Photo Lennart Nilsson / Albert Bonniers Publishing Company

Unable to locate copyright owner

Unable to locate copyright owner

Unable to locate copyright owner

Unable to locate copyright owner

Unable to locate copyright owner

Unable to locate copyright owner

Unable to locate copyright owner
Unable to locate copyright owner
Unable to locate copyright owner
Unable to locate copyright owner
Unable to locate copyright owner
Unable to locate copyright owner
Unable to locate copyright owner
Photography Paul Cruz, Maternity Clothing JWO (Japanese Weekend, Inc.), http://www.japaneseweekend.com
Photograph Paul Cruz, Maternity Clothing JWO
Photography Paul Cruz, Maternity Clothing JWO
Unable to locate copyright owner
Unable to locate copyright owner
Copyright Gilles Bensimon
Copyright Gilles Bensimon
Copyright Gilles Bensimon
Courtesy of the Library of Congress
Courtesy of the Library of Congress
Courtesy of the National Library of Medicine, Bethesda, Maryland
Courtesy of the National Library of Medicine, Bethesda, Maryland
Courtesy of the National Library of Medicine, Bethesda, Maryland
Courtesy of the National Library of Medicine, Bethesda, Maryland
Courtesy of the National Library of Medicine, Bethesda, Maryland

CHAPTER SIX

Photo Lennart Nilsson/Albert Bonniers Publishing Company
Unable to locate copyright owner
Unable to locate copyright owner
Unable to locate copyright owner
Copyright Annie Leibovitz/Contact Press Images
Copyright Annie Leibovitz/Contact Press Images
Copyright Annie Leibovitz/Contact Press Images
Photographed by Carolyn Jones. Paintbox photo illustration by Phillip Heffernan. FCL/COLORSPACE.
Unable to locate copyright owner
Unable to locate copyright owner
Copyright Mary Ellen Mark
Unable to locate copyright owner
Copyright Annie Leibovitz/Contact Press Images
Copyright Annie Leibovitz/Contact Press Images
Copyright 1993 James Balog
Copyright Jill Gussow

Copyright Jill Gussow

Copyright Aida Laleian

Copyright Michael Zide

Photo Lennart Nilsson/Albert Bonniers Publishing Company

Copyright Tom Wagner/SABA

EPILOGUE

Courtesy of the Estate of George Platt Lynes

Unable to locate copyright owner

Copyright Joyce Tenneson

Reprinted by permission of David R. Godine, Publisher, Inc. Copyright 1985 by Ronald W. Wohlauer

Photo Lennart Nilsson/Albert Bonniers Publishing Company

Unable to locate copyright owner

Copyright Jon Lomberg/SPL/Photo Researchers Inc.

Copyright Tanya Marcuse

Copyright Robin Lasser, from "How's My Mothering?" series 1995–1997

Courtesy of the artists (Renee Cox, Maggie Hadleigh-West, Jenny Polak and Juana Valdes).

Index